CW00552924

CLARENDON LAW SERIES

Edited by
PAUL CRAIG

CLARENDON LAW SERIES

LAW AND GENDER

JOANNE CONAGHAN

OXFORD
UNIVERSITY PRESS

OXFORD
UNIVERSITY PRESS

Great Clarendon Street, Oxford, OX2 6DP,
United Kingdom

Oxford University Press is a department of the University of Oxford.
It furthers the University's objective of excellence in research, scholarship,
and education by publishing worldwide. Oxford is a registered trade mark of
Oxford University Press in the UK and in certain other countries

Published in the United States of America by Oxford University Press
198 Madison Avenue, New York, NY 10016, United States of America

British Library Cataloguing in Publication Data
Data available

Library of Congress Control Number: 2013937762

ISBN 978–0–19–959292–0

To Paddy, with love and gratitude

ACKNOWLEDGEMENTS

This book combines my strange but undeniable love for the law with a lifelong interest in and engagement with the nature and significance of gender in legal operations. It has provided me with a welcome opportunity to engage in sustained reflection about issues which have occupied my mind for many years, and I am profoundly grateful to the University of Kent for giving me the time and solace to pursue my dream project. It is perhaps of some value that I have arrived at this juncture at a fairly advanced stage of my academic career for it has allowed me to draw upon a rich stock of insights shared by friends and colleagues I have encountered along the way. It may be a truism to remark that scholarship is always and unavoidably 'a collective enterprise but it is a truism worth repeating, particularly in a cultural and political context which fosters an understanding of academic endeavour in relentlessly individualist terms.

A number of people have helped me particularly with gathering sources and/or formulating ideas. These include Rosemary Auchmuty, Maria Drakopoulou, Peter Fitzpatrick, Nicola Lacey, Linda Mulcahy, Steve Pethick, Nick Piska, Erika Rackley, Janice Richardson, Kunal Parker, and Ngaire Naffine. Rosemary, Steve, and Erika, along with Paddy Ireland, have kindly read portions of the text in draft and provided useful and constructive feedback. Matt Howard has provided wonderfully reliable and encouraging research assistance throughout. I have also been fortunate to benefit from having spent many years in an intellectual environment in which gender and law issues have been pleasingly and conspicuously to the fore. To my colleagues at Kent Law School, and particularly those with whom I worked for many years on the editorial board of *Feminist Legal Studies*, I express my heartfelt thanks and appreciation.

Much of the text was written in Ireland. I had the rare privilege of being able to squirrel myself away in the Donegal countryside for long periods to pursue my ideas with little or no distractions save for occasional straying livestock and (for longer than I would have liked) a friendly mouse called Bernard. None of this would have been possible without the support and forbearance of my friends and family and they have my eternal gratitude. I am especially grateful to my youngest son, Edward, who put up with my absences uncomplainingly (although he has certainly developed a new and enthusiastic appreciation of his mother's culinary skills). A special thanks also to Sharon, friend, colleague, and PA extraordinaire, who has been with me all the way with friendly words of wisdom and advice through the miracle of email.

    Above all, I want to thank my husband, Paddy, who has given so generously of his time by assuming the lion's share of family duties for a not inconsiderable period and allowing me to indulge in the rare and almost forgotten luxury of having time to myself. I know it is a gift of love, but I am very grateful all the same.

Joanne Conaghan
Culdaff, Co Donegal

CONTENTS

LIST OF ABBREVIATIONS

CA	Court of Appeal
CJ	Chief Justice
CLJ	*Cambridge Law Journal*
CLRC	Criminal Law Revision Committee
CLS	*Critical Legal Studies*
DPP	Director of Public Prosecutions
EU	European Union
Fam LQ	*Family Law Quarterly*
HC	House of Commons
HL	House of Lords
HMSO	Her Majesty's Stationery Office
JLS	*Journal of Legal Studies*
L	Lord/Lady
LJ	Lord/Lady Justice
LQR	*Law Quarterly Review*
L Rev	*Law Review*
MLR	*Modern Law Review*
NYU	New York University
OJLS	*Oxford Journal of Legal Studies*
QC	Queen's Counsel
UK	United Kingdom
UN	United Nations

TABLE OF CASES

European Court of Human Rights

European Court of Justice

Scotland

United States of America

TABLE OF STATUTES

1

THE INCONGRUITY OF LAW
AND GENDER

1.1 INTRODUCTION: IN WHICH
WE DISCOVER THAT LAW HAS
A FEMININE SIDE

We are here to do homage to our lady of the common law; we are her
men of life and limb and earthly worship.[1]

In October 1911, the famous Oxford jurist, Sir Frederick Pollock, delivered a series of lectures at Columbia University Law
School entitled *The Genius of the Common Law* in which the
common law is depicted as a medieval lady surrounded by her
knights. As the seven lectures unfold, Pollock recounts how 'our
lady of the common law' confronts 'giants and gods', 'enemies in
the gate', and 'ransom and rescue', over all of which she triumphs
either by 'alliance or conquest'.[2] By the time the lectures conclude, she has become a 'shrewd old lady'[3] whom the men of
law are encouraged to revere in the hope of catching sight of her
'most benignant smile'.[4] Pollock finishes this extraordinary
eulogy with an exhortation designed to ignite the aspirations
and stoke the nobler ambitions of anyone who chooses the path
of legal practice, declaring: 'There is no more arduous enterprise
for lawful men, and none more noble, than the perpetual quest
of justice laid upon all of us who are pledged to serve our lady of
the common law'.[5]

Pollock's image of the common law as a lady has been picked
up by other jurists. Benjamin Cardozo, for example, in an address

---

[1] Sir Frederick Pollock, *The Genius of the Common Law* (New York: Columbia University Press, 1912), 2.

[2] Pollock, *Genius of the Common Law*. The phrases in quotations correspond
to the titles of lectures two, four, five, and six respectively.

[3] Pollock, *Genius*, 54.

[4] Pollock, *Genius*, 62.   [5] Pollock, *Genius*, 125.

to the first graduands of St John's Law School in 1928, offers a quasi-sexual presentation of our lady of the common law as a beauty and insatiable flirt.[6] More recently, Lord Justice Laws of the English Court of Appeal borrowed Pollock's sobriquet for the title of a public lecture in which he describes our lady of the common law as a 'hard mistress to please'.[7] Nor have the quasi-religious connotations of the imagery gone unnoticed. Cardozo's speech was notably reproduced in the *Catholic Lawyer*. Our lady of the common law is also the subject of an address by John Hu to the American Guild of Catholic Lawyers in 1953 in which the portrayal is somewhat more restrained. According to Hu, the common law is like 'a patient and kindly housewife who knows how to make, stitch by stitch, a seamless tunic for you to wear',[8] the seamless tunic representing the continuity and coherence of common law principles.

The depiction of the common law variously as a medieval lady, beauty on a pedestal, incorrigible flirt, patient housewife, and shrewd old lady may seem to capture a surprisingly diverse array of images of femininity but the personification of law and more particularly justice, as a woman is neither new nor unusual. Indeed, Justitia or Lady Justice is perhaps the most ubiquitous representation in legal iconography. While her name and precise status may vary, Lady Justice is transnational, transcultural, and transhistorical, as at home among the goddesses of Ancient Greece as upon the rooftops of suburban courthouses. Today Justitia may be found perched on or near almost any place of law or government, whether the Old Bailey, Dublin Castle, or Amsterdam Town Hall.[9] She almost invariably carries a sword and scales, is sometimes blindfolded, and is

---

[6] B Cardozo, 'Our Lady of the Common Law' (1972) 18 *Catholic Lawyer* 276; originally delivered in 1928.

[7] Lord Justice Laws, 'Our Lady of the Common Law' (Incorporated Council of Law Reporting, 1 March 2012) <http://www.iclr.co.uk/images/iclr/documents/2011transcript.pdf> accessed 28 May 2012.

[8] J C H Hu, 'The Natural Law and our Common Law' (1954) 23 *Fordham L Rev* 13, 30.

[9] For a comprehensive survey of images of justice, see J Resnick and D Curtis, *Representing Justice: Invention, Controversy and Rights in City-States and Democratic Courtrooms* (New Haven: Yale University Press, 2010).

often accompanied by additional objects including snakes, dogs, books, skulls, and a variety of other things. Linda Mulcahy explains the symbolic value of these props in the following terms:

> The sword depicts the power of the state, the scale the balancing of right and wrong, the blindfold her impartiality, the book her association with the written law, the lector rods are a Roman emblem, the globe suggests her universality, the serpent is associated with evil and provides a contrast with the friendship and loyalty of the dog, and the skull represents human mortality from which justice does not suffer because it is eternal.[10]

While the image of justice as female is so prevalent as barely to attract a glance and rarely any sustained reflection, the idea of representing law in female form seems intuitively odd. After all, for large parts of its history, law served as a bastion of male privilege and female subjection. There is ample evidence, historical but to some extent still current, of the collusion of law in the support of a patriarchal social order in which women were positioned as (at best) different from men and therefore occupying a separate social sphere, or (at worst) inferior and therefore cast in the role of serving or amusing men or constituting objects of their property. Upon marriage, women slipped below the legal radar almost entirely: under the common law doctrine of coverture, a wife's personhood became legally absorbed in that of her husband so that a woman's entry into the married state was tantamount to a form of 'civil death'.

In legal education and practice, women have long been positioned as outsiders. Until the late 19th and early 20th century, they were completely excluded, legal knowledge and practice evolving over centuries on the premise that law was an unreservedly masculine enterprise. Even after securing entry into the legal profession (in England in the early 20th century) women were for the most part consigned to the margins of legal practice, facing particular challenges in reconciling their

---

[10] L Mulcahy, 'Imagining Alternative Visions of Justice: An Exploration of the Controversy Surrounding Stirling Lee's Depictions of Justitia in Nineteenth Century Liverpool' (2011) *Law, Culture and the Humanities* 1, 12, n59.

professional aspirations with the undertaking of domestic duties. In 1930 the English barrister, C P Hawkes commented that:

Men–Barristers in general desire to treat their learned (lady) friends with fairness and generosity; but it would seem as though a married lady-Barrister would have to forgo the joys of family life and mother-hood, for the law is a jealous lover and admits of no divided allegiance.[11]

Law thus took its modern shape and form not under conditions of gender-neutrality but in the context of a legally sanctioned gender hierarchy. It is hardly surprising that in 1996 Margaret Thornton observed that women continued to be 'fringe-dwellers in the legal community'.[12] One only has to reflect upon the current gender composition of the United Kingdom Supreme Court, or indeed the judiciary more widely, to recognize that this description has considerable purchase even today.

The irony then of feminized images of justice, let alone juristic appeals to our lady of the common law, cannot fail to strike anyone familiar with the long and difficult struggle women had to sustain to become fully and equally recognized in law. When late 19th and early 20th century feminists invoked the common law to support the entry of women into the legal profession as well as other public and professional offices, 'our lady' was anything but welcoming to her sisters. Indeed, as Albie Sachs and Joan Hoff Wilson observe, in rejecting a succession of claims made on women's behalf, the common law served as the judicial weapon of choice: 'The English common law which had so often been extolled as being the embodiment of human freedom ... in fact provided the main intellectual justification for the avowed and formal subordination of women'.[13]

The personification of law and justice in female terms also jars with a tendency in modern feminist legal scholarship to

[11] C P Hawkes, *Chambers in the Temple: Comments and Conceits 'in Camera'* (London: Methuen & Co Ltd, 1930), 75.

[12] M Thornton, *Dissonance and Distrust: Women in the Legal Profession* (Oxford: OUP, 1996).

[13] A Sachs and J H Wilson, *Sexism and the Law: A Study of Male Beliefs and Judicial Bias* (Oxford: Martin Robertson, 1978), 41 and generally ch 1, discussing a series of cases collectively known as 'the persons cases'.

characterize law as in some respect *male*, for example, as reflecting male values and interests or as embodying a particular logic and structure which is male-created and reinforced.[14] During the course of the last few decades, feminist scholars around the globe have subjected law and legal discourse to extensive, in-depth excavation. An extensive body of scholarship has now accumulated asserting not only that the content of law often reflects and reinforces gendered social and cultural norms but also that gender is implicated in the very forms of law, in the logic and structure of legal concepts and classification schemes and in the practices and assumptions which underpin legal reasoning. Yet, such claims notwithstanding, gender is still far from regarded as a significant concept within the legal scholarly mainstream. Why is the role of gender in law not afforded more mainstream attention? What are the jurisprudential implications of recognizing gender as a significant legal concept? And, while we are asking questions: why *is* justice almost always portrayed as a woman?

This book sets out to answer such questions and more by exploring the relationship between law and gender. It is surely curious that gender, while figuring so centrally in the construction and organization of social life across virtually all societies and civilizations is nevertheless barely visible in the conceptual armoury of law. In the jurisprudential imagination, law occupies a self-consciously artificial and gender-devoid world in which the individual legal subject is presumed to be without gender, although as feminist analysis has shown, 'he' is generally male by default.[15] This is not because women are absent from law or indeed not subject to it. Historically, and even in modern times, the very fact that women are thought to be different from men has provided grounds for their distinct regulation and governance. It is rather to suggest that in the legal conceptual framework gender tends to be understood at best as a matter of

---

[14] See eg L Finley, 'Breaking Women's Silence in Law: the Dilemma of the Gendered Nature of Legal Reasoning' (1989) 64 *Notre Dame L Rev* 886; R West, 'Jurisprudence and Gender' (1988) 55 *University of Chicago L Rev* 1.

[15] See eg N Naffine, *Law of the Sexes: Explorations in Feminist Jurisprudence* (Sydney: Allen & Unwin, 1990).

content not form, as part of the legal bricks and mortar rather than a structural feature or principle of architectural design. After all, the concept of law (to invoke the title of Hart's famous work[16]) has been endlessly interrogated in terms which do not admit the relevance of gender. As a consequence, the possibility that gender has some deeper, closer relation to law may not have been fully explored.

This is not to say that legal scholarship has ignored gender; indeed the trend is clearly to be increasingly attentive to its significance and operations in legal contexts. There remain few areas of law and legal scholarship today in which gender has not been accorded some consideration. Moreover, once looked for in law, gender seems manifestly everywhere. Consider the many issues of law with a gender dimension which have occupied the sphere of political and legal debate in recent years. In the UK, these include: a range of criminal justice concerns around rape, domestic violence, prostitution, and sex trafficking; extensive contestation in family law and policy over parental rights and responsibilities; a succession of unique and often highly complex regulatory dilemmas arising from the development and application of new reproductive technologies; and the increasing importance attributed to 'family-friendly' initiatives in labour, welfare, and even tax law, contributing to the reconstitution of family life and the gendered order therein. Nor are these kinds of issues a focus of legal policy and debate only in the UK; they are also matters of concern in many other jurisdictions. Moreover, in the sphere of international law and human rights, growing apprehension about violence against women and issues of gender inequality, particularly in situations of conflict or post-conflict, mirror the increasing prominence of sex and gender considerations in a domestic legal setting.

While sex and gender considerations are now at the forefront of legal and policy agendas, the scope and focus of gender-informed debate is radically changing, challenging simplistic assumptions that gender issues concern only women or are of marginal importance politically, legally, and ethically. Increasingly, questions of

[16] H L A Hart, *The Concept of Law*, 3rd edn, edited by P Bulloch and J Raz (Oxford: OUP, 2012).

sex and gender have become entangled in broader debates about sexuality rights and regulation. They have also figured prominently in discussions around equality and social justice. In the opening decade of the 21st century, Britain has extended statutory anti-discrimination protection to gays and lesbians and recognized transgender identities. It has offered same-sex couples the opportunity to form civil partnerships with the same basic legal consequences as (heterosexual) marriage and advanced measures to tackle homophobic hate crimes. It has also taken substantial steps towards the development of a much more inclusive and effective legal equality regime.

It is against this background of the enhanced visibility of sex/gender in legal policy-making and debate, alongside the continued adherence of mainstream legal discourse to a conceptual and normative framework in which formally gender has no place, that this book has developed. What *is* the place of gender in law? Is it merely a matter of legal content or does it play a role—explicit or implicit, conscious or unconscious—in the construction and formal ordering of law? Does gender contribute significantly to the constitution of legal concepts and structures of liability and/or to the rules which come into play in the context of such constitutive operations? If so, how should we understand and theorize this constitutive process and relation? To what extent is law as a discipline premised upon unarticulated but nevertheless deeply operative gendered assumptions and viewpoints and what are the consequences for legal theory of acknowledging this? Most importantly, how and why does legal theory adhere so resolutely to a discursive framework in which gender officially has no place?

Feminist scholarship has been raising these kinds of questions for some time. While much of the existing body of work has been rightly directed at substantive legal content and on the ways in which particular laws or bodies of law produce unequal gendered outcomes and effects, there is also a clear concern in the feminist literature to interrogate the basic forms and underpinnings of law, to tease out the presence of gender not just in the legal detail but in the overall purpose and design. According to Nicola Lacey, the idea that the 'structure and method of modern law is hierarchically gendered' has emerged as a key contention of feminist legal theory.[17] Ngaire Naffine asserts that 'a problem of sex is built into the very forms of law'.[18] Reg Graycar and Jenny Morgan set out to expose the 'hidden gender of law' by eschewing traditional doctrinal categories and reconfiguring legal doctrine around women's lives and practical experiences.[19] Martha Chamallas and Jennifer Wriggins argue that the structure of contemporary tort law '... tends to reflect and reinforce the social marginalization of women and racial minorities'.[20] The thrust of these arguments is to suggest that law is gendered in a fairly fundamental way; that the relation between law and gender goes beyond the still occasional manifestation of gender bias in content or operation. The thrust of these arguments is that gender is a crucial part of what law *is* or *does*.

And yet, for the most part, legal scholarship continues to hold on to the view that gender plays little or no role in the conceptual make-up, normative grounding, or categorical ordering of law. The official position is that the *idea* of law and legal fundamentals are, and certainly ought to be, gender-independent. This book puts such long-held assumptions to the test by subjecting the relation between law and gender to sustained scrutiny. The aim is to offer an accessible, critically engaged account of law and legal scholarship which takes gender as a core analytical concept and interrogatory tool. The focus is less on matters of substantive legal content and more on how law is conceptualized, organized, articulated, and legitimated; how it is given meaning in legal texts, doctrine, and practices; and, most particularly, how gender is able to operate *within* law while simultaneously appearing to be *outside* it.

Because this is an engagement with legal concepts and ideas, the jurisdictional reach is potentially quite broad. This is not a book about English law, although English law provides most

<hr/>

[17] N Lacey, *Unspeakable Subjects: Feminist Essays in Legal and Social Theory* (Oxford: Hart Publishing, 1998), 2.
[18] Naffine, *Law of the Sexes*, x.
[19] R Graycar and J Morgan, *The Hidden Gender of Law*, 2nd edn (Sydney: Federation Press, 2002).
[20] M Chamallas and J B Wriggins, *The Measure of Injury: Race, Gender and Tort Law* (NY: NYU Press, 2010).

although not all of the context and examples from which I draw. Moreover, the analysis is informed and enriched by the work of an abundance of scholars from around the world and across the fields of gender, sexuality, feminism, and law. I do acknowledge a not unsurprising affinity with the jurisprudential literature and traditions of the common law world and the commentaries thereon. Inevitably, the main concerns of the book are shaped and constrained by my own knowledge, experience, priorities, and predilections. I hope it nevertheless proves useful to others who consider the interrelation of law and gender to be a subject worthy of consideration, and, more broadly, that the analysis goes some way towards advancing current understandings of and engagements with law and legal theory.

Before proceeding further, it is useful to offer a brief sketch of the general theoretical terrain within which the enquiry is located by exploring the key notions of law and gender against the background of the book's broader context, purposes, and concerns. I will then conclude with a short elucidation of the book's central thesis along with the structure and organization of the arguments to follow.

1.2 LAYING DOWN THE LAW

The word 'law', in Middle English 'lawe', originally derives from Old Norse and has the same etymological root as the words 'lay' or 'lie'.[21] Thus, from its linguistic origins, the notion of law has long been associated with that which has been laid down, fixed, or prescribed. One may talk about law in general or about particular laws or areas of law, such as contract law or the law of tort. The term 'law' may also be used in contexts which are not strictly legal, as, for example, when we invoke the notion of a moral law or the laws of nature or physics. In this context we summon the idea of law to capture both the fixity and normativity of the moral or natural order. Conceived in this

---

[21] The etymological root is *log* (pl. *lag*) signifying 'to put in place or order' (R K Barnhart (ed), *Chambers Dictionary of Etymology* (London: Chambers 1988)). The Latin term *lex* is also thought to derive from Old Norse although some associate it with the Latin *legere* meaning 'to read'.

way, law may be understood in broad terms as a normative regime brooking little or no deviation and/or carrying a general mandate to comply.

This is indeed how law is conceived and experienced by most new law students; it is a conception to which they become quickly and easily attuned. Students come to their studies fully expecting to encounter a formal system comprised of rules, rubrics, and clear principles of demarcation and they have a surprising appetite for predictability, orderliness, and similitude. Students learn quickly that the rightness or wrongness of a legal decision depends not on any social, moral, or political standard of measurement but upon the degree of conformity to the prescribed doctrinal framework. They are quick and keen to grasp distinctions: between different sources of law (for example, judge-made law and legislation); between different spheres of legal operation (criminal/civil, public/private, common law/ equity) and between particular legal categories and concepts (for example, persons and property, ownership and possession, *mens rea* and *actus reus*). By contrast, students are slow to see— often resistant to—unruliness in law. Their expectations, combined with the practicalities of getting to grips with the first year curriculum, encourage an almost wilful blindness to the blurred lines and conceptual fudges which linger unheeded amidst the pursuit of doctrinal purity and schematic coherence. It is the rationality and order of law which tends to hold students' appeal. They have little taste for any contrary aesthetic.

Why is the promise of order so compelling? Costas Douzinas and Adam Gearey suggest that 'law attests to the inherently conflictual form of social life'.[22] It is this widely shared belief in the inescapability of social conflict which generates the anxious desire for legal order, based not upon mechanisms of tyranny or dictatorship but upon rationally accessible, widely accepted values and norms. Understood in this modern liberal democratic sense, law is the desired outcome of an imaginary consensus most commonly expressed in the political philosophical tradition of

---

[22] C Douzinas and A Gearey, *Critical Jurisprudence: the Political Philosophy of Justice* (Oxford: Hart Publishing, 2005), 40.

social contractarianism but also evidenced in the early legal sociological work of Henry Maine, in which law's development from
primitive to modern form is portrayed as a movement from
relations of status to contract.[23] This familiar and comforting
ideal easily supports a presentation of law as a fair, unbiased,
and essentially scientific system for the resolution of disputes,
an aspiration to which we hold fast even when law itself self-
evidently falls short.

The systematicity of law, expressed in the close alignment of
norms of generality, consistency, and deference to tradition,
together combining to produce a discrete, unified, and coherent
whole, is central to the credibility and effectiveness of law as a
neutral arbiter in the face of social contestation. We do not wish
to see law as a space of chaos and confusion and acknowledge its
fallibility rarely and reluctantly. We welcome the idea that law
transcends the muddle of everyday life, occupying a separate,
untainted realm which is peculiarly legal and almost entirely
self-legitimating. While we expect law to mirror, albeit in a
legally distilled form, the practicalities and challenges of social
living, we do not apprehend legal norms first and foremost as
social constructions. We much prefer to see law as distinguished
by special features which elevate it above and beyond the social
context from which it derives and in which it operates. To this
end, much jurisprudential effort has been devoted to identifying
appropriate lines of demarcation between law and everything
else, and to representing law as a relatively closed space within
which specifically legal operations are performed. This is a view
of law *unadulterated*, expressed in its most extreme form in Hans
Kelsen's articulation of a 'pure theory of law',[24] and generally
associated with the theoretical tradition of legal positivism.
While it is commonplace today to express scepticism about the
continued purchase of this approach and to point to trends in
legal scholarship and education away from a view of law as a

[23] H Maine, *Ancient Law* (London: Dent & Sons, 1917).
[24] H Kelsen, *Introduction to the Problems of Legal Theory: A Translation of the First Edition of the Reine Rechtslehre or Pure Theory of Law 1934*, trans B Litschewski Paulson and S Paulson (Oxford: Clarendon Press, 1992).

discrete and autonomous field,[25] the idea of law as a special and distinctive way of ordering and interpreting human conduct still holds considerable appeal. Moreover, the notion of law as an uncontaminated space of purely legal operations exercises a far greater grip on how law is presented in textbooks and in the classroom than we are inclined to acknowledge. In turn this ensures the reproduction of adherence within legal scholarship and practice to the notion of a sphere of the 'strictly legal', expressed in the somewhat tautological proposition that what is law, and only what is law, determines what counts as law.[26] In this way, the 'what is law?' question, famously posed by Hart at the beginning of *The Concept of Law*, continues to remain at the centre of the enterprise of legal scholarship and education.

Granted, it is now widely recognized that, historically and cross-culturally, law is far more implicated in its social, political and cultural contexts than this jurisprudential ideal would have us believe. The growth of socio-legal, critical, and interdisciplinary approaches to legal scholarship and the general acceptance of much greater diversity in the legal scholarly field is undeniable. Legal theory today encompasses feminism, postmodernism, queer theory, deconstruction, critical legal theory, critical race theory, Foucauldian genealogy, cultural studies, and the myriad other approaches to the study of law and legal phenomena, many of which are now included in standard jurisprudential texts. The scope of legal theoretical enquiry has widened considerably, going some way to dislodge the tenacious grip of legal positivism and giving way to theorizations in which law is conceived in very different terms.

In particular, the various manifestations of what might broadly be described as critical legal theory, from the law and society movement to feminist and postmodernist perspectives on law, can be said to unite on a number of concerns. These include: enquiring more closely into law's social and political purposes, operations, and effects; probing the implication of law

---

[25] B H Bix, 'Law as an Autonomous Discipline' in P Cane and M Tushnet (eds), *The Oxford Handbook of Legal Studies* (Oxford: OUP, 2005), 975.

[26] See N Naffine, *Law's Meaning of Life: Philosophy, Religion, Darwin and the Legal Person* (Oxford: Hart Publishing, 2009), particularly ch 3.

in relations of power and privilege; tracing the hidden narratives in legal texts; re-presenting law as a discursive site or practice; and exploring the processes through which law confers meaning and structures experience. What these approaches have in common is precisely a refusal to position law as a discrete focus of enquiry, an insistence upon an interpretative lens in which the boundary between law and non-law is blurred if not dissolved, and, most importantly, a reframing of the theoretical field in such a way that the premises, purposes, and preoccupations of traditional jurisprudence seem fundamentally undermined.

But are they? Margaret Davies suggests that conventional legal theory has been 'decapitated'; it has 'lost its distinct identity, its subjectivity and its focus upon the essential nature, spirit or rationale of law'.[27] This she views as a positive development because it paves the way for 'a proliferation of new [theoretical] life forms—new species, not mere clones'.[28] The notion that conventional legal theory has comprised a succession of mere clones is perhaps unfair. Even in a discipline in which conservatism is almost a methodological prerequisite, one must allow for some degree of evolution. In any event, I do not think the decapitation thesis is really borne out by the evidence. Indeed, measured in terms of the level of continued engagement with traditional themes, albeit in more diverse and innovative ways, the field of legal theory might well be said not only to be alive but to be generally flourishing.[29]

A considerable amount of legal scholarship is still devoted to general jurisprudential enquiry, to what James Penner, David Schiff and Richard Nobles characterize as 'law with a capital L'.[30] This kind of scholarship is interested in producing generalities about law not with interrogating the legal detail; it is very

---

[27] M Davies, *Asking the Law Question*, 3rd edn (Sydney: Lawbook Co, 2008), 30.

[28] Davies, *Asking the Law Question*, 30.

[29] This is the assessment of the editors of a recent three volume compendium of essays on legal theory: M Giudice, W Waluchow, and M Del Mar (eds), *The Methodology of Legal Theory 1 (Library of Essays in Contemporary Legal Theory)* (Farnham: Ashgate, 2010), ix.

[30] J Penner, D Schiff, and R Nobles, *Jurisprudence and Legal Theory: Commentary and Materials* (London: Butterworths, 2002), 3.

much engaged with *ideas* of law, its various conceptualizations and imaginings. This includes consideration not only of the more traditional kinds of concerns about how law is authenticated and how it is distinguished from non-law—but also giving attention to the structural configurations and internal workings of law. How, for example, do we account for the systematization of law, its self-replication, and general mechanical functioning? Upon what does law draw for sustenance and support? What are its primary modes of alteration and how are they initiated and brought into effect?

As a statement of the jurisprudential mission this is broader than it looks and in principle includes explorations which seek to trouble—even dissipate—the boundaries of the legal and non-legal. In practice, however, the tendency is to look for—and therefore generally to find—some formal frontiers to law; to identify, however imprecisely, a realm of the strictly legal. Indeed, it is in the nature of the discursive conventions which govern legal thought to do precisely this. Every law student is encouraged to learn how to know and authenticate legal doctrine, articulate and apply it with precision, and locate it within a broader doctrinal framework. Cultivating legal formalist techniques, understood not in terms of some crude caricature of unyielding adherence to logic and deduction but rather as the practical acceptance that 'doing law' requires an ability to deploy legal justifications, which are acceptably and readily distinguishable from non-legal justifications,[31] is a necessary skill that we seek to impart to our students. We may do so reluctantly, sceptically, and subject to extensive qualification, but the lesson is inevitably learned.

Traditional jurisprudence helps to make sense of these contradictions experienced by the students and scholars of law. For some, jurisprudence assumes the status of a quest for a golden formula that will unlock law's secrets and bring it clearly and unambiguously into view. Its draw here is immense. It is expressive of an ethics and aesthetics which appear natural and proper to the lawyer. Critical legal scholars may lambast such an

---

[31] To deploy the understanding of legal formalism adopted by R M Unger, 'The Critical Legal Studies Movement' (1983) 96 *Harvard L Rev* 561.

approach as 'morally impoverished' because it effects the strict separation of fact and value and encourages scholars to concern themselves primarily with making law coherent and intelligible rather than with making it just.[32] However, that is to miss its moral and ethical appeal as a way of resolving disputes without recourse to the murky waters of uncertainty, subjectivity, and judicial choice. Nor can it fairly be said that traditional jurisprudence is not concerned with justice. Indeed within the analytical philosophical tradition, justice has been an important theoretical focus. Legal positivists, for example, give considerable attention to questions of justice although they are more likely to be conceived in procedural than substantive terms and viewed within a discursive frame in which a formal demarcation governs the space of law and morality. The point is, however, that within the (still) dominant tradition of legal scholarship and within the field of jurisprudence which supports and legitimates it, law continues to be apprehended not in terms of content but in terms of adherence to form. The predominant (or perhaps, more accurately, default) tendency is to engage with law as if it is, or aspires to be, a discrete and systemized framework of norms which can be comprehended independent of the wider context from which it emerges, and navigated through the effective deployment of a methodologically neutral approach understood as legal reasoning.

In this respect, Penner, Schiff, and Nobles, in a jurisprudential text devoting considerable space to non-traditional perspectives, draw an interesting distinction between traditional jurisprudence—by which they mean 'the lawyers' understanding of law'—and 'legal theory', which they cast in quite different terms:

What unites legal theorists is that they take law, or indeed theorising about law, as *a point of departure* for exploring any and all types of issues of many different kinds.[33]

---

[32] Douzinas and Gearey, *Critical Jurisprudence*, 4–6.
[33] Penner et al, *Jurisprudence and Legal Theory*, 4 (my italics).

The language used here is quite striking; the notion of departure telling. There is a sense in which critical legal theory at a certain point can be said simply to vacate the space, leaving the jurisprudential head well and truly on its shoulders. It is true, Penner et al acknowledge, that much legal theory (of the 'departure' type) is devoted to trying to disrupt the self-understanding of law which lawyers adopt and cultivate, but this does not really seem to have occurred. Notwithstanding the wholesale assault of critical legal scholarship, the spirit of law as an intelligible and self-legitimating field of vision is remarkably resilient, still directing and informing much of the work produced by new generations of legal scholars. More importantly, it continues to have cultural and political purchase.

Critical legal scholars account for this persistence variously. Pierre Schlag suggests we are enchanted by reason.[34] Duncan Kennedy thinks we are all in denial.[35] Others, such as Margaret Davies and Douzinas and Gearey, offer alternative jurisprudential narratives in the hope of displacing the authority and influence of the dominant account. I want to take the dominant account seriously and address it to the extent that it is possible on its own terms. It is striking, I think, that although feminism and critical legal theory have together produced vast reams of literature which contest virtually every aspect of how law is traditionally conceived, mainstream legal scholarship remains strangely immune to the contamination which such a challenge presents. How is it possible for legal scholars simply to continue as if nothing of significance has been said? What weight *should* we attribute to that cluster of ideas and suppositions about law which continue to hold sway notwithstanding the alleged decapitation of legal theory? And how and why have these ideas remained so apparently resistant to the infusion of a gendered analysis?

---

[34] P Schlag, *The Enchantment of Reason* (Durham, NC: Duke University Press, 1998).

[35] D Kennedy, *Critique of Adjudication: Fin de Siècle* (Cambridge, Ma: Harvard University Press, 1997).

1.3 INTERROGATING GENDER

> In grammar, gender is understood to be a way of classifying phenomena, a socially agreed upon system of distinctions rather than an objective description of inherent traits.[36]

'Gender' is a term very much in common usage. However, its precise meaning and relation to the associated term 'sex' is the subject of considerable debate and contestation. As with any concept, understandings and deployments of gender have changed and developed over time. Indeed, as a word to denote a person's sex or sex-based differences, the deployment of 'gender', until fairly recently and certainly until the second half of the 20th century, has been quite limited. Mary Wollstonecraft, for example, in her *Vindication of the Rights of Woman*, published in 1792, writes exclusively about men and women in terms of 'sex', as does John Stuart Mill in the *Subjection of Women* in 1869. Even in the late 1920s, Virginia Woolf in her iconic set of essays, *A Room of One's Own*, makes no reference to gender even though her focus is very much upon differences in the situation of men and women with respect to the pursuit of artistic and creative activities. This is not to say that the usage of gender as a surrogate for sex was unheard of in earlier times. In *Some Reflections upon Marriage*, published in 1700, the famous feminist essayist, Mary Astell, occasionally refers to the 'feminine gender' while Charles Dickens, in *A Tale of Two Cities* published in 1859, makes a similar kind of reference.

Etymologically, 'gender' derives from the old French, *gendre*, from the Latin stem, *genus*, meaning 'kind or sort'.[37] In this sense gender is associated with modes of categorization, with the need to sort and distinguish things which are perceived to be different from each other. The most obvious example here is the use of gender in languages as a classification scheme from which particular grammatical rules may be derived. Although we may be tempted to associate the linguistic classification of nouns as

---

[36] J W Scott, *Gender and the Politics of History*, 2nd edn (NY: Columbia University Press, 1999), 29.

[37] *Chambers Dictionary of Etymology*. Cognates include 'genetic', 'genius', and 'genital' ('things we treat differently because of inherent differences').

'masculine' and 'feminine' with masculinity and femininity understood as indicators of sexual difference, there is in fact no necessary correlation.[38] This is because, etymologically speaking, sex is only an example of the broader purchase of gender in the context of classification.

That said, there can be little doubt that the primary understanding of gender today is as an extension of or supplement to 'sex'. In particular, 'gender' is commonly used in opposition to 'sex' to signal social as opposed to natural or biologically-based sex difference. While sex is understood to be biologically derived and therefore (relatively) fixed and immutable, gender is recognized as the product of social and cultural institutions, practices, and beliefs which change over time and, moreover, are subject to challenge and negotiation. This is the most common understanding of gender in feminist theory as well as in other disciplines such as sociology and anthropology: gender is seen as a social category superimposed upon a sexed body. Moreover, gender differences are widely recognized as normatively imbued, carrying social and cultural meanings which have practical, distributional effects. Viewed in this way, gender is often characterized in disciplinary terms, that is, as a way in which 'men' and 'women' are brought into being discursively: socially and culturally constructed gendered norms act upon subjects to compel their compliance with gendered expectations within the broader context of social arrangements in which gender features as a category of significance.

The dichotomization of sex and gender, effectively as nature and nurture, is generally attributed to sociological and psychological literature from the mid-20th century. In particular, in 1968, psychiatrist, Robert J Stoller developed and systemized the distinction between sex and gender in terms of biology on the one hand and social/psychological construction on the other.[39] Following this, Ann Oakley, in *Sex, Gender and Society*, published in 1972, a book which quickly assumed the status of

---

[38] For a general discussion of gender and language, see M Warner, *Monuments and Maidens: the Allegory of the Female Form* (London: Random House, 1985), ch 4.

[39] R J Stoller, *Sex and Gender* (London: Hogarth Press, 1968).

feminist classic, drew directly from Stoller's classification to offer a feminist-informed sociological account of sex and gender. Stoller's study, as well as the views of a number of leading feminist theorists in the 1970s (for example, Juliet Mitchell and Nancy Choderow) was strongly influenced by Sigmund Freud. His investigations into the formation of sexual identity are significant not because of the precise details of the Freudian account into how sexual identity develops (which is much contested within and beyond feminism) but in the general recognition that sexual identity *is* formed, that is, that we do not arrive, fully fashioned, as gendered subjects.[40] The point is that much of what we characterize as masculine or feminine behaviour, values, and attributes are the product of social and psychological influences. It is in this sense that Simone De Beauvoir famously pronounces: 'One is not born but rather becomes a woman'.[41]

By the late 1970s and early 1980s, it had become common-place in feminist scholarship to understand gender as a social and cultural construct in contrast to sex which was a biological essence. This was no less the case in feminist legal studies. For example, Katherine O'Donovan, in her path-breaking mono-graph in 1985, clearly distinguishes between sex and gender in these terms.[42] The analytical and strategic value of the distinc-tion is undeniable, enabling feminists to argue, on the one hand, that in some (albeit limited) ways women are biologically differ-ent from men and thus in need of legal or political accommo-dation, for example, in the context of pregnancy and childbirth, while, at the same time, insisting that many of the perceived differences between men and women, often enshrined in legal texts and discourses, are socially constructed and, therefore, neither the proper basis for legal distinctions nor indeed immune to challenge or alteration.

---

[40] See especially S Freud, *Three Essays on the Theory of Sexuality*, originally published 1905 (New York: Basic Books, 2000).

[41] S De Beauvoir, *The Second Sex Book 2 (Vintage Classics)*, originally pub-lished in 1949 (London: Random House, 1997), 295.

[42] K O'Donovan, *Sexual Divisions in Law* (London: Weidenfeld & Nicolson, 1985), 60–2.

Such strategic advantages notwithstanding, the sex/gender distinction was no sooner adopted than it became vulnerable to challenge. One of the earliest critiques came from feminist philosopher, Moira Gatens. In an essay first published in 1983, Gatens expressed concern that the sex/gender distinction encouraged feminists to ignore or downplay the significance of bodies in processes of meaning and value conferral. She argued that by focusing on the way in which gender, understood as a socially constructed hierarchy, shaped and informed perceptions, attitudes, and beliefs, feminists were presupposing a passive or neutral body with no causal significance or agency. In this sense, the sex/gender distinction simply reproduced the separation of mind and body associated with Cartesian dualism: gender became aligned with the realm of the ideal and sex was reduced to raw, unmediated materiality.

In advancing her critique, Gatens was responding to a particular stance popular among feminists at the time—including Oakley and Choderow—which advocated a process of mass resocialization as the route to women's emancipation. Gatens described this strategy as 'degendering'.[43] It was premised on the assumption that because gender was socially constructed, women's disadvantages could best be countered by challenging and eliminating gender-based differentiations, in other words by pursuing gender-neutrality. Gatens believed that this approach failed adequately to recognize the social significance of bodies, in particular, the significance of material differences between bodies. Her argument was not simply that 'biology was destiny', an approach which most feminists sought to discredit by highlighting the social significance of gender over sex. Gatens was *not* claiming that bodily differences necessarily produced fixed and determinate social effects. However, that they produced some effects in social contexts, she contended, was undeniable and for this reason if no other, feminists could not afford to ignore bodies in their theoretical efforts. In accounting for and challenging women's disadvantage, it was necessary to consider bodies, how they functioned, how they were perceived socially

---

[43] M Gatens, 'A Critique of the Sex/Gender Distinction' in *Imaginary Bodies: Ethics, Power and Corporeality* (London: Routledge, 1996), 16.

and culturally, how they interacted with and impacted upon wider material and discursive processes, and, especially, how they were socially valued. Put simply, Gatens' contention was that bodies *matter* and the sex/gender distinction, as at that time deployed by feminists, tended to assume that they did not. One of the points that Gatens was endeavouring to make was that sex as well as gender is subject to processes of social and cultural construction or, to put it another way, nature and nurture are not as easily disentangled as the sex/gender distinction would imply. Interestingly, a study by Thomas Laqueur has demonstrated significant historical variations in the way in which men and women's bodies have been apprehended and analytically portrayed.[44] Pre-modern conceptualizations tended to posit the female body either as a *part* of the male body, as in the Biblical account of Eve's creation from Adam's rib, or as a defective version of the male body, as in Aristotle's pronouncement that '...the female is, as it were, a deformed male'.[45] A conception of male and female bodies as separate from one another and as fundamentally *different*, what Laqueur describes as the 'two-sex' rather than 'one-sex' view of the human body, does not really emerge as dominant until the 18th century. There is also evidence that some cultures have adopted a 'three-sex' (or more) classification of bodies.[46]

The point here is not to suggest that sex is purely the product of social and cultural construction or that real differences between men and women's bodies do not exist. Rather it is to emphasize that how we know or apprehend bodies and the differences between them is inevitably socially and culturally mediated. In this sense, asserting a sharp and definitive line between sex and gender or indeed between nature and nurture is misleading as it tends to suppose that what falls into the former category (sex/nature) is biologically fixed and determined and

[44] T Laqueur, *Making Sex: Body and Gender from the Greeks to Freud* (Cambridge, Ma: Harvard University Press, 1990).
[45] Aristotle, *Generation of Animals*, trans A L Peck (Cambridge, Ma: Harvard University Press, 1943) 175 (Book 1:3).
[46] G Herdt, *Third Sex, Third Gender: Beyond Sexual Dimorphism in Culture and History* (New York: Zone Books, 1993).

what is assigned to the latter (gender/nurture) is socially and culturally negotiable. The result is to shield from scrutiny the social and cultural dimensions of understandings of nature and biology.

All this calls into serious question the explanatory value of the sex/gender distinction as it has been commonly deployed in the scholarly literature. Indeed some feminist philosophers, for example, Judith Butler (whose work has been particularly influential in recent feminist theory), reject the distinction entirely. Thus Butler observes:

If the immutable character of sex is contested, perhaps that construct called sex is as culturally constructed as gender; indeed perhaps it was always already gender with the consequence that the distinction between sex and gender turns out to be no distinction at all.[47]

Butler contends that sex, understood as a natural, 'pre-discursive' category, is a product of gender, that is, that gender yields sex and not, as is often thought, the other way round. Butler's arguments around this point are complex (and not aided by a propensity to write in an inaccessible and convoluted style). Moreover her views are frequently recast by others in overly simplistic terms in which both sex and gender are considered wholly through the lens of social construction and completely divorced from their embodied contexts. At which point we find ourselves back within a Cartesian frame in which the body is sidelined and materiality is located beyond the reach or warrantable attention of theory.[48]

Given these concerns, I do not regard the common distinction between sex and gender in terms of nature and nurture (or body and consciousness) as either useful or tenable. Therefore, for the rest of this book, I will be using 'sex' and 'gender' loosely and interchangeably, occasionally linking or separating them by a forward slash (as in 'sex/gender') to emphasize their interconnectedness but with gender—understood inclusively—as the default term (as it should be understood in the title of this

---

[47] J Butler, *Gender Trouble* (NY: Routledge, 1990), 10.
[48] Butler seeks to address this problem in a subsequent publication, *Bodies that Matter* (NY: Routledge, 1993) although not entirely successfully.

book, *Law and Gender*). There are times when I am required to invoke the sex/gender distinction in the more conventional sense outlined above because that is the sense in which it figures in the work of a particular scholar or scholarly field. However, this should be evident to the reader from the context (and is generally indicated). In adopting an approach which effectively collapses the sex/gender distinction, I do not wish to imply that sex/gender is solely the product of language or discourse, that it does not also have a significant material including biological dimension which actively shapes how we apprehend and value a sexed/gendered social world. I do take the view that our access to the material and our apprehension of the biological is inevitably mediated by social and cultural understandings of the same: knowledge is never 'pure' and a clear line between the material world and the ideas and concepts through which we perceive that world cannot really be drawn.

How then do I deploy gender in the context of what follows? The approach of this book is to take gender as a category of analysis, that is, as a conceptual tool with which to probe and interrogate understandings of law and legal phenomena. There is nothing privileged about the decision to focus on gender. I could equally have chosen to analyse law through the lens of race or class or some other category of significance in the social, cultural, and political order. It might be suggested that to analyse the place of gender in law without simultaneously taking into consideration these other categories is neither a tenable nor useful approach. This is both true and not true in the sense that everything depends on how gender is being used in the analytical process and how, more broadly, it is understood. I should emphasize at the outset that, notwithstanding a predisposition within contemporary feminist scholarship to invoke gender in terms of identity, in my view gender is better understood as relational, that is, an expression of (often oppressive) social relations rather than social identity.[49] Thus understood, gender is not located in individual subjects but in the patterns

---

[49] This is not to say that it is not possible to approach gender as an aspect of identity or subjectivity but rather to suggest that it is not always, or even often, useful to do so.

and practices which gendered social relations produce: gender functions here as a category of social ordering and can therefore be deployed as an analytical tool to interrogate particular social relational configurations and their effects. Of course, the relations which constitute gender do not operate in total isolation from other social relational forms, based, for example, on race or class. In its many materializations, gender tends to feature in the broader context of, and often interlocking with, these other relational forms to produce patterns and regularities with distributional and cultural/symbolic consequences. In endeavouring to understand how and why gender is so deeply imbricated in patterns of inequality (whether in or beyond law), I would agree that it is not possible to generate useful answers without recognizing the ways in which multiple inequalities work through and sometimes against each other to produce unjust outcomes. However, this book is not directly concerned with addressing problems of inequality, although I would hope that my analysis helps to shed light on legal operations which have equality or inequality as a focus. My concern here is with gender as a feature of social ordering, that is, as an expression of a particular relational form—albeit the character and content of which is neither fixed nor static—which is significantly implicated in the shaping and organizing of the social world and, one might surmise, in the conceptual and normative ordering of law. I believe there is value to be had in engaging gender as a discrete category—one which functions fairly meaningfully and effectively in our lives, although not always consistently or coherently—in jurisprudential analysis, including analysis of the more traditional sort. I am also very interested in the processes, practices, and presuppositions which render gender irrelevant in such contexts.

At which point we come back to my central question: where exactly do we locate gender in law? Is it there in the background, operating unseen? If so, why is it invisible and how do we bring it into view? We will see later that there are some contexts in which 'sex', and more recently 'gender', operate as explicit categories in law. However these contexts are relatively rare; indeed, even when legal rules or doctrines are expressly predicated on sexual difference, law only infrequently pauses to consider the content or meaning of sex/gender for legal purposes. More often than not, sex/gender is a taken-for-granted background fact or a wholly unarticulated aspect of legal thought and deliberations. At the same time, a lot of (mainly feminist) attention has been paid to the ways in which law shapes our understanding of gender; gender roles, values, attributes, assumptions, and relations are often argued to be, at least indirectly or partially, the product of legal norms and their discursive or distributive effects. Less attention has been given to how gender acts upon law: how it functions in the context of conferring legal meanings; how it informs the content, organization, and apprehension of law and legal knowledge; and how it serves to legitimate law or reinforce particular legal outcomes. Moreover, identifying the various ways in which gender acts upon and influences law is not the end of the matter. What is most interesting is that it consistently appears *not* to do so. Law and gender, it seems, are simply not comfortable occupying the same space; they make a somewhat odd and incongruous pairing. In what follows, I try to uncover how and why this is so.

1.4 STRUCTURE, ORGANIZATION, AND CENTRAL THESIS

The rest of the book proceeds in a fairly straightforward manner. In Chapter Two I take a close look at two leading English law cases separated by half a century in which gender considerations feature strongly. My purpose here is to illustrate and tease out in a concrete contextual setting many of the themes and issues which will be later explored. At the very least, the analysis should engage the readers and, hopefully, persuade them that the issues raised bear further enquiry. Chapter Three lays out and elaborates upon the primary ways in which the relationship between gender and law has been theorized to date. It is an exercise which is part survey, part critique, bearing in mind the overall aim of advancing understanding of the relation between gender and law. Having explored the field as it currently stands, I then move towards a closer analysis of the operation(s) of gender in law and, more particularly, in legal scholarship. In this context, my analysis is driven by two primary enquiries: first, what is the place of gender in law and second, why does it appear to have little or no place at all? The content and organization of the rest of the book is particularly determined by my efforts to answer the second question. It is based on a tentative thesis, sketched briefly here but elaborated in further detail in subsequent chapters. What I suggest is that in explaining the place of gender in law and, in particular, its seeming categorical irrelevance, attention must be paid to a number of discursive conventions which support and infuse the discipline of law and place gender in a position of apparent exteriority. These conventions are familiar to anyone engaged in legal study or practice. The first relates to the formal exclusion of gender as a category of relevance through the adherence to concepts and doctrines which adopt a gender-neutral form, including but not limited to the concept of legal personhood. This formal exclusion of gender from law tends to operate alongside its informal incorporation and is supported by a historical narrative which emerged in the late 19th and early 20th century, a narrative which presents legal development in terms of unerring progress towards an ideal notion of general abstract rules applied without reference to the particular circumstances (including sex) of individuals or groups, in essence, the rule of law ideal.

The second convention concerns the way in which the field of law is envisaged and its borders maintained. I have already suggested there remains a strong impetus within legal discourse to self-identify as a discrete and autonomous field of discourse, perception, and practice which is distinct from, for example, the domains of the social, political, and cultural. In this way, law is able to maintain what Naffine and others describe as a realm of the 'strictly legal'[50] within which arguments puts forward and positions adopted carry special weight and validity. By contrast, arguments which appear to proceed from outside the realm of the strictly legal have far less, and sometimes no, weight or validity in legal contexts. Many legal judgments bear witness to skirmishes at the borders of the strictly legal and those borders are constantly in a process of renegotiation. In this context, the

---

[50] Naffine, *Law's Meaning of Life*, ch 3.

introduction of gender-explicit arguments or appeals often serves to place an advocatory stance outside the boundaries of the strictly legal. This is in part because of the first convention articulated above. However it is also because law tends to privilege arguments 'from immanence', that is arguments which proceed upon the basis that whatever is being legally contended for is already there. Many legal reconstructive projects successfully adopt this form. However, the seeming incongruity of gender in a legal context, against a historical backdrop in which the only legal precedents for taking account of gender are uncompromisingly patriarchal and legal progress is measured against an ideal standard of gender-neutrality, make it extremely difficult to present gender-explicit arguments which do not appear to invoke 'extra-legal' considerations. To put it another way, gender-based arguments in law are likely to have less weight and validity because they do not fit comfortably into the boundaries of the strictly legal while arguments from immanence can only appeal to a legal interiority which is historically unreceptive to gender other than as an aspect of a patriarchal social and legal order from which law has rightly progressed.

The third discursive convention to which I will refer here is the tendency to view legal argument as a neutral and objective exercise premised upon ideas of rationality. The result is the production of a discursive form which is self-consciously detached from context and adheres excessively to tenets of consistency and coherence. Coherence is understood here in terms of a propensity to relate data, norms, and concepts to one another in an abstract, orderly, and intelligible fashion accompanied by an understandable investment in the support and maintenance of the conceptual structures and classificatory schemes which emerge as a result. Coherence is the process, purpose, and product of legal reasoning, playing a vital role in authenticating and legitimating law and presenting it as an intelligible and unified field. In these ways coherence confers and is testament to the *integrity* of law which in turn helps to support the idea of a realm of the strictly legal.

The argument I advance is not one which necessarily supports the eschewal of coherence as a value to which law should aspire. At the same time, unmitigated investment in the maintenance of

existing categories, classifications, and normative and conceptual
structures generates an inbuilt doctrinal reluctance to adopt new
ideas and frameworks which disturb the underlying legal architecture, an architecture which has emerged from a gendered
legal past and may well serve to import unacknowledged aspects
of that past into the legal present. History leaves its trace not
only on substance but on form and an unreflective adherence to
existing doctrinal categories and structures in the face of challenge may, as some feminist legal scholars have demonstrated,
mask the operation of legal norms that produce problematic
gendered consequences with a troubling degree of regularity.[51]

Chapters Four, Five, and Six set out to tackle these concerns in
a gendered legal context. Although the argument is cumulative,
these chapters, along with Chapters One to Three are framed in
a way which also allows 'dipping in'. The chapters do not have to
be read sequentially to be intelligible. Chapter Four explores the
continued potency of the past in shaping and containing the
operation of gender in law. Chapter Five, building, inter alia, on
the centrality of tradition highlighted in Chapter Four, considers
understandings and conceptualizations of law in the jurisprudential imagination with a view to highlighting both the role of
jurisprudence in the construction of a realm of the strictly legal
and the gendered implications of so doing. Chapter Six follows
through by focusing on the final discursive convention identified
above in the context of a broader survey of the idea of legal
reason and its relation to and implications for the place of gender
in law. The book concludes in Chapter Seven with a brief
traditional summation of the main arguments put forward
throughout, the identification of and reflection upon new
research questions which the analysis might suggest, and a return
to one of the questions posed at the book's outset—why is justice
a woman?—as a way of rounding off the argument, pulling
together some key themes which underpin it, and (I hope)
whetting the reader's appetite for further exploration of what
I suspect is a rich but still relatively untapped field of legal
theoretical endeavour.

---

[51] See eg Chamallas and Wriggins, *The Measure of Injury*.

2

A TALE OF TWO CASES

2.1 INTRODUCTION: MY RUDE AWAKENING

In the winter of 1949, in the wake of a horrible accident to her husband at work, Julia Best brought an action against his employers, Samuel Fox & Co Ltd, for interference with her right to her husband's consortium. Mr Best, who had already succeeded in a negligence action, had been rendered sexually impotent by the accident. As a consequence, Mrs Best, at the tender age of twenty-five, unsurprisingly felt severely aggrieved and afflicted: normal marital relations had been permanently impaired, as had any opportunity to have children in the future.

It is interesting to speculate upon what prompted Mrs Best to bring such an action. While a husband's action for loss of his wife's consortium was well established, indeed could be traced back to medieval times, no corresponding claim had yet been recognized as vested in a wife. Did she perhaps benefit from the advice of a forward-looking lawyer or was she herself the person who decided to launch the claim? Of course we do not know. What we do know is that Julia Best's claim was a resounding failure; it was rejected at the court of first instance, again on appeal and, eventually, in the House of Lords.[1] As a consequence, the formal inequality between women and men with regard to the right of access to a loss of consortium claim continued in the UK until the action was abolished by the Administration of Justice Act 1982, just at the point when I first encountered it in my own legal studies.

Best v Fox is now rarely read by law students. I imagine I was one of the last generation for whom it was prescribed as necessary reading in tort law. However, I still recall the simultaneous excitement and disappointment I felt when I first came across it

---

[1] *Best v Fox* [1951] 2 KB 639 (CA); *Best v Fox* [1952] AC 716 (HL).

while studying the law of negligence. I had by then spent a good deal of my study time scouring the cases I was obliged to read in hopeful anticipation that among the stories (or 'facts' as I had learned to regard them) I would find some female protagonists with whom I could relate, empathize, or otherwise identify as having had an influence upon the resolutely male world into which I had strayed. Of course I read *Best v Fox* as a brave attempt by the female plaintiff to invoke legal rationality on behalf of women and was dismayed to find the views of their Lordships pointing so strongly in a different direction. At the time I imagine that my emotionally infused reaction to the gender dimension in *Best* did not find particular favour with my tutor. As Otto Kahn-Freund, commenting almost contemporaneously with the *Best* decision though in a broader legal context observes:

> Emotional abhorrence of a legal principle . . . carries us nowhere. We must see how it originated, on what argument it was based, whether anything can be done to change the law without legislation and, if not, on what lines legislation might possibly be developed.[2]

Looking back now with the practised eye of legal scholar of some experience, and endeavouring to apply Kahn-Freund's exhortation, it is not difficult to tease out the doctrinal uncertainties bubbling beneath the surface of the judgments in *Best* to yield the kinds of arguments which might, had they been sympathetically received, have secured a different result. Interestingly, the House of Lords judgments are relatively short and fairly unanimous in concluding that as the action for loss of consortium was no longer consistent with 'modern' understandings of the marital relation, it made little sense to extend it further and certainly not without the intervention of Parliament.[3] The Court of Appeal decision is longer, the arguments more doctrinally complex and there is somewhat less unanimity

---

[2] O Kahn-Freund, 'Inconsistencies and Injustices in the Law of Husband and Wife Part II' (1953) 16 *MLR* 34, 35; see also (1952) 15 *MLR* 133 (Part 1) and (1953) 16 *MLR* 148 (Part III).

[3] *Best v Fox* (HL), 728 per L Porter, 733 per L Goddard, and 735 per L Morton.

between the judges. Although all three judges agree that Mrs Best should not succeed, the decision appears to turn primarily on the doctrinally dubious principle that an action can only lie where the loss of consortium is total, not just partial or subject to interference. While the defendant's negligence had deprived Mrs Best of full sexual relations with her husband (and thereby, as Lord Asquith concedes, the 'capacity to bear children in wedlock'), other aspects of consortium—'companionship, love, affection, comfort, mutual service'—remained intact.[4] Upon this slender distinction, the legal authority for which, as we shall see, appears thin,[5] was the case disposed of by the Court of Appeal.

Reading *Best v Fox*, one is struck by the fact that no fewer than nine judges united in opposing what effectively amounted to an application for the extension of formal equality to women with respect to the consortium action. Yet at no time did the courts appear to endorse anything other the principle that women were and ought to be equal before the law. Here we have a plainly unequal outcome sitting comfortably alongside repeated judicial affirmations of the principle of gender equality and unequivocal expressions of disapproval with respect to the historically subordinate position of women. How such a remarkable outcome is achieved is just one of the questions this chapter will explore. By engaging in a close analysis of the reasoning deployed I hope to throw some light on how gender features in law and particularly in judicial reasoning. In so doing, I want to consider *Best* alongside another House of Lords case decided fifty years later. In *R v R*,[6] the House of Lords took the momentous step of recognizing the possibility of rape in marriage notwithstanding apparent legislative and doctrinal authority to the contrary. Immediate points of comparison spring to mind: both cases must attempt to cope with the legal implications of substantial and wide-ranging changes in women's social status and role; both confront the historical legacy of women's subordination; and each faces squarely the dilemma of whether

[4] *Best v Fox* [(CA), 669 per Asquith LJ; see also 533 per Birkett LJ.
[5] See eg 'Note: *Best v Fox*' (1952) 11(2) *CLJ* 299 and E Todd, 'Reflections on *Best v Fox*' (1952) 15(2) *MLR* 246.
[6] [1992] 1 AC 599 (CA and HL).

to intervene judicially to right a perceived wrong or to invite legislative action, coming to diverging conclusions on this point. There are also clear points of contrast. *R v R* is not so easily framed as an issue of formal equality, although equality is certainly a concern, at least implicitly. One might also speculate that more is at stake: the practical consequences of *R v R* for men and women are surely greater than those of *Best*. This in itself might be enough to explain why the judges felt compelled to act in one case and not in the other. And of course more time has passed; it was perhaps more difficult for the judges in *R v R* to resist the tide of social change around gender relations than their predecessors nearly half a century earlier.

In any event, let us take a considered look at both cases in the context of the broader set of issues which animate this enquiry.

2.2 MRS BEST'S MISFORTUNE

It is perhaps worth saying a little about the social and legal background to *Best*. The facts of the case took place just after the Second World War. Mr Best's accident occurred in 1946, which was a time when men were returning to full-time employment, often ousting working women who had kept industry going during wartime. The period also witnessed the final consolidation of the British welfare state, including the creation of a National Health Service and the official promulgation of a 'cradle to grave' conception of social insurance. In the legal arena, the decade before the war had witnessed the beginning of the development of the modern law of negligence, triggered by the decision in *Donoghue v Stevenson*.[7] This was followed by legislative reform of various aspects of tort law during the 1930s and 1940s.[8] Indeed, one might be tempted to view the period as a time of tort modernization. Clearly too, it was a time of change for women but equally of challenge. While considerable gains had been made in women's legal and social status during the inter-war years, and while the war itself

---

[7] [1932] AC 562 (HL).

[8] See eg, the Law Reform (Married Women and Tortfeasors) Act 1935 and the Law Reform (Contributory Negligence) Act 1945.

had provided women with further opportunities to enter and succeed in a male world by filling the employment gap left by fighting men, the end of war and the adoption of a male breadwinner family model to undergird the new welfare state (in which social insurance was premised upon a family norm consisting of a husband engaged in paid work and a wife who stayed at home to look after children), heralded new risks and uncertainties in terms of progress towards gender equality.

The consortium claim was part of a family of civil actions collectively known as the domestic torts.[9] Together these actions provided the patriarchal head of the family with a considerable legal arsenal with which to 'protect' those under his guardianship and care. Thus, a husband could seek damages from another for enticing his wife to leave him.[10] Derived from an ancient writ of ravishment, the action for enticement was abolished in England and Wales in 1970.[11] Similarly a husband could sue anyone who harboured his wife without lawful justification. To 'harbour' a wife was to give her shelter after a demand by her husband to deliver her up. Devlin J described the object of the action as 'submission by starvation':[12] deprived of shelter elsewhere, a wife would be forced to return to her husband's protective arms.

Of particular interest to scandalmongers and popular broadsheets was the antiquated action for criminal conversation known colloquially as 'crim-con'. This conferred a right on the husband to sue where his wife had engaged in adultery with another, although the action was against the adulterous third party and not against the wife herself.[13] In part this was because, until at least the late 19th century, a wife could not sue

[9] See generally R F V Heuston and R Buckley, *Salmond and Heuston on the Law of Torts*, 21st edn (Sweet & Maxwell 1996), ch 15.

[10] eg *Place v Searle* [1932] 2 KB 497 (CA).

[11] Law Reform (Miscellaneous Provisions) Act 1970, s 5.

[12] *Winchester v Fleming* [1958] 1 QB 259, 266; see also *Salmond and Heuston on Torts*, 349.

[13] eg *Norfolk (Duke of) v Germaine* (1692) State Trials 929. The old action for criminal conversation was abolished in 1857. Thereafter, the right to claim damages for adultery could still be made by way of petition in matrimonial proceedings until its final abrogation in the Law Reform (Miscellaneous Provisions) Act 1970, s 4.

or be sued in her own right, her legal personhood being absorbed in that of her husband through the common law doctrine of coverture.[14] Lord Melbourne was notoriously subject to a criminal conversation suit in 1836 while he was a serving Prime Minister although the action eventually failed.[15] Finally, the action *per quod consortium amisit* or *servitium amisit*, the action invoked in *Best*, allowed a husband to sue another if, by virtue of a tort committed against his wife, he was deprived of her society and/or services.[16] The action, which was available for negligent as well as intentional interferences, originally arose under the writ of trespass but eventually could be made by way of case stated.

Because these actions were presumed to derive from the common law assumption that a wife's person and, in particular, her services were part of her husband's property, no corresponding right was vested in the wife—and of course during the period when the actions were most utilized she lacked the legal standing to sue in any event. However, after the passing of the Married Women's Property Acts in the 1870s and 1880s, women did begin to test the legal waters with respect to the domestic torts. In particular, by the 1930s a line of authority had developed recognizing the possibility of a claim of enticement by a wife.[17]

It is against this background, social and legal, that Mrs Best launched her claim, relying on a cause of action which could hardly have been typical fare for her solicitors, WH Thompson (now Thompson solicitors), a Yorkshire firm specializing in industrial injury claims. Mrs Best's case was first heard at Leeds Assizes by Croom-Johnson J who, according to the headnote preceding the Court of Appeal report, denied the claim on the ground that 'the plaintiff had failed to show a total loss of her

---

[14] See generally, W Blackstone, *Commentaries on the Law of England in four volumes*, 15th edn (London: A Strahan, 1809), Vol 1, ch xv.

[15] For further details, see Chapter Four.

[16] eg *Hambrook v Stokes* [1925] 1 KB 141.

[17] See eg *Gray v Gee* [1923] 39 TLR 429; *Newton v Hardy* [1933] All ER 40 (HC). An action by a wife for the harbouring of her husband was denied in *Winchester v Fleming*, decided some years after *Best*.

consortium'.[18] A contemporaneous case note[19] offers a slightly different account, suggesting that Croom-Johnson J's decision was based at least in part on a finding that no duty of care arose because the defendant neither knew of Mrs Best's existence nor intended her harm. The circumstances were therefore distinguishable from those characterizing the enticement cases in which a wife's cause of action against a third party for enticing her husband away from her had been legally recognized.

2.2.1 BEST v FOX: COURT OF APPEAL

On appeal, counsel for Mrs Best argued that pre-existing authority supported a wife's right to the consortium of her husband. Counsel relied upon two related lines of case law: first, on the group of fairly recent cases culminating in judicial recognition of a wife's claim to sue for enticement; and second, on a 19th-century authority, *Lynch v Knight*, in which the majority of judges who heard the case took the view that an action by a wife for loss of consortium could lie in the circumstances alleged.[20] Taken together, they appeared to offer not inconsiderable authority in support of Mrs Best's claim.[21] By contrast, counsel for Fox & Co sought to tie the consortium action as tightly as possible to a historical conception of the marital relationship in terms of a husband's proprietary interest in the *servitium* (services) of his wife. This, it was argued, was the true basis of the consortium action and was necessarily

[18] *Best v Fox* [1951] 2 KB 639 (CA).

[19] 'Note: *Best v Fox*', 117.

[20] *Lynch v Knight* (1861) 9 HLC 577 (HL). A wife brought an action for loss of consortium after she was cast aside by her husband because of slanderous remarks about her virtue made by a third party. The wife's action was upheld by the Irish Exchequer Chamber but rejected by the House of Lords on the ground that the damages were too remote.

[21] See also *Place v Searle*, which, although an action for enticement brought by the husband, included judicial dicta recognizing the right of a wife to her husband's consortium, eg 'It seems to be clear that at the present day a husband has a right to the consortium of his wife, and the wife to the consortium of her husband, and that each has a cause of action against a third party who, without justification, destroys that consortium' (per Scruton LJ at 513).

non-reciprocal as a wife had no corresponding interest in her husband's services. While acknowledging that such a conception did not gel with modern social attitudes, the respondent maintained that changes of public opinion with regard to a wife's status 'cannot give her a right which she never had'.[22] In this way, respondent's counsel signalled the novelty of the appellant's claim against a doctrinal background which suddenly looked a lot less sympathetic. The respondent also pushed the argument that had found favour with the court at first instance, namely that an action for loss of consortium—even at the suit of the husband—can only lie where the loss alleged is total and not merely interfered with or impaired. In what hindsight reveals to be a grave strategic error, counsel for the appellant gave little attention to this argument, no doubt because the authorities did not really support it.

Lack of authority notwithstanding, two of the three Court of Appeal judges endorsed this approach in rejecting Mrs Best's appeal. In the absence of case law, Birkett LJ deploys a form of consequentialist reasoning which warns against the perils of a position other than the one he wishes to adopt: 'if consortium is capable of separation into many and extremely diverse elements, so that the impairment of any element, however, slight, will give a cause of action, then the prospects are overwhelming'.[23] It is difficult to know quite what to make of this argument. It hints at a concern that the net of liability may be cast too wide to include all sorts of minor rights infringements; but there is also a sense in which Birkett LJ is simply uncomfortable with a conception of consortium which is divisible and, in particular, which invites the courts to pry into the intimate sexual details of married life.[24] Asquith LJ is also clearly exercised about the consequences of recognizing a claim for partial rather than total loss of consortium

[22] *Best v Fox* (CA), 650.

[23] *Best v Fox* (CA), 665.

[24] The view that the sexual relations should not be scrutinized in the courts clearly informs the case although it is never explicitly articulated except by respondent's counsel in the House of Lords: 'the court will not hold an inquiry into the sexual relations of husband and wife save in proceedings for nullity of marriage or in respect of cruelty . . .' *Best v Fox* (HL), 721.

arguing that 'disengag[ing] a particular strand in the consortial bond . . . finds no support in the precedents and leads to insoluble problems in practice'.[25] He illustrates his concerns by appealing to hyperbole:

Is a wife to be entitled to sue her husband's employer because through his negligence her husband has been lamed, and hence that element of their consortium which consisted in long country walks which they used to share has perished?[26]

Pronouncing 'extreme perplexity and complication'[27] to be the probable result of conceiving of consortium as anything other than a unified abstraction, Asquith LJ thus relies upon a practical, common sense approach to the resolution of Mrs Best's claim.

Only one of the three Court of Appeal judges is not prepared openly to align himself with the contention that an action for loss of consortium can only lie where the loss is total. Cohen LJ is careful to avoid the issue, preferring instead to base his decision on the 'anomalous' nature of the husband's consortium right and the undesirability, therefore, of further extending it. In reaching this conclusion Cohen LJ is influenced by the respondents' efforts to tie the action to a medieval conception of a wife's services as a husband's property. While acknowledging that this view of the position of a wife is now 'entirely obsolete',[28] the historical basis of consortium in the notion of *servitium*, he argues, precludes recognition of a similar claim in the wife.

Notwithstanding the unanimity of outcome, there is an interesting divergence of opinion in the Court of Appeal on the question of whether it is in the power of the courts to bring the law into line with the principle of gender equality or whether that task should fall to Parliament. Birkett LJ, who, as we have seen, denies the wife's claim because her loss of consortium is not total, has no apparent hesitation (albeit *obiter*) in recognizing in principle a wife's claim in the same circumstances as a husband:

---

[25] *Best v Fox* (CA), 669.   [26] *Best v Fox* (CA), 669.
[27] *Best v Fox* (CA), 670.   [28] *Best v Fox* (CA), 666.

... So long as the husband is given the cause of action, I cannot see any good reason why the wife should be deprived of it. I am of the opinion, therefore, that today the rights of husband and wife in the consortium are fully mutual and *completely equal, before the law,* and the wife is entitled to bring an action when she has been deprived of her consortium by the negligent act of a third person (my italics).[29]

By contrast, Asquith LJ adopts a more conservative view, drawing upon case law in the United States where the vast majority of states had rejected claims to extend the right of consortium to a wife in the context of negligent injury to her husband.[30] This allows him to underscore the novelty of Mrs Best's claim and the need for a considered legislative approach: '... The husband's right being deeply entrenched in authority and the wife's never having been affirmed, I think the intervention of the legislature would be needed to produce equality ...'.[31]

At which point Mrs Best turned her sights to the House of Lords.

2.2.2 *BEST v FOX:* HOUSE OF LORDS

In the House of Lords, Mrs Best's counsel introduced an interesting new argument. Insisting that either party to a marriage had a right of action for loss of consortium and citing no less than seventeen cases in support (the earliest dating to 1618), Pritt QC contended that the reason for the relative rarity of consortium actions initiated by wives was not because a wife did not have such a right in substance but rather that procedurally, until the Married Women's Property Act 1882, she was precluded from bringing a legal action without joining her husband as plaintiff. Pritt QC also sought to draw a distinction between *consortium* and *servitium,* both in an effort to free the action from any necessary association with 'services' and to make it easier to defend a claim for partial loss or impairment. On this latter

---

[29] *Best v Fox* (CA), 664.
[30] The exception being the state of New York which had only very recently recognized a wife's consortium action in *Hitaffer v Argonne Co* 183 F 2d 811 (1950).
[31] *Best v Fox* (CA), 669.

point Mrs Best's counsel were unequivocal: 'since a husband can recover for partial loss of consortium there is no reason why a wife should not be able to do so to'.[32] This was supported by an extensive and etymologically-inflected trawl of the relevant case law by Pritt's junior in which it was also suggested that the *servitium* element in a husband's claim was quite a recent invention.[33] In summing up, counsel called upon the evolutionary nature of the common law tradition to support a favourable outcome for Mrs Best, asserting: 'Ours is a living law, adapting itself to the needs of our times'.[34]

The respondent's counsel also shifted their argument slightly, conceding, on the strength of the enticement cases, that a wife did have a right to sue where the loss of her husband's consortium was knowingly and deliberately inflicted. However, Paull QC continued, because a wife's right to consortium, unlike a husband's, was not based on any proprietary interest, an action for damages could not lie where the loss was not deliberate.[35] In any event, consortium was indivisible and no action lay for its impairment. It was a relation in the nature of a partnership and only the dissolution of the partnership would result in a loss of consortium. The overall thrust of counsel's argument here was to show that 'the rights and obligations of husband and wife are, and always have been, essentially different'.[36] Thus, while a husband was under an obligation to support his wife, no corresponding obligation was vested in the wife. By appealing to a logic of 'equal but different', respondent's counsel were able to support a view of the rights and obligations within the marital relation as non-reciprocal without adopting a stance which was blatantly anti-egalitarian.

---

[32] *Best v Fox* [1952] AC 716 (HL), 719.

[33] See eg *Brockbank v Whitehaven Junction Railway Co* (1862) 7 H & N 834 cited to support the argument that *servitium* was traditionally an aspect of the master/servant relationship which had been imported into the marital relationship at a fairly late stage.

[34] *Best v Fox* (HL), 725.

[35] Paull QC explained the enticement cases in terms of analogy with *Lumley v Gye* (1853) 2 El & Bl 216 in which a tortious action for deliberately inducing a breach of a contract was first recognized.

[36] *Best v Fox* (HL), 724.

All five law lords agreed that Mrs Best's appeal should be dismissed. However, the approach taken differs from the Court of Appeal in that the emphasis is not on the indivisibility of consortium and the inability to bring a claim for partial as opposed to total loss, but rather on the anomalous nature of the action in a modern social context and the imprudence, therefore, of further extending it.[37] On the former point, none of their Lordships unequivocally endorse the Court of Appeal approach and at least one, Lord Reid, is quite adamant that a claim *could* lie where the loss is less than complete: 'I do not think it open to doubt that an impairment of the wife's capacity to render assistance to her husband was enough to found a cause of action'.[38] Lord Reid is also dismissive of the notion that consortium should be viewed as a unified abstraction which cannot be broken down into particular elements, including the ability to engage in sexual relations. By contrast, Lord Goddard declares himself to be in agreement with the Court of Appeal in viewing consortium as an abstraction which is mainly if not exclusively concerned with *servitium*, expressing doubt as to whether interference with sexual relations without more is even within the scope of the action. He observes:

Sexual relations are doubtless a most important part of the marital relation but if age or illness of even disinclination impairs the potency of either of the spouses who continue to live together as husband and wife, I do not think the consortium is affected. It would only be if on this account one of them withdrew and decided to live apart.[39]

Once again here a judicial distaste for subjecting the most intimate aspects of marriage to legal scrutiny is revealed.

Steering the case away from the murky waters of damaged sexual relations and dubious doctrinal principle, their Lordships prefer to determine the matter by relying on the tried and tested practice of exercising judicial restraint. Mrs Best's claim, they maintain, is novel and unprecedented; is founded upon an action the basis of which is quite out of line with modern

[37] See *Best v Fox* (HL), 728 per L Porter and 731–2 per L Goddard.
[38] *Best v Fox* (HL), 736.
[39] *Best v Fox* (HL), 733–44.

sensibilities; and which, consequently, is best left to Parliament to sort out. The novelty of the claim is established by drawing a clear line between loss of consortium resulting from knowing and wilful interference with the plaintiff's rights and loss resulting from negligence. The enticement cases, they argue, fall into one category; Mrs Best's claim into another (although why the wife's claim is confined to wilful harm while the husband's is not is never really explained other than in terms of the absence of principle or authority). Their Lordships find support for their position in a decision of the Australian High Court, *Wright v Cedzich*,[40] in which a wife's action for loss of consortium resulting from negligence was denied. Thus, by invoking a distinction between negligent and intentional harm, their Lordships are able confidently to dismiss the relevance of the vast bank of authorities in support of the claim assembled by Mrs Best's counsel.

Reframing the claim effectively as negligence, or more specifically, as occupier's liability because the original accident suffered by Mr Best occurred on premises controlled by the respondent,[41] their Lordships are also able to deny the claim on the grounds that no duty of care arises. This approach is adopted both by Lord Goddard and Lord Morton. Lord Goddard emphasizes the lack of proximity between Mrs Best and her husband's employer and the employer's lack of knowledge of her (and therefore of foresight of harm). He analogizes the wife's position with that of a servant, pointing out that if a master is killed by another's negligence, a servant has no claim against the tortfeasor even if he suffers loss as a result in the form of loss of employment.[42] Lord Morton identifies the respondent, Fox & Co, as an invitor (using the pre-statutory terminology governing occupiers' liability) asserting a total absence of support for liability of an invitor in such circumstances: 'It has never been the law

---

[40] *Wright v Cedzich* (1930) 43 CLR 493 although in *Best v Fox* (HL), 727, L Porter acknowledges the 'vigorous opposition' of Isaac J in *Wright*.

[41] At that time, occupiers' liability was governed solely by common law and therefore more closely aligned doctrinally with negligence. Legislative reform did not occur until later in the decade (Occupier's Liability Act 1957).

[42] *Best v Fox* (HL), 731.

of England that an invitor, who has negligently but unintentionally injured an invitee, is liable to compensate other persons who have suffered'.[43] This is probably not quite true, as presumably a husband would have a claim against an invitor who negligently injured his wife in such circumstances. Certainly neither of their Lordships seems concerned that a claim is vested in a husband here, lack of duty notwithstanding.

The novelty of the case is further underscored by according particular weight to the passing of time. While the husband's claim is 'firmly established',[44] 'founded on old authorities',[45] and 'too late to deny,'[46] the claim of a wife is said to be based on 'the circumstances prevailing today',[47] and to be a product of social change inviting corresponding change in the common law. In this way, the issue is presented in terms of a pre-existing legal state which persists until law decides to give way to public opinion. But *ought* law always to give way and in what circumstances? Lord Porter is doubtful that the case for legal change has been established here:

I do not think it possible to say that a change in the outlook of the public, however great, must inevitably be followed by a change in the law.... The common law is a historical development rather than a logical whole, and the fact that a particular doctrine does not logically accord with another ... is no ground for its rejection.[48]

Lord Goddard says something similar, acknowledging that the husband's right is anomalous, but at the same time observing that 'English law is free neither of some anomalies nor of everything illogical, but this is no reason for extending them'.[49] The narrative here is essentially one of tradition trumping rationality (albeit regretfully). It is ironically the very adaptability of the common law in the context of social change which supports this argument. Because law is a process of historical development and *not* a purely rational construction, pockets of

---

[43] *Best v Fox* (HL), 734–5.   [44] *Best v Fox* (HL), 735 per L Morton.
[45] *Best v Fox* (HL), 735 per L Morton.
[46] *Best v Fox* (HL), 733 per L Goddard.
[47] *Best v Fox* (HL), 727 per L Porter.
[48] *Best v Fox* (HL), 727.   [49] *Best v Fox* (HL), 733.

illogicality are as foreseeable as they are inevitable. Therefore 'the fact that a particular doctrine does not logically accord with another or others is no ground for its rejection'.[50]

Time serves both to expose the anomaly of the husband's action and endorse it. Time also allows their Lordships to confirm the origins of the action in a husband's proprietary interest in his wife's services. Thus Lord Morton describes the husband's claim as 'exceptional', an 'anomaly at the present day', and as 'founded on old authorities decided at a time when the husband was regarded as having a quasi-proprietary right in his wife'.[51] Lord Goddard observes that the 'highest' legal authorities (for example, Bracton, Blackstone, and Holdsworth) confirm that the action 'is founded on the proprietary right which from ancient times it was considered the husband had in the wife', going on to explain that the action is based on the same grounds giving a master a right to sue for injury to his servant.[52] In Lord Goddard's view, the weight of authority in support of a position which—it is fully acknowledged—is quite out of keeping with modern times is such that the actions of Parliament and nothing else are required to put matters right.[53] In other words, their Lordships' hands are sadly tied.[54]

There is a final dimension to their Lordships' reasoning here which bears attention. Underpinning at least some of the judgments is an unarticulated belief in a certain natural order with respect to relations between husbands and wives in which the husband is the master and financial provider and the wife is his helpmate, effectively his servant. This comes out particularly in the arguments of Lord Goddard in which, as we have seen, the relationship between is husband and wife is expressly analogized with that of master and servant. However, it is also manifest in more subtle ways. For example, Lord Porter, in passing, observes that the damages a husband receives for loss of his wife's consortium correspond with the expenses he incurs, usually the costs of medical treatment and any costs associated with replacing his

---

[50] *Best v Fox* (HL), 727 per L Porter.   [51] *Best v Fox* (HL), 735.
[52] *Best v Fox* (HL), 731–2.
[53] *Best v Fox* (HL), 733 per L Goddard and 735 per L Morton.
[54] See eg *Best v Fox* (HL), 728 per L Porter.

wife's domestic services while she is injured. As, he continues, such expenses fall upon a husband and not a wife (who is, after all, financially dependent on her husband) 'it is *natural* that he should recover and she should not'.[55] Lord Goddard also articulates this view:

> There is this about it that is neither anomalous nor illogical, *still less unjust*; a husband nowadays constantly claims and recovers for medical and domestic expenses to which he has been put owing to injury to his wife.... I think his claim really lies in his legal obligation to provide proper maintenance and comfort, including medical and surgical aid, for his wife.[56]

Both Lord Porter and Lord Goddard take for granted a particular gender division of labour while depicting the marital relation as one in which different obligations are owed by either party. The 'natural' asymmetry of the marital relationship means that no real injustice is done in denying Mrs Best's claim. Of course, it is true that her claim is not primarily for medical expenses but for the distress and suffering she experienced as a result of the loss of sexual relations with her husband and the loss of the opportunity to bear children in the future. However, these kinds of harm, Lord Goddard suggests, should not really concern the law: 'it is to the protection of such material interests [ie the financial costs incurred by a husband when his wife suffers injury] that the law attends rather than mental pain or anxiety [the harm suffered by the wife]'.[57]

Thus was the tragedy which had beset young Mrs Best dismissed by their Lordships as not within the purview of legal redress.

2.2.3 SITUATING GENDER

How should we understand the role of gender in *Best v Fox*? Is it relevant to the decision-making process? In one sense, of course,

---

[55] *Best v Fox* (HL), 728 (emphasis added).

[56] *Best v Fox* (HL), 733 (emphasis added).

[57] *Best v Fox* (HL), 733; L Goddard cites L Wensleydale in *Lynch v Knight* in support of this point.

gender is central. This is a case in which a woman challenges the inequality of law on its face, taking on centuries of patriarchal tradition in support of women's right to equal protection under the law. In another sense though, in a formal doctrinal sense, gender is barely relevant to the decision at all. Neither the term 'gender' nor 'sex' appears anywhere in the judicial reasoning. Moreover, in determining the legal outcome, the courts take no formal account of the gender inequality they confront. Obviously the judges did not apprehend gender equality as a principle of law. *Best v Fox* predates sex discrimination law, European equality law, and the institutionalization of human rights and at the time *Best* was decided the European Convention of Human Rights was still in a process of becoming.[58] While the 1948 United Nations Declaration of Human Rights predates the litigation and includes reference to sex equality in Article 2 and the right to equal recognition under the law in Article 6, this instrument had only moral not legal effect. Nor had a body of jurisprudence, international or domestic, yet emerged around sex equality. The Convention on the Elimination of All Forms of Discrimination against Women (CEDAW) was not adopted by the UN General Assembly until 1979. One can detect no consciousness of human rights or international obligations within the legal deliberations and while reference is made to some overseas case law—from Australia and the United States—this is very much within the contours of doctrinal practice in which the decisions of higher courts in other common law countries may have persuasive value but are in no sense binding on British courts.

Gender itself is clearly a category of practical relevance in determining the scope of the consortium claim in that it informs the legal conceptualization of husband and wife and the marital relationship. However, the legal constitutive role of gender here is not acknowledged as such. While all of the judges clearly understand the marital relation in terms of a formal legal union between a man and a woman, this is assumed to be beyond

---

[58] The Convention was drafted by the Council of Europe (of which Britain was a founding member) in 1950 and came into force in 1953. Britain allowed the referral of cases to the European Commission of Human Rights from 1966.

contestation or the need for supporting legal authority. *Best v Fox* thus embodies a particular juridic conception of family relations which is historically specific and socially and culturally inflected. Moreover, it is a conception which privileges the attitudes and beliefs of those in a position to inject their particular knowledge and experience into the veins of the common law. This knowledge and experience is neither presented nor understood as situational. Rather it is assumed to be wholly uninfluenced by the position of the knower, an objective representation of the empirical world which law is called upon to regulate and govern.

This reliance upon an objective social reality exterior to law allows the judges to acknowledge and call upon gender without conceding its legal status or conceptual relevance. Gender occupies the sphere of the social upon which law acts but from which it is presumed to be formally detached. The narrative which emerges is one of social change and legal adaptation in which the patriarchal premises of the consortium action are acknowledged by all, as is the present day unacceptability of conceiving a wife's services to be part of a husband's property. The discursive underpinning of legal argumentation is generally one of slow and steady social progress towards equality between men and women, peppered with approving references to reforming legal enactments such as the Married Women's Property Acts. Yet, at the same time, as we have seen, the judges reveal themselves as holding views about marital relations and gender roles which belie their rhetorical gestures towards formal gender equality. This is particularly evident in the judgments of Lords Porter and Goddard, who clearly viewed marriage as an asymmetric partnership in which the different roles and responsibilities are both sexually determined and naturally occurring. It is clear too that within this partnership or 'semi-contract', that one party is considered superior to and master of the other. This is evidenced by the frequent judicial analogizing of the husband and wife relationship in terms of master and servant.

Within this implicitly hierarchal framing of the marital relation there also emerges a private realm which is seen as not properly subject to legal interference. The sphere of sexual relations in particular is regarded as beyond legal reach. Sex between a man and wife (or the lack thereof) is considered non-justiciable as are other 'non-material' aspects of this peculiar partnership. The unarticulated invocation of a public/private divide serves not only to protect the most intimate aspects of the marital relation from the probing scrutiny of law; it also contributes to the creation of a hierarchy of harms in which material and financial harm attract far greater legal attention than emotional and psychological damage. As a result, both the nature and extent of harm suffered by Mrs Best were lost from judicial view; and the law was revealed to offer no form of redress to a young woman in her prime who through another's negligence faced a sexually unfulfilled future with no practical prospects—bearing in mind the social and technological realities of the time—of having (further) children. Indeed, it is striking that at no point in the judgments is it made clear whether the Bests already had any children. It is possible they did not, as the accident to Mr Best occurred in 1946, presumably just after his return from the war. In any event, the inability to have children, while attracting the sympathy of the judges, was nowhere conceived in terms of actionable harm.

All of this suggests that the role of gender in the decision-making process, while clearly significant, is not easily unravelled or articulated, certainly not within the contours of existing doctrinal conventions. Indeed there is something much more subtle and covert going on. At the very least, judicial perceptions of men and women in terms of difference and complementarity allowed the judges to feel more comfortable about the justice of their final decision. Yet this process of taking gender into account is all but hidden behind a doctrinal form in which it appears quite extraneous. Through a series of distinctions, between total and partial loss, negligent and intentional harm, material and non-material injury, the wife's claim to equality is rendered more and more remote from the core of legal authority she has called upon in support. As a consequence, her position becomes that of petitioning the court to extend the doctrinal scope beyond what is deemed to be the current position; Mrs Best was not arguing what the law *is* but rather what it *ought* to be; the is/ought distinction worked here to relocate her arguments outside the sphere of law proper. This position is made explicit by Asquith LJ in the Court of Appeal who observes 'I do not believe that at present the wife has such a cause of action as is claimed. Whether she ought to is, of course, quite another question'.[59] A position of exteriority is aided by yet a further distinction—between law and 'public opinion'—once again conjuring up a sharp divide between the legal and social spheres. This artificial distinction disguises the fact that law is replete with concepts and categorizations which are as deeply imbricated in the social as the legal. Indeed, it is by treating the social and ideological content of categories such as 'husband' and 'wife' as legally fixed and beyond interrogation that the judges are able to import—albeit largely unconsciously—a particular gendered ideological conception of the marital relation (in terms of hierarchically ordered complementarity) into the legal argument.

2.3 OF FICTIONS AND FUDGES

The deliberations in *Best v Fox* necessitated legal consideration of gendered ideas and attitudes which, while enshrined in law for many centuries, were increasingly out of line with modern social practices and sensibilities. Yet, one of the most striking features of *Best* is how the legal argumentation compelled the adoption and promulgation of those very same ideas and attitudes by at least some of the participants in the litigation process. Repackaging the ideological remnants of the past as legal authority becomes a way in which ancient and outmoded ideas continue to exercise a grip on present realities, in this context on the family life and future plans of Mr and Mrs Best.

Indeed, even as the 20th century was drawing to a close, misogynistic echoes of the past still rebounded on the walls of English courtrooms, this time in the pronouncements of Sir Matthew Hale, a 17th-century English jurist and author of the posthumously published *The History of the Pleas of the Crown*. Widely regarded as one of the founding fathers of common law thinking, Hale also enjoys the dubious privilege of contributing to the development of rape law in ways which have blighted the lives of women for over 300 years. It is Hale who is credited

---

[59] *Best v Fox* (CA), 669.

with the infamous assertion that '[rape] is an accusation easily to be made and hard to be proved, and harder to be defended by the party accused, tho never so innocent',[60] forming the doctrinal foundation of the corroboration rule governing sexual offences in many common law jurisdictions.[61] Perhaps even more significant are Hale's remarks about rape within marriage:

But the husband cannot be guilty of rape committed by himself upon his lawful wife, for by their mutual matrimonial consent and contract the wife hath given up herself in this kind unto her husband *which she cannot retract.*[62]

Remarkably, when the House of Lords, for the first and final time, came to consider the marital rape exemption in 1992, they found little authority before Hale in support of this principle. An exemption which had long been taken for granted across the common law world was thus discovered to rest upon pretty insubstantial foundations. How it prevailed for so long and was so little contested is perhaps as intriguing a question as why, after so many years and without clear evidence of legislative consensus, their Lordships finally decided to act, although it is the latter question which forms the focus of the enquiry here.

Again, before examining the arguments in *R v R*,[63] it is useful to set the scene more broadly. During the course of the 1970s and 1980s violence against women became of increasing social and political concern in many Western jurisdictions. This was largely a result of the efforts of women's organizations, supported by feminist-informed research, revealing a level of violence and abuse—including against wives—which could no longer safely be ignored by policy-makers.[64] Rape was at the

---

[60] M Hale, *Historia Placitoruma Coranae: Vol I* (first published 1736, Sollom Emlyn 1800), 634 ('*The History of the Pleas of the Crown*').

[61] In England and Wales, the corroboration requirement was abolished in the Criminal Justice and Public Order Act 1994.

[62] Hale, *History of the Pleas of the Crown*, 628 (emphasis added).

[63] *R v R* [1992] 1 AC 599 (CA and HL).

[64] Influential studies included R Dobash and R Dobash, *Violence Against Wives* (NY: Free Press, 1983); D Russell, *Sexual Exploitation: Rape, Child Sexual Abuse and Workplace Harassment* (California: Sage, 1984); and D Russell, *Rape in Marriage*, 2nd edn (Bloomington: Indiana University Press, 1990).

forefront of these attentions, particularly the investigation of rape and the treatment of rape victims within the criminal justice system.[65] In a number of countries, including Canada, Australia and various US states, the legal rules governing sexual offences underwent significant statutory reform.

In England in the mid-1970s, the decision in *DPP v Morgan*,[66] in which the House of Lords held that a man who honestly but unreasonably believed that a woman was consenting to sexual intercourse was not guilty of rape, created a public outcry. Universally condemned by feminists (although many legal academics considered it to be a correct application of *mens rea* principles[67]), the government responded by establishing a committee chaired by Mrs Justice Heilbron.[68] This eventually led to the Sexual Offences (Amendment) Act 1976 which, while changing aspects of rape law, did not affect *Morgan*. Nor did the Act address the marital rape exemption which, curiously, Heilbron barely considered. During the early 1980s the Criminal Law Revision Committee[69] further deliberated about rape law reform, including the marital exemption, although no additional legislation was forthcoming until the Criminal Justice and Public Order Act 1994 (after the decision in *R v R*). Meanwhile, legal scholars began to question both the authority and rationality of the marital exemption[70] and empirical studies on the trauma of rape, including rape within marriage and in the context of intimate relationships, began to accumulate. Against this background of social, political and intellectual concern about violence again women, *R v R* came before the courts.

---

[65] See eg G Chambers and A Millar, *Investigating Sexual Assault* (Scottish Office Central Research Unit, 1983); I Blair, *Investigating Rape: A New Approach for Police* (London: Police Foundation, 1985).

[66] [1976] AC 182 (HL).

[67] See eg J Sellars, '*Mens Rea* and the Judicial Approach to "Bad Excuses" in the Criminal Law' (1978) 41 *MLR* 245, 248. Civil liberties groups such as the National Council of Civil Liberties also supported the decision.

[68] Home Office, *Report of the Advisory Group on the Law of Rape* (Cmnd 6352, 1975).

[69] CLRC, *Working Paper on Sexual Offences* (London: HMSO, 1980); CLRC, *Sexual Offences* Cmnd 9213 (London: HMSO, 1984).

[70] See eg M Freeman, 'But If You Can't Rape Your Wife, Whom Can You Rape?: The Marital Exemption Re-examined' (1981) 15 *Fam LQ* 1.

The facts of the case are simple: the defendant and the victim had been married for five years, had a four-year-old son, and had experienced intermittent marital difficulties. Eventually the wife left her husband and, with her son, moved in with her parents. Subsequently and by telephone, she discussed with her husband the possibility of divorce, communicating her clear intention to go down that road. However, no formal legal proceedings were initiated. In November 1989, about a month after the wife left her husband, the latter broke into his parent-in-laws' home, attacked his wife and tried to force himself upon her.

The defendant came before Leicester Crown Court in July 1990 where Owen J rejected a submission that the offence of rape was not known to law where the defendant was the husband of the victim. Consequently, the defendant pleaded guilty to attempted rape and assault occasioning actual bodily harm. Subsequently however he appealed the conviction for attempted rape.

2.3.1 *R v R*: COURT OF APPEAL

The arguments in *R v R* are marked by a surprising degree of doctrinal spareness. Unlike *Best v Fox*, there were no antiquated decisions to dig up, no competing lines of case law to distinguish or reconcile. The authority of the marital exemption, it appeared, rested upon a couple of juristic pronouncements by early treatise writers,[71] a muddled 19th-century decision not even on point,[72] and a plethora of cases in which the courts for the most part sought to avoid the exemption rather than apply it. As a result, and notwithstanding the fact that the appeal was heard by a bench of five—an indication that the court held the matter to be of great importance—there is only a single judgment delivered by the Chief Justice, Lord Lane, on behalf of the court.

---

[71] In addition to Hale, the Court of Appeal and House of Lords both cite Archbold's *Pleading and Evidence in Criminal Cases* (1822), 259. The House of Lords also refer to a reproduction of Hale's statement in East, *Treatise of the Pleas of the Crown: Vol 1* (1803) 446.

[72] *R v Clarence* (1888) 22 QBD 23 (HC).

While reaching what some might regard as a radical result, this judgment is in form a model of legal convention. Lane CJ begins by identifying the issue in the following terms:

... the question which the judge had to decide was whether ... despite her refusal to consent to sexual intercourse, the wife must be deemed by the fact of the marriage to have consented.[73]

From the outset then the marital exemption is framed by the court as conveying the idea that a wife's irretractable consent to sexual intercourse is a necessary incidence of marriage. This of course is the precise basis of Hale's articulation which, Lane accepts, was at the time of utterance most likely an accurate representation of the common law although, in fact, there is little contemporaneous case law to support it and, as Freeman has pointed out, at least one authority from that period can be read against it.[74]

Lane does not make reference to these reservations or demonstrate an awareness of them. His examination of the case law begins with the 19th-century decision of *R v Clarence*, in which a husband who suffered from gonorrhoea had sex with his wife without informing her of his condition, thus knowingly infecting her. He was charged and convicted, inter alia, of assault and the question of the wife's consent to intercourse, given her lack of knowledge of his condition, inevitably became an issue. In the course of deliberation the Crown Cases Reserved (comprising a court of thirteen judges) considered the marital exemption *obiter*, coming to different views as to its standing. However, at least two judges, Lane CJ notes, questioned whether sufficient authority existed to support it.[75] Thereafter the principle does not appear to have been directly considered in a reported case

---

[73] *R v R* (CA), 603.

[74] See *R v Audley (Lord)* (1631) 3 State Trials 401 (discussed by Freeman, 'If You Can't Rape Your Wife') in which the defendant was convicted of rape after forcibly holding his wife down while she was raped by another. Freeman asks why, if the marital exemption was at that time good law, it was not invoked to prevent Audley's conviction at least for rape? (Indeed, the exemption principle does not appear to have been considered in the case at all.) For a contrasting view, see also J L Barton, 'The Story of Marital Rape' (1992) 108 *LQR* 260.

[75] *R v Clarence* (see the judgments of Wills and Field JJ).

until *R v Clarke*[76] in which Byrne J held it did not apply where a legal order providing that the wife should no longer be bound to cohabit with her husband had been made. *Clarke* signalled the beginning of a process of diluting the doctrinal potency of the exemption through judicially-created exceptions.[77] This process of attenuation, Lane CJ observes, continued for some decades, with only one case applying the exemption to absolve a husband of raping his wife.[78]

R v R came to the Court of Appeal amidst a spate of recent trial court decisions evidencing increased judicial dissention around the applicability and scope of the marital exemption. Lane CJ highlights two English decisions[79] as well as a decision by the Scottish High Court of Justiciary in which the Lord Justice-General, Lord Emslie, rejected the marital exemption outright as part of the law of Scotland.[80] The Scottish decision was relied upon by Simon-Brown J in *R v C* who, viewing the marital exemption to be indefensible, tossed the legal gauntlet into the ring when he pronounced: 'The position in law today is, as already declared in Scotland, that there is no marital exemption to the law of rape. That is the ruling I give'.[81] By contrast, Rougier J in *R v J* determined that the exemption still applied; indeed was statutorily enshrined by the inclusion of the term 'unlawful' in the Sexual Offences (Amendment) Act 1976, s 1(1) of which reads 'For the purposes of section 1 of the Sexual Offences Act 1956 (which relates to rape) a man commits

---

[76] *R v Clarke* [1949] 2 All ER 448 (Assizes).

[77] See eg *R v O'Brien (Edward)* [1974] 3 All ER 663 (consent revoked by granting of a decree nisi which effectively terminated the marriage); *R v Steele* (1977) 65 Cr App R 22 (CA) (exemption did not apply where a husband had given an undertaking to the court not to molest his wife as this was the equivalent of a court-imposed injunction); *R v Roberts* [1986] Crim LR 188 (CA) (exemption did not apply when an ouster and non-molestation order were in place notwithstanding the absence of a non-molestation clause in the formal deed of separation).

[78] *R v Miller* [1954] 2 QB 282 (Assizes).

[79] See *R v C (Rape: Marital Exemption)* [1991] 1 All ER 755 and *R v J (Rape: Marital Exemption)* [1991] 1 All ER 759.

[80] *S v HM Advocate* (1989) SLT 469. Note the primary Scottish authority is Hume not Hale (*Hume on Crimes: vol I* (1797), ch 7).

[81] *R v C*, 758.

rape if—(a) he has *unlawful* sexual intercourse with a woman who at the time of the intercourse does not consent to it . . .' (emphasis added). Rougier J concluded that 'unlawful' in this context should properly be construed to mean 'outside the bounds of matrimony'. Rougier J also ruled that as a consequence further judicial encroachment upon the exemption without parliamentary intervention was precluded.[82]

The existence of such division at trial court level—taking account too of the trial court decision in *R v R*—allows Lane CJ to frame the issue in terms of a division of approach at trial court level, requiring the strong and steady hand of the Court of Appeal to provide direction. Lane CJ identifies three approaches emerging from the relevant case law:[83] 'the literal solution' which he attributes to *R v J*; 'the compromise solution' of the trial court judge in *R v R*; and 'the radical solution' of Simon-Brown J in *R v C*. Lane CJ proceeds to dismiss the literal solution on the grounds that to adopt it would effectively overrule previous judicial encroachments on the exemption principle, an outcome Parliament surely did not intend. He considers the compromise solution to be not unreasonable but concludes that as the list of exceptions to the general rule continues to grow, an undesirable degree of uncertainty is created, inviting complex and invidious judicial line-drawing exercises. While paying lip-service to the alleged drawbacks of the radical solution—it may be said to go beyond the legitimate bounds of judge-made law and raises social considerations around the privacy of marriage—it is already clear that this is the direction the Chief Justice wishes to take. Posing the question 'what should be the answer?' and noting with approval the process of judicial encroachment to date, Lane CJ continues:

There comes a time when the changes are so great that it is no longer enough to create further exceptions restricting the effect of the proposition, a time when the proposition itself requires examination *to see whether its terms are in accord with what is generally regarded today as acceptable behaviour.*[84]

---

[82] *R v J*, 767 per Rougier J (relying on *R v Chapman* [1959] 1 QB 100 (CA)).
[83] *R v R* (CA), 609.   [84] *R v R* (CA), 610 (emphasis added).

Lane CJ thus uses the exceptions to make the case against the rule, a classic judicial manoeuvre. At the same time, he engages in a slightly more devious move. Testing the authority of a long established legal principle against what is deemed acceptable to contemporary public *mores*, Lane CJ invites the historical weight of the principle to work against itself, to make the case for the eschewal of tradition in light of changes in modern times. Stemming the flow of further contestation, he castigates the principle of irretractable consent as flimsy and unrealistic: 'It can never have been other than a fiction and fiction is a poor basis for criminal law . . . [which] no longer even remotely represents the true position of the wife in present day'.[85]

It is worth pausing for a moment here over the Chief Justice's pejoration of the marital exemption principle as a 'fiction'. The legal fiction is of course a well-known and widely used technique of the common law. Fuller describes it as a 'pretense' invoked in law with consciousness of its falsity for purposes of legal or practical expediency.[86] Examples of legal fictions include the doctrine of corporate personality (by which the corporation is deemed to be a legal 'person') and the constructive trust (which supposes a trust to have arisen without having been consciously created by a trustor for the benefit of a trustee). Other features of legal argumentation, for example, the imposition of implied terms and the operation of doctrinal or evidentiary presumptions, also rely upon the creative deployment of fictional devices, allowing the courts to proceed *as if* circumstances are as the courts imagine them to be. Moreover, it is sometimes helpful to approach legal fictions as metaphors which over time come to assume a technical legal meaning. Fuller cites as examples 'the *merger* of estates . . . the *breaking* of contracts . . . the *ripening* of obligations';[87] he continues by observing that 'the legal language of today is in part composed of the dead shells of former pretenses'.[88]

One could perhaps view the fiction of marital unity which underpins the common law doctrine of coverture, as a

[85] *R v R* (CA), 610.
[86] L Fuller, *Legal Fictions* (Stanford: Stanford University Press, 1967), ch 1.
[87] Fuller, *Legal Fictions*, 10.   [88] Fuller, *Legal Fictions*, 20.

metaphorical expression of the nature of the bond which the legal institution of marriage creates, an unbreakable and irrevocable merger of two into one from which the notion of irretractable consent appears naturally to flow. However this does not explain why the wife's personhood is lost in the husband's and not the other way round. Nor does it explain why the law empowers the husband to enforce the marital bond but does not allow the wife to do so. It is as this point that practicality and expedience come into play, for of course the fiction of irretractable consent, like the fiction of marital unity which undergirds it, is present in law because it serves—or at one time served—a useful purpose (where useful is defined in terms of who is empowered to do the using).[89]

This pragmatic, utility-dependent dimension to the legal fiction gives it an uncertain and vaguely reprehensible status in law. According to Fuller 'we may liken the fiction to an awkward patch applied to a rent in the law's fabric of theory'.[90] While acknowledging the fiction as a less than ideal instrument, Fuller sees its virtue to lie in an ability to bridge conceptual gaps in order to maintain the unity and integrity of law. Others view the fiction much more negatively, most notably Bentham, who compares the legal fiction to a disease, tainting and corrupting the law with its 'pestilent breath'.[91] Generally, there is a sense in the scholarly literature that fictions are at best necessary evils which must not be invoked too lightly or too frequently. Moreover, their persuasive power is very much dependent upon how they are invoked and deployed. A fiction can be presented as a well-established doctrine or principle, the authority of which is plainly unquestionable or it can be exposed as a falsehood which brings the law into discredit and must be eschewed. Moreover, the fictional status of legal fictions is always open to debate. For example, in the present context one can argue that the notion of irretractable consent is a fiction

[89] See M Doggett, *Marriage, Wife-Beating and the Law in Victorian England* (London: Butterworths, 1992), especially ch 3.

[90] Fuller, *Legal Fictions*, viii.

[91] J Bentham, *The Works of Jeremy Bentham: Vol I* (London: William Tait, 1843), 235.

because in the real world (the world outside law), wives frequently choose to withdraw their consent to sexual intercourse with their husbands, whether temporarily or permanently. On the other hand, it might be contended that the legal state of marriage creates *real* juridic relations which encompass a wife's irretractable consent. It is in this sense that one might say that, given the specifically legal nature of the matrimonial relation, a husband cannot rape his wife; this may not be a factual truth but is it not—at least until *R v R*—a juridic one?

This ontological ambiguity around the status of legal fictions endows them with discursive flexibility but also provides a basis for their shady reputation. Moreover it begs an unarticulated theoretical question: what is—or ought to be—the relationship between law and real life? The denigration of legal fictions is usually linked to their lack of correspondence with perceived empirical truths. Thus, in justifying his rejection of the marital exemption, Lane CJ invokes the contemporary reality of modern marriage in which wives simply do *not* give their irretractable consent to sex with their husbands; therefore, the law is wrong to deem that they do. The juridic truth becomes an empirical falsity requiring the courts to act to correct the lack of correspondence between law and the real.

Why is this important? Well, one reason is that the credibility of law as 'an unassailable field of knowledge'[92] might well be thought to require a high degree of propinquity between law and truth. Indeed, Carol Smart argues that the power of law lies less in its capacity to require compliance and more in its potency to aver truths which, because they are enshrined within a specialized professional discourse, are not easy to contest.[93] At the same time, whenever law is seen to diverge too far from reality—from *how things really are*—this potency risks compromise. In addition, the functionality of the legal fiction will often require a close correspondence between law and reality, although this is not always the case. Indeed it has been argued that, certainly in a commercial context (which might be said to

[92] N Lacey, *Unspeakable Subjects: Feminist Essays in Legal and Social Theory* (Oxford: Hart Publishing, 1998).

[93] C Smart, *The Power of Law* (London: Routledge, 1989).

encompass aspects of marriage as a legal institution), law should
be free to develop whatever concepts work best regardless of
their correspondence with 'facts'.[94]

At the same time, the discursive juxtaposition of law and the
real, whether in terms of correspondence or divergence, belies
the fact that law plays a vital role in constituting what we
understand as real—law is an important lens through which
we see and interpret the world around us, operating cognitively
to shape our perceptions, as well as prescriptively, to impose
norms. This cognitive function is implicitly denied when law is
called to account for failing to fit the facts. The idea that law
mirrors reality rather than constitutes it allows the skilled legal
rhetorician to move with relative ease between discourses of
'ought' and 'is' without appearing to undermine the fact/value
distinction. In *R v R*, what begins as a normative enquiry—what
ought the court to do—subtly shifts, through the Chief Justice's
discursive appeal to the reality of modern social conditions as
against the fictional basis of the marital exemption, into a declaration of what *is* in *fact* the *true* legal position. By so doing, Lane
CJ no longer looks so radical. Rather he looks to be articulating
the right and proper solution by exposing and discarding the
false empirical basis upon which the marital exemption struggles
to stand.

This makes it a lot easier for him to forestall the need for
legislative intervention. He simply asserts the duty of the court
to act appropriately where ancient rules no longer accord with
modern times.[95] That Lane CJ is pursuing the proper path of
common law evolution and not engaging in any illegitimate
law-making is underscored in the final paragraphs of his judgment: 'We take the view that the time has now arrived when
the law should *declare* that a rapist remains rapist . . . irrespective
of his relationship with his victim'.[96] The passage of time is
prayed in aid here to absolve the court of doing anything

---

[94] F H Lawson, 'The Creative Use of Legal Concepts' (1957) 32 *NYU L Rev*
907, 911.
[95] *R v R* (CA), per Lane CJ: 'it is the duty of the court is to take steps to alter
the rule if it can legitimately do so . . .' 610.
[96] *R v R* (CA), 611 (emphasis added).

more than declaring what has now become the true position, while the 'rapist' trope prompts an emotive sense of virtue and righteousness which assures us that justice is being done.

And in the moment when we are reminded of the gravity of the issue at stake, the Chief Justice disposes, almost casually, of a crucial legal concern. The decision to jettison the marital exemption, he argues, does not create any new offence but merely removes an 'anachronistic and offensive common law fiction'.[97] In three short lines, Lane CJ anticipates and deftly deflects what was later to become a central argument before the European Court of Human Rights, that is, that *R v R* represented an illegitimate exercise in retrospective law-making which usurped the function of the legislature.[98] After wisely covering the court's position by indicating that had they decided other than that the exemption had no legal effect, the court would have held the immunity to be lost where a wife withdrew from cohabitation after making clear she regarded the marriage as at an end, Lane CJ concludes by dismissing the appeal.

Leave to appeal was granted immediately, the point of law of general public importance formulated in stark and simple terms: 'Is a husband criminally liable for raping his wife?'

2.3.2 *R v R*: HOUSE OF LORDS

In the sole judgment of the case, Lord Keith of Kinkel also proceeds formally, confronting directly the question of legal support for the marital exemption principle, whether by virtue of principle, weight of authority, or as a consequence of legislative intention or enactment. With regard to principle, he adopts almost wholesale the reasoning of Lord Emslie in *S v HM Advocate* (which is reproduced at some length), to endorse a

---

[97] *R v R* (CA), 611.
[98] *CR v UK* (1996) 21 EHRR 1. The European Court of Human Rights eventually endorsed the decision of the UK courts in *R v R* holding that no breach of Article 7 of the European Convention on Human Rights (which embodies the principle of non-retrospectivity) had occurred because judicial evolution along these lines was appropriate and wholly foreseeable.

conclusion that the marital exemption is without principled justification. Lord Emslie had emphasized the dramatic changes in the status of women, particularly married women in the 20th century, stating that, in a modern marriage, husband and wife were now 'equal partners'. Moreover, a 'live system of law' had to have regard to this contemporary reality.[99] In these circumstances, Lord Emslie continued, the fiction of implied and irretractable consent was wholly unsustainable:

... a wife is not obliged to obey her husband in all things nor to suffer excessive sexual demands on the part of her husband ... nowadays it cannot seriously be maintained that by marriage a wife submits herself irrevocably to sexual intercourse in all circumstances.[100]

This is a view with which Lord Keith unequivocally concurs, emphasizing, as did Lord Emslie, the incompatibility of the marital exemption with other legal developments in the course of the 20th century. The picture thus presented is one in which the exemption appears out of line not just with contemporary social realities but also with the general shape and tenor of the framework governing marriage as a legal institution. A century of legal change in family law had therefore swept away any principled underpinning upon which the exemption might be said to rest, rendering the legal fiction, as Lord Emslie observes, to be without useful purpose. For a legal device which is reliant upon utility as the measure of its worth, this is compelling grounds for its abandonment.

If there is no case in principle to support the marital exemption, what is the weight of legal authority? Lord Keith offers a dutiful account of the same case law considered by the Court of Appeal, adding a few recent decisions that allow him to illustrate the absurd lengths to which judges have to resort to reconcile the exemption with the application of a just result.[101] Painting a picture of doctrinal distortion and judicial disquiet added new

---

[99] *R v R* (HL), 617 per L Keith (citing L Emslie in *S v HM Advocate*, 473).

[100] *R v R* (HL), 618 per L Keith (citing L Emslie in *S v HM Advocate*, 473).

[101] See eg *R v Caswell* [1984] Crim LR 111; *R v Kowalski* (1987) 86 Crim App R 339 (CA); and *R v H* (HC, 5 October 1990) per Auld J. The thrust of these decisions appears to be that acts which are not part of the normal process of sexual intercourse, such as *fellatio*, are outside the scope of the exemption.

urgency to the issue before the House, requiring judicial action even in the face of legislative irresolution. Like Lane CJ in the Court of Appeal, Lord Keith presents the disarray in the lower courts as a compelling reason for judicial intervention. In any event, the lack of consensus in the case law alongside increasing evidence of contorted judicial reasoning offered a poor base in authority for retaining the exemption.

At this point all that was left in the armoury of the appellant's advocates was the argument based on legislative enactment. This was effectively two-pronged, comprising, firstly, a claim that Parliament intended to retain the exemption by including the word 'unlawful' in s 1(1) of the 1976 Act and/or secondly, an assertion that abolition of the exemption constituted new law and required parliamentary intervention. On the former point, Lord Keith concludes that the interpretation propounded by appellant's counsel—that 'unlawful' on the basis of *Chapman* should be read as 'outside marriage'—simply did not hold up to scrutiny.[102] Some of the accepted judicial exceptions to the marital exemption, Lord Keith points out, come well within the marital bond and it could not be believed that Parliament intended to abolish them. He also observes, not unreasonably, that sexual intercourse outside marriage would not ordinarily be described in modern times as unlawful. He therefore concludes that there are no rational grounds for interpreting the term as the appellant contends. Like the Court of Appeal, Lord Keith concludes that the term 'unlawful' should be treated as 'mere surplusage' in the 1976 Act.[103]

Finally, Lord Keith considers whether the eschewal of the exemption goes beyond the proper scope of judicial decision-making. He concludes not, largely reproducing the reasoning of Lane CJ in the Court of Appeal to support his position: the decision to declare the marital exemption to be no longer part of English law involved not the introduction of something new but the removal of something old and anachronistic.[104] This is presented as disposing unequivocally of any suggestion that their

---

[102] *R v R* (HL), 623 per Lord Keith, discussing *R v Chapman*, 105 per Donovan LJ.
[103] *R v R* (HL), 621–3.   [104] *R v R* (HL), 623.

Lordships are engaged in illegitimate law-making. And yet, while few people today would disagree with the substantive outcome of *R v R*, fewer still would deny that the decision to reject the marital exemption was anything other than a radical alteration of the then existing legal position. In this sense the judicial claim that *R v R* introduced nothing new is the ultimate legal fiction, a sophisticated version of the declaratory theory of the common law which allows judges to engage in law-making without acknowledging that they do so. The decision in *R v R* brought about a long awaited change in the law of rape which, had it been enacted by the legislature would only have applied prospectively. To maintain the legal fiction which underpins the declaratory theory, the courts must proceed *as if* the law was always as they declare it to be.[105] The temporal context of *R v R* is necessarily suspended by an act of mass judicial deceit in which we are all invited to join.

R v R is a decision which is memorable not just because it disposed of a very objectionable legal principle but for sheer judicial daring. It was, if you like, a gamble that—perhaps surprisingly—paid off; surprising because aspects of the decision render it less than convincing as an exercise in judicial decision-making. One cannot help, for example, but be underwhelmed by the thinness of the doctrinal content and the homogeneity of the historical narrative. Can such a well-established common law principle really rest upon such a vague, undeveloped, and mostly unconsidered doctrinal base? According to some commentators, *R v R* does not really tell the full 'story' of the marital rape exemption. Pointing out that the origins, elaboration, and rationale of the *debitum conjugale* lie in ancient canon law, John Barton paints a picture of a reciprocal sexual obligation owed by both spouses which was by no means absolute or unqualified. Absolving Hale of any personal responsibility for 'inventing' the marital rape exemption, Barton intimates an unexplored doctrinal hinterland in which sexual obligations within marriage were 'worked out' by canon lawyers in a detailed, rigorous fashion.[106]

---

[105] See further, R Tur, 'Time and Law' (2002) 22 *OJLS* 463.
[106] Barton, 'The Story of Marital Rape', 260.

Equally unsatisfactory is the way in which the judges in *R v R* dealt with the small problem of the legislature. It takes a brave—almost reckless—court to determine that a word included in a fairly recent legislative enactment is 'mere surplusage'. For a number of reasons this conclusion does not add up. Contemporaneous legal commentaries reveal that even feminist legal scholars understood the term 'unlawful' to be doing the work of carrying forward the marital exemption after 1976.[107] It is also undisputed that the exemption received repeated policy scrutiny in the years preceding *R v R*, producing no firm resolution but rather endless vacillation. In a Working Paper of the Criminal Law Revision Committee in 1980, a majority had proposed that rape within marriage should be a recognizable crime but in deference to the social considerations involved, any prosecution should require the consent of the Director of Public Prosecutions.[108] In the final report of 1984, the majority position had changed to one more in line with the then current status quo.[109] The matter was then passed to the Law Commission which produced a Working Paper in 1990 provisionally recommending abolition of the exemption and inviting public comment.[110] This was the state of play when *R v R* came before the courts. None of it adds up to evidence of a policy, let alone legislative consensus at the time. Even more striking is the fact that neither the Court of Appeal nor the House of Lords considered evidence of the legislative intention at the time when the 1976 Act was being debated. Had they done so, they would have discovered that a proposal at parliamentary committee stage expressly to reject the principle of implied consent had been jettisoned, as had other suggestions to make explicit judicially crafted

---

[107] See eg J Temkin, 'Towards a Modern Law of Rape' (1982) 45 *MLR* 399, 407; K O'Donovan, *Sexual Divisions in Law* (Weidenfeld & Nicolson 1985), 120.

[108] CLRC, *Working Paper* (1980).

[109] CLRC, *Sexual Offences* (1984).

[110] Law Commission, *Working Paper: Rape within Marriage* (Law Com no 116, 1990) and Law Commission, *Criminal Law Rape within Marriage* (Law Com no 205, 1992).

exceptions to the exemption.[111] Effectively what the court had done, rather than determine through the usual process of statutory interpretation how the term 'unlawful' should be understood, was to proceed *as if* the legislature intended it as mere surplusage. The courts had done away with one fiction only to replace it with another.

A sense of unease about *R v R* is evident even in feminist commentary. Jennifer Temkin acknowledges that academic concern about the judicial usurpation of Parliament's law-making function in *R v R* is not wholly without merit. She concludes that given the level of uncertainty around the application and scope of the exemption principle at the time 'the Court of Appeal and the House of Lords did what had to be done. If the methodology was faulty, the result was not'.[112] In other words, she intimates, the courts had to act because Parliament had singularly and reprehensibly failed to do so. *R v R* thus emerges not so much as a triumph of judicial ingenuity over an antiquated but nevertheless authoritative body of legal doctrine but as a political and legal fudge in which the right result is reached but not necessarily in the right way or for the right reasons.

2.3.3 SITUATING GENDER

In *R v R*, as with *Best v Fox*, gender is simultaneously everywhere yet nowhere. Rape of course is a gendered crime. It is gendered empirically, socially, and culturally. In the UK it is gendered explicitly in the sense that a penis is expressly required for the commission of the act.[113] British women cannot be rapists. This is in contrast to a number of other jurisdictions.

---

[111] Parl Deb HC (5th ser), vol 911, cols 1952–1980, as discussed by Barton, 'The Story of Marital Rape', 269. The conclusion of the House of Commons debate (21 May 1976) was to refer the issue to the CLRC.

[112] J Temkin, *Rape and the Legal Process*, 2nd edn (Oxford: OUP, 2002), 84–5.

[113] Sexual Offences Act 2003, s 1(1)(a) [text headed 'rape'] states: 'a person commits an offence if he intentionally penetrates the vagina, anus or mouth with his penis'. The inclusion of orifices other than the vagina allows for the possibility of male-on-male rape. See also Sexual Offences (Scotland) Act 2009, s 1.

For example, in Australia, most states have adopted a gender-neutral conception of sexual offences and the crime of rape has given way to various forms of sexual assault in which the penis is only one of a number of possible instruments of unlawful penetration.[114] This shift to gender-neutrality represents a concrete strategic move on the part of the state to take gender, or more specifically sex, out of rape law; to repackage it as a crime of violence not sex. It is hoped that by so doing, rape will be taken more seriously, viewed less as an extension of 'normal' heterosexual relations and more as anti-social and criminal behaviour. Many feminists support this conceptual shift. Others however argue that to lose sight of the gender dimension in rape is to lose sight of what rape is really about, that is, women's sexual subordination to men. Rape, it is argued, is not, cannot be, gender-neutral; it is rather wholly gender-imbued. Moreover, rape, and sexual violence more generally, are deeply implicated in the persistence of gender inequality. Rape, it is contended, has to be viewed as part of this wider, more pervasive picture.

In fact the judges in *R v R* do make the connection between sexual (in)equality and the marital rape exemption: changes in women's social and legal status—specifically their elevation to 'equal partner' in the matrimonial bond—provide reason for jettisoning the principles behind the exemption, rendering its continued application no longer justifiable. This is as a clear indication as we are likely to get that the courts share the view repeatedly expressed by feminist scholars that the marital exemption 'expresses and legitimizes a view of unequal power relations in marriage'.[115] In this sense *R v R* represents a rare instance of judicial willingness to penetrate the ideological veil of implied consent cloaking the gendered hierarchy lurking beneath. In *Best*, the judges used notions of consent and reciprocity to justify a plainly unequal outcome, suggesting that continued legal recognition of a husband's consortium action

---

[114] P Rush, 'Criminal Law and the Reformation of Rape in Australia' in C McGlynn and V Munro (eds), *Rethinking Rape Law: International and Comparative Perspectives* (London: Routledge, 2010), 239.

[115] Lacey, *Unspeakable Subjects*, 70; see also O'Donovan, *Sexual Divisions*, 119.

while denying a wife's was fair in the practical context of the 'deal' struck by men and women on marriage, in which men provide the financial support and women the care and nurturing. The judges in *R v R* viewed the matrimonial deal quite differently. It was the social practice of equality in marriage—or at least the prevalence of a social belief in that practice—that led the courts to reject a well-established legal rule. Moreover, unlike in *R v Miller*[116] (decided in 1954, almost contemporaneously with *Best*) in which the court effectively held that the *fact* of retraction of consent to intercourse by a wife was of no legal significance unless supported by an order of the court, in *R v R*, the social reality of a wife's retraction was suddenly and unprecedentedly vested with formal legal consequences.

Nevertheless, in common with *Best v Fox*, the judgments in *R v R* did not formally call upon any legal principle of gender equality, notwithstanding that by the early 1990s such a principle was much more visibly manifest in law through the combined effects of European Community equality law and the growing jurisprudence of the European Court of Human Rights. At this stage the potency of sex equality as a legal norm had not yet been fully recognized (although within a decade a member of the House of Lords would be describing equality as no less than a 'constitutional principle' of English law).[117] *R v R* then was not so much about achieving equality as ensuring an appropriate correspondence between law and reality. It was the lack of fit between legal principle and social practice rather than gender inequality per se which was both the trigger and the proffered rationale for judicial action. Interestingly such a lack of fit was not viewed as sufficient to displace the weight of past authority in *Best v Fox*. In *Best*, time worked very differently to thwart efforts to bring law into line with present realities, even when illogicality was the result, while in

---

[116] Although the wife in *Miller* had presented a petition for divorce, formal legal proceedings had not yet begun. Lynskey J, affirming the correctness of Hale's principle, held that the wife's implied consent could only be revoked by an order of the court.

[117] L Steyn, 'Democracy through Law' (2002) *European Human Rights L Rev* 723, 731.

R v R, deference to history easily gave way to a greater imperative, the need to ensure law's continued legitimacy and respect.
Such was the threat to law of retaining the marital exemption
that the courts were prepared to ride fairly roughshod over legal
convention to bring about its demise.

From a gender perspective, the decision in *R v R* is hugely
significant. However, this significance lies not so much in opening the way for criminal prosecutions against husbands who rape
their wives. Notwithstanding an increased willingness by
women to report rape, there continue to be substantial difficulties in securing convictions where rape is alleged between intimates. There is a symbolic and ideological dimension to *R v R*,
certainly. The decision sends out a clear and unambiguous signal
of judicial endorsement of a social conception of marriage as a
'partnership of equals'. In this sense *R v R* is not so much a
decision about rape as it is a legal reconstitution of marriage. The
real significance of *R v R* lies in its practical contribution to
reshaping the gendered social order so that marriage can remain
at its heart. Law operates here as a site of the production,
renegotiation, and validation of particular gendered understandings of the social world; it actively participates in processes
through which notions of gender and gender difference acquire
substantive meaning and operative effects. Law then is not so
much *gendered* as *gendering*: it is gender as verb not noun or
adjective which best captures the relationship between law and
gender here. What one sees in *R v R* and in *Best* is the working
through of a concept of marriage fit for legal purpose, in the
context of gendered social change which threatens the functionality of marriage as an organizing category. Within this
process the instability and volatility of social and legal concepts,
including gender, and the porosity of the social/legal boundary
is clearly revealed. Marriage emerges simultaneously as a technical legal category comprising a complex unity of legal norms and
as an important regulatory tool which orders and privileges
particular relations, attitudes, and ways of life. This is not just a
process of prescription but cognition; after *R v R*, we can no
longer see any truth in the assertion that a man cannot rape his
wife. The tension between the legal and social reality has been

resolved and in the process a new gendered truth, a new empirical reality of the marital relation, has emerged.

2.4 CONCLUSION

Although this chapter has focused only on two cases fifty years
apart, the questions considered and the issues discussed have
been fairly wide ranging. This has not been a narrow excavation
of judicial reasoning in pursuit of gender bias or discrimination.
The idea rather has been to bring to the fore some of the issues
with which this book seeks to engage and to place them within a
familiar doctrinal context in which the legal moves and motives
are readily recognized and understood. Among other things the
analysis has served to demonstrate the formal, that is, conven-
tion-compliant, nature of legal argument, the presentation of
judicial decisions as rational and preordained, and the extent to
which these formal features help to mask legal uncertainty and
the exercise of judicial discretion. The analysis has also high-
lighted the processes and techniques through which judges
promote or resist legal change and the various ways in which
time is deployed in these contexts. The tensions between principle and practicality and between rationality and tradition are
also evident, as is the lack of a consistent approach to their
resolution. The particular world views and ideological outlooks
of the judicial actors also make their inevitable appearance, albeit
within the constraints of discursive conventions which the legal
community generally recognize and endorse.

So where is gender in all of this? What role does it play? As an
analytical approach, gender allows us to root around below the
surface of legal discourse to get at the layers underneath. It is a
tool of critique, a spotlight which helps to illuminate the dark
corners and murky regions of doctrinal argumentation. It is also
particularly adept at flushing out the interpenetration of the legal
and the social; the porosity of conceptual and ideological
boundaries which are both contingent and contrived. Looking
at law through a gender lens is a way of seeing what might
otherwise be obscured; it tells a different story and, by so doing,
reminds us that, in the course of law, stories are being told.

But is there more going on? Does gender have a particular significance in law which requires investigation and theorization? And why does a gender perspective allow us to see law differently? Why does it appear on the outside of legal discourse rather than within? And what does it mean to say that law is 'gendered' or that it 'genders'? In what sense is law a gendering activity? In the chapter that follows I address these questions directly.

3

THEORIZING THE RELATIONSHIP BETWEEN LAW AND GENDER

3.1 INTRODUCTION: THE OFFICIAL POSITION

When H L A Hart sat down to write about the concept of law in the middle of the last century, the idea of gender was far from his conscious mind. Purporting to offer a descriptive account of key features of a modern legal system, Hart presents a legal world in which gender has no apparent place and in which differences between women and men are without theoretical significance. Hart is not directly concerned with legal subjects, that is, with the governed; nor is he interested in critiquing the content of law or challenging developments in legal policy. Rather, his purpose is to contribute to 'the clarification of the general framework of legal thought'[1] by adopting an approach which simultaneously engages with (while not necessarily purporting to endorse) a central preoccupation of analytical jurisprudence—namely, the question of the nature or essence of law—while at the same time presenting law as a fundamentally social phenomenon, as a matter of social fact.

Of course one should not be surprised at the absence of attention to gender in *The Concept of Law*. It is, after all, entirely in keeping with the legal scholarly tradition at the time. Nor was law in any way different from other disciplines in attaching little or no theoretical significance to sex/gender considerations. The very notion of scholarship was, and for many still is, predicated upon the possibility of abstract universal reason and the power of a mind severable from and wholly uncontaminated by its embodied context. In the aftermath of the horrors of the Second World War, the need to hold on to a belief in the transcendental

---

[1] H L A Hart, *The Concept of Law*, 3rd edn, edited by P Bulloch and J Raz (Oxford: OUP, 2012), vi.

power of reason undoubtedly assumed even greater urgency, as did the idea that law should be understood without reference to differences between particular groups or categories of people. In a passing vignette in her autobiography, Hart's wife, Jenifer, tells us that her husband was unreceptive when she complained of being slighted by other Oxford academics because of her sex; Herbert, she observes, 'was antagonistic to thinking in terms of women and men'.[2] Thinking for Hart was an activity upon which gender has no bearing.

And yet interestingly, the text of *The Concept of Law* is littered with gendered references to 'men', 'Englishmen', 'educated men', and so on. Hart does not pause for breath as he paints a picture of law in which men come literally to mind. Of course at the time of writing the academic convention was that 'man' and 'men' were general terms, assumed to be inclusive of women unless otherwise stated. The contemporaneous reader would not have attributed any gendered significance to the repeated use of the male pronoun. To the modern ear, however, Hart's constant invocation of a masculine subject, perhaps more than any other feature of this jurisprudential classic, makes manifest its temporality. Nor is it easy to allay the suspicion, once entertained, that when Hart makes reference to men, it is because men are in fact his envisaged readership. Feminists have argued, convincingly in my view, that the linguistic practice whereby references to the masculine were assumed unless otherwise indicated to have general application, often functioned to conceal the conceptualization of a male subject as the a priori model of humanity. Indeed, this linguistic fiction is surely deeply implicated in the patriarchal fabric of the Western intellectual tradition. There is no reason to think that Hart differed from his scholarly contemporaries in adopting a worldview which, while dismissive of gender as a category of intellectual significance, was nevertheless implicitly premised upon a gendered social order.

Putting these reservations to one side, it cannot be contested that Hart's depiction of law, a depiction which, as Nigel Simmonds, observes, 'has played such a large part in establishing

---

[2] J Hart, *Ask Me No More* (London: Peter Halban, 1998), 164.

the categories and assumptions in terms of which jurisprudential debate is now generally constructed'[3] is self-consciously and resolutely gender-less. Hart's iconic text is an emblematic example of the official position within mainstream legal thought that gender is theoretically irrelevant. Whether we focus on jurisprudence at its narrowest, glibly encapsulated in the 'what is law?' question, or conceive the field more broadly to encompass aspects of political or moral philosophy and even legal sociology, the terms of debate, parameters of discussion, key contestations and challenges, are, for the most part, framed and explored without gender in mind. As in Hart's text, this is not so much a stated as an assumed position. Nor is it without qualification, particularly in the context of the markedly increased diversity in legal theoretical approaches in the last few decades. However, the notion that gender has some general significance for law is far from widely accepted and there remains a vast body of literature in the field of legal scholarship in which sex/gender considerations are not visibly present.

Taking the position of the jurisprudential status quo, this poses no problem. Sometimes gender is relevant to law, sometimes not. However, if one is to adopt the view, as some feminists do, that gender is an inherent aspect of law, or assert that law is in some general sense gendered, or even merely speculate that the relationship between law and gender may, in the context of broader intellectual enquiry, be of greater theoretical importance than the scholarly orthodoxy acknowledges, the relative neglect of gender in legal scholarship does seem to invite explanation. For the most part this task has been undertaken by feminist legal scholars in which context the analytical gaze has been filtered through a lens predominantly concerned with gender injustice and solutions thereto. Thus, feminists have explored how gendered hierarchies are constructed and reinforced by law; they have probed the unstated assumptions about masculinity and femininity which operate unseen beneath the patina of legal formalism to influence legal decision-making; they have given extended consideration to the

---

[3] N Simmonds, *Law as a Moral Idea* (Oxford: OUP, 2007), 4.

potency of law as a progressive tool to eradicate gender injustice and advance gender equality. In these contexts, the deployment of gender as an investigative tool has been a function of a broader critical enquiry into the implication of law in women's disadvantage and, inevitably, the normative and political dimensions of the feminist project have infused the investigative process. At the same time, the emergence of other political and theoretical concerns with a gender dimension—for example, around sexuality, transgender identity, and masculinity—along with an increasing tendency to view gender as part of a much more complex matrix of interlocking inequalities encompassing race, class, disability, religion, and so on, has widened the cast of gender as an analytical frame well beyond a focus on women's disadvantage or gender injustice per se. As a consequence, the intellectual and political ties between gender as an analytical starting point and feminism as a critical project have loosened, yielding a normatively and conceptually more diverse range of approaches to issues of gender and law.

This chapter does *not* set out to explore the relation of gender and law in terms of the theoretical developments sketched briefly above. I am not proposing to offer a chronology of approaches to gender and law. Nor am I presenting an account of feminist legal theory or considering how gender intersects with race, class, and other factors in the production of inequality and injustice. These are all important issues and concerns with which I, among many others, have previously engaged.[4] My purpose here is different and, in a sense, more narrowly focused (although, arguably, by reframing the enquiry as I do, new avenues for exploration are opened up). In any event, the object is to tease out and explore the range of ways in which the

---

[4] See eg J Conaghan, 'Reassessing the Feminist Theoretical Project in Law' (2000) 27 *JLS* 351; J Conaghan, 'Feminist Legal Studies: General Introduction' in J Conaghan (ed), *Feminist Legal Studies: Critical Concepts in Law*, Vol 1 (London: Routledge, 2009), 1; J Conaghan, 'The Making of a Field or the Building of a Wall? Feminist Legal Studies and Law, Gender and Sexuality' (2009) 17(3) *Feminist Legal Studies* 303; J Conaghan, 'Intersectionality and the Feminist Project in law' in E Grabham, D Cooper, J Krishnadas, and D Herman, *Intersectionality and Beyond: Law, Power and the Politics of Location* (London: Routledge-Cavendish, 2008), 21.

relation between law and gender has been presented within the literature and to gauge the extent to which extant accounts establish gender as a category of general relevance in the context of legal scholarly enquiry. To this end I draw upon a loose, tentative, and non-prescriptive taxonomy of approaches adapted from an earlier essay in which I reflected on what might be entailed by feminist assertions that law is 'male'.[5] The masculinity of law has been a common theme in feminist legal scholarship although, as a position, it is perhaps most closely associated with the work of Catharine MacKinnon.[6] In my earlier analysis I considered three ways in which we might understand the claim that law is male. First, the claim might be predominantly historical and/or empirical, in the sense of acknowledging that, historically, law was made by and for men and that, to an empirically determinable extent, continues to produce legal outcomes which privilege male interests and concerns. Alternatively (or in addition) it might be contended that law is *ideologically* male in that a masculine bias inheres in the values and assumptions law endorses and the priorities and interests it privileges. Another way of saying this is to assert that law reflects and supports what is really a male point of view. Finally, it might be suggested that law is symbolically male, that is, while not directly or substantively incorporating a male point of view, law valorizes or is valorized through symbolic and metaphorical associations with maleness and masculinity. This is a less commonly articulated approach which, in the context of my analysis at the time, found particular resonance in feminist philosophical engagements with the idea of reason and with symbolic and representational associations of reason with masculinity.

Nowadays, feminist scholars rarely attempt to put forward the claim that law is male as it recognizably relies upon a fixed and

---

[5] J Conaghan, 'Tort Law and the Feminist Critique of Reason' in A Bottomley (ed), *Feminist Perspectives on the Foundational Subjects of Law* (London: Cavendish, 1996), 47.

[6] See eg C A MacKinnon, *Towards a Feminist Theory of State* (Cambridge, Ma: Harvard University Press, 1989), 161–2: 'The state is male in the feminist sense. The law sees and treats women the way men see and treat women'.

unitary conception of masculinity in terms of a core set of
features which serve as an appropriate indicator of maleness.
Such an essentialist and reductionist approach has increasingly
given way to an understanding of masculinity, and indeed
gender categories more generally, as complex, pluralistic, and
unstable.[7] This makes it much more difficult to talk in a meaningful way about law as male. A further difficulty with characterizing law as male is that it may be taken to imply a
masculine bias in law which is absolute and unqualified. Yet, it
cannot be denied that there are times when law benefits and
empowers women. Moreover as Carol Smart has observed, law
develops unevenly and not always consistently in terms of the
interests it upholds and the outcomes it produces.[8] The resulting
distributive configurations are complex and often cut across
gender categories. If law *can* be said to favour one particular
group more than others, whether in terms of distributive outcomes or general standpoint, it is probably white, middle-class,
heterosexual, able-bodied men who are favoured, but to
acknowledge this is far from establishing that law is resolutely
and unconditionally male. While it may be apparent that gender
is a feature of the power relations mediated and supported by
law, and indeed, that it is a category of significance in terms of
legal distributional patterns, this does not, without more, sustain
a claim that law is male.

It makes more sense therefore to speculate that law is *gendered*
and certainly, in the context of considering whether, and to
what extent, gender is a category of significance in law, it is
surely useful to explore the historical, ideological, and/or symbolical dimensions to such a claim. Again, it must be emphasized
that the analytical frame deployed here is designed to serve the
practical function of organizing the enquiry in an accessible and
intelligible way, in particular, to aid the apprehension of differences in approach to the theorization of the law–gender relation.
The template I adopt is neither authoritative nor exhaustive.
Moreover, in their practical manifestation, the approaches

---

[7] See eg R Collier, *Men, Law and Gender: Essays on the Man of Law* (London:
Routledge-Cavendish, 2011).
[8] C Smart, *Feminism and the Power of Law* (London: Routledge, 1989).

I distinguish are closely related and, more often than not, present as inextricably entangled elaborations of one other. In teasing them apart, however artificially, the idea is to get a clearer picture of the nature and implications of existing theorizations of law and gender, and thereby come to a better understanding of the significance of gender in law and legal thought.

3.2 GENDER AS HISTORICAL TRACE

In decisions such as *Best v Fox*[9] and *R v R*,[10] considered in detail in the previous chapter, the judicial tendency is to approach instances of gender bias in law as remnants of a patriarchal legal past which law is gradually casting off. In this kind of analysis, gender features as a historical aberration, a mistake to be corrected within the context of a conception of law as an essentially benign and progressive institution, albeit, as the product of human design, prone to error. This is a teleological idea of law in pursuit of itself, as moving inexorably towards its own self-realization as a neutral, objective, and fundamentally rational mechanism for the resolution of disputes in a just and civilized society. At the normative heart of this ideation is formal legal equality, the principle that 'every man, whatever be his rank or condition, is subject to the ordinary law of the realm', identified by the 19th-century jurist, Alfred Venn Dicey, as a core feature of the Rule of Law.[11] Unsurprisingly, this principle is a common feature of judicial oaths, in a British context expressed in a sworn commitment to 'do right to all manner of peoples after the laws and usages of this Realm without fear or favour, affection or will'.[12] It is also widely regarded as an essential precondition of individual freedom. Economist and political theorist, Friedrich Hayek, explains the significance of formal equality in the following terms:

---

[9] [1952] AC 716.   [10] [1992] 1 AC 599.

[11] A V Dicey, *Introduction to the Study of the Law of the Constitution*, 6th edn (London: Macmillan & Co, 1902), 189.

[12] 'Judicial affirmation' (Judicial Office, 2012) <http://www.judiciary.gov.uk/about-the-judiciary/introduction-to-justice-system/oaths> accessed 30 July 2012.

... When we obey laws in the sense of general abstract rules laid down irrespective of their application to us, we are not subject to another man's will and are therefore free. It is because the lawgiver does not know the particular cases to which his rules apply ... that it can be said that laws and not men rule ... as a true law should not name any particulars so it should not especially single out any specific person or group of persons.[13]

This deference to formal equality is at the heart of the neglect of gender (as well as race, class, and other socially significant categories) in conventional legal theory. Through the invocation of the maxim of equality before the law, sex/gender is effectively removed from legal theoretical consideration while adherence to a gender-neutral account of law emerges as a virtue by conforming to the rule of law ideal.

And yet, one of the most striking features of this aspect of rule of law ideology is that it comfortably co-existed with the formal disqualification of women from many aspects of legal person-hood and entitlement. Dicey himself, in almost the same breath that he extols the virtues of the rule of law, acknowledges that the call for women's political suffrage is viewed by many as against the nature of things.[14] By contrast, John Stuart Mill rails against the legal regimes which deny women equal protection under the law: 'The disabilities of women are the only case ... in which laws and institutions take persons at their birth and ordain that they shall never in all their lives be allowed to compete for certain things'.[15] In *The Subjection of Women*, Mill effectively calls upon law to deliver on its promise of formal equality which he regards as a natural and logical corollary to human liberty.[16] Law is thus required to 'perfect' itself by removing such disqualifications and distinctions between persons as are

[13]   F Hayek, *The Constitution of Liberty* (Chicago: University of Chicago Press, 1960), 153–4.

[14]   A discussion of the issue of women's suffrage can be found in a revised introduction to the 8th edition of Dicey, *Introduction to the Law of the Constitution*, published in 1915.

[15]   J S Mill, *The Subjection of Women*, first published 1869, edited by S M Okin (Indianapolis: Hackett Publishing Inc, 1988), 20. On the legal situation of women in 19th-century Britain, see further Chapter Four.

[16]   J S Mill, *On Liberty* (Harmondsworth: Penguin, 1976) first published 1859.

inconsistent with the commitment to legal equality. In this way, the misconceptions and partialities of the past may be put to rest and law can present itself as truly universal, with gender an irrelevant characteristic of which law should properly take no account. It is in this sense that Richard Wasserstrom, in his classic exposition of the principle of formal equality, maintains that race and gender should be as irrelevant to law as eye colour.[17]

Formal legal equality provides the traditional frame within which the relationship between law and gender is located and explored, and it is certainly that to which the legal mainstream remains most receptive. Espousing the principle of formal equality also accommodates recognition of the fact that while gender *ought* to be irrelevant to law, in terms of historical development and, to some empirically determinable extent, contemporary application, it is not. From this starting point, an analytical perspective on law and gender, broadly captured within the rubric of liberal feminism, has emerged. It begins with recognition that, as a matter of historical fact, law was crafted by men in their own image and that this historical legacy struggles to erase itself from the topography of modern law. This remains empirically evident in legal practice and institutions: notwithstanding the vastly increased representation of women lawyers, men still enjoy far better career prospects within the legal profession and women continue to complain of an institutional culture in which they feel marginalized and often sexualized.[18]

During the late 19th and early 20th centuries, liberal feminism was deeply invested in challenging the 'disabilities' which law imposed upon women, preventing them from entering the professions, holding public office, or participating as full citizens in the political and commercial spheres. Over time, however, it became clear that excising all traces of the patriarchal inheritance from law required more than the eradication of formal, gender-based distinctions. The social and political order with which law

---

[17] R Wasserstrom, 'Racism, Sexism and Preferential Treatment: An Approach to the Topics' (1977) 24(3) *UCLA L Rev* 581.
[18] U Schulz and G Shaw (eds), *Women in the World's Legal Professions* (London: Hart Publishing, 2003).

had long been associated was gendered to the core and the adoption of a position of gender-neutrality in the application of legal rules could do little to unsettle deeply embedded social hierarchies and widely shared cultural attitudes and beliefs. Moreover, in a context in which access to power and resources remained very unevenly spread, the practical, distributive effect of legal rules adhering to a gender-neutral form was often simply to inflict new disadvantages upon women. The legal rules regarding the disposition of property in the context of the breakdown of intimate relationships serve as a good example here. It cannot be denied that the married women's property reforms of the late 19th century (particularly when taken in conjunction with the legal drift towards greater and more equal access to divorce), at the time represented a considerable advance by recognizing women's legal status as separate from their husbands and empowering them to hold property in their own right.[19] Such reforms serve as a classic example of the removal of the gendered legal 'disabilities' which Mill and others decried. However the reforms also yielded significant, unanticipated, practical disadvantages for women in the context of relationship breakdown. While women were now entitled to keep their own earnings and inheritance on divorce, so also were their husbands; and as married women had very limited opportunities to earn and few inherited, women often found themselves with little or no property in the aftermath of divorce. These concerns were not really addressed by law until the 1970s[20] and even today non-earning cohabitees remain financially vulnerable in the context of relationship breakdown.[21]

As the need to eliminate formal gender distinctions from law began to diminish, the limits of formal equality as a feminist strategy became increasingly apparent and the nature of feminist

---

[19] See eg Married Women's Property Act 1870 and 1882; Matrimonial Causes Act 1857 and 1923. These developments are considered further in Chapter Four.

[20] See especially Matrimonial Proceedings and Property Act 1970 and the Matrimonial Causes Act 1975.

[21] Law Commission, *Cohabitation: The Financial Consequences of Relationship Breakdown* (Law Com No 307, 2007).

engagement with law underwent change. In particular, greater attention was paid to the potential of law as a progressive tool which might be wielded on women's behalf. At the same time, because the application of formally equal laws to people who were already differently situated was proving as likely to exacerbate as alleviate gender inequality, some feminists began to challenge the allegiance of law to formal equality and argue for differential or 'special' treatment for women to accommodate differences between the sexes.[22] In other words, instead of insisting that gender be disregarded by law, the position became one of calling upon law, at least in some instances, expressly to take gender into account.

Disagreement about whether law should treat women in the same way as men or take account of women's difference has been a recurring theme in feminist legal engagement.[23] A particular example is the debate which emerged around pregnancy and maternity rights in the 1980s. On the one hand, some feminists argued that pregnancy at work should be subject to the same legal regime governing other kinds of workplace incapacity or absence, that is, as part of some generic sickness or disability scheme. On the other hand, many feminists maintained that such an approach made it impossible for women to compete in the workplace on equal terms with men and that the pursuit of gender equality required recognition of special, sex-specific rights and protections for pregnant workers. At the heart of such disagreement was contention around the ideal of equality in law: did equality require women to be treated in the same way as men or should differences between men and women (natural or social) mandate differences in treatment in order to produce more equal outcomes (what became known in feminist legal scholarship as 'the equal treatment/special treatment debate').[24]

---

[22] See eg E Wolgast, *Equality and the Rights of Women* (Ithaca, NY: Cornell University Press, 1980).

[23] O Banks, *Faces of Feminism: A Study of Feminism as a Social Movement* (Oxford: Basil Blackwell, 1981).

[24] J Sohrab, 'Avoiding the Exquisite Trap: a Critical Look at the Equal Treatment/Special Treatment Debate in Law' (1993) 1(2) *Feminist Legal Studies* 141.

Eventually feminists figured out that the dilemma was normatively loaded in that, whether or not a sameness or difference approach was adopted, the reference point remained constant: women were effectively being measured according to their degree of correspondence with, or deviation from, men. Behind the benign façade of neutral legal rules lurk norms tailored—historically and empirically—to the needs, interests, and lifestyles of men. In a workplace environment in which men have traditionally dominated, the pregnant worker emerges as a low priority, her needs easily cast as a form of 'special' pleading. In conceiving of pregnancy in terms of 'difference', legal debate around pregnancy and maternity rights is premised upon a corporeal norm to which the capacity to give birth does not conform. That it is the *capacity* to give birth which is considered atypical, not the *incapacity* to do so, speaks volumes about the metaphysical model underpinning the legal subject in play here: the 'disembodied' subject of labour law is revealed to be endowed by somatic features which are unequivocally male; and what becomes clear is that the residual effects of social and legal arrangements historically premised on women's exclusion and/ or subordination are not so easy to erase.

Formal legal equality fails as a feminist ideal because, against the historical backdrop of a gendered social order, it requires women to behave like men, to conform to values and be judged by measures which were largely developed with men in mind. For the same reason, formal legal equality offers an inadequate and misleading account of the place of gender in law. The simple solution of 'adding' women to the privileges of legal personhood by removing formal distinctions and disqualifications from law has not resulted in any great leap towards substantive gender equality. Nor, it seems, has it succeeded in eliminating gender from legal operations. What it does is to render less visible gendered aspects of those operations particularly when law is viewed through a formalist frame in which legal and non-legal considerations are assumed to be readily distinguishable: a truly gendered analysis turns out to require a layer of investigation not generally considered to be part of legal enquiry. Unearthing the normative premises which support legal rules and doctrines, and considering their impact and effects in a wider social, political and cultural context requires a penetration of the boundaries of the strictly legal and a reframing of the legal landscape in terms which threaten the integrity of law as a discrete sphere of operation.

Nevertheless, this is the direction which gender-led analyses have taken, the concern that law fulfils its liberal promise gradually being replaced by a suspicion that patriarchal values and assumptions about women's inferiority and social role are knitted into the very fabric of liberal legal thought. A particularly influential critique in this context is Carole Pateman's now classic text, *The Sexual Contract*.[25] Taking as her focus the social contractarian theories of 17th and 18th century political thought (in particular the work of Hobbes, Locke, and Rousseau), Pateman argues that built into the social contract upon which the political order is imagined to rest is an implicit sexual contract effecting and legitimating the power of men over women. What Pateman is suggesting is that the civil society envisaged by social contract theory not only assumes but depends upon women's subordination.

As a study of texts, Pateman's arguments are compelling, although not without their critics.[26] More importantly, however, they do go some way to explaining how rule of law ideology could co-exist comfortably with women's formal exclusion from political and legal citizenship. A key conceptual device in this context is the public/private distinction: political theorists such as Locke expressly distinguished between the public world of political power and the private world of familial (or, as Locke described it, 'paternal') power[27] as a way of justifying differences in approach to the regulation of the two spheres, the former being deemed to be based on agreement, the latter resting explicitly upon gendered hierarchy. In the same

[25] C Pateman, *The Sexual Contract* (London: Polity Press, 1988).

[26] For a critical overview of engagements with Pateman, see J Richardson, *Selves, Persons and Individuals: Philosophical Perspectives on Women and Legal Obligations* (Farnham: Ashgate, 2004), chs 5 and 6.

[27] J Locke, *The Second Treatise of Civil Government* (1690, Ascot). Locke argued that while political power was subject to the social contract, paternal power—the power of the husband and father over his family—was naturally occurring.

way, law has often sought to explain and justify differences in the application of legal standards through the designation of particular spheres of regulation as public or private. Challenging the apparent failure of law adequately to address violence against women in the home, for example, feminist scholars have high-lighted liberal reliance upon notions of privacy to account for the reluctance of law to 'intervene' in family life.[28] Ngaire Naffine takes this argument further, arguing that there is a contradiction at the heart of law which reflects a tension in liberalism between the public (or as Naffine describes it *Gesell-schaft*) values of the marketplace and the private (or *Gemeinschaft*) values associated with belonging to a family or a social group. Law and society, Naffine contends, assign to women the role of 'holding the two worlds [of *Gemeinschaft* and *Gesellschaft*] together'.[29] The liberal contradiction is thus resolved, but at women's expense. By locating women in the private sphere, engaged in caregiving and community support, men are freed to pursue the benefits of active political and economic citizenship. It thus becomes possible to conceive of the universal subject of law as rational, self-interested, fully mature, and largely unencumbered by responsibility for others yet still ensure that necessary arrangements are in place for social production and reproduction.

These insights provide feminism with particular challenges. For example, is it possible to rehabilitate liberalism, to produce a version thereof which does not depend upon a gendered division of labour and an accompanying model of political and legal citizenship? This is a particularly pertinent question to ask in relation to law because, certainly in its Anglo-American

---

[28] F Olsen, 'The Myth of State Intervention in the Family' (1985) 18 *University of Michigan Journal of Law Reform* 835, and see generally K O'Donovan, *Sexual Divisions in Law* (London: Weidenfeld & Nicholson, 1985) and M Thornton (ed), *Public and Private: Feminist Legal Debates* (Melbourne: OUP, 1995).

[29] N Naffine, *Law and the Sexes: Explorations in Feminist Jurisprudence* (Sidney: Allen & Unwin, 1990), 149. The German terms *Gemeinschaft* (literally meaning 'community') and *Gesellschaft* (literally meaning 'association') were originally deployed by the sociologist, Ferdinand Tonnies, to distinguish different forms of social relations.

manifestations but also to a varying degree in jurisdictions around the world, law is so deeply infused with liberal values and ideals. Returning the focus to how best to conceive the relationship between law and gender, does the claim that gender is theoretically irrelevant to law now depend upon erasing the vestiges of patriarchy from liberal legal thought? And (how) can this be done?

In recent years, feminist theorists have begun to re-engage more positively with liberal ideas and values. Martha Nussbaum, for example, has argued strongly in favour of a return to universal values and has subjected the feminist critique of liberalism to a similarly trenchant critique of her own, the thrust of which is that feminists have oversimplified liberalism and failed to recognize that it comes in many varieties, not all of which are encompassed within the contours of feminist censure. Nussbaum proceeds to mount a fairly defiant defence of individual autonomy as a key liberal value which too many women across the world are denied.[30] Similarly, Drucilla Cornell argues that the feminist turn away from universal values is erroneous. Cornell calls upon feminism to embrace equality and freedom as desirable legal ideals which, with certain minimum guarantees, allow each of us to pursue our own particular project of becoming a person.[31] Finally, Vanessa Munro has subjected feminist legal theory to the wholesale scrutiny of a rehabilitated liberal lens.[32] Like Cornell, Munro is attracted to liberalism because it offers the possibility of articulating universal principles which are not dependent upon essentialist invocations of sex/gender. Given the complexity and problematicity of sex and gender as categories, the very *sexlessness* of liberalism, once for feminists its principal weakness, in this context becomes a key strength.

---

[30] M Nussbaum, *Sex and Social Justice* (Oxford: OUP, 1999), especially ch 2.

[31] D Cornell, *The Imaginary Domain: Abortion, Pornography and Sexual Harassment* (New York: Routledge, 1995). See especially ch 1. See also D Cornell, *At the Heart of Freedom: Feminism, Sex and Equality* (Princeton: Princeton University Press, 1998).

[32] V Munro, *Law and Politics at the Perimeter: Re-evaluating Key Debates in Feminist Legal Theory* (Oxford: Hart Publishing, 2007).

The attractions to feminism of a return to liberal values are undeniable. One does not get far politically or ethically without norms and the normative appeal of liberalism is as compelling as it is comforting. In particular, the reinstatement of a discourse of the universal does seem to be an indispensable prerequisite of any argument premised on gender equality. The difficulty however, from the perspective of an enquiry into the place of gender in law, is that liberalism already *is* the language of law; and, the language of law as we have seen, is one in which gender has no formal or acknowledged place. Feminist legal engagements with liberalism tell us what the place of gender *ought* to be in an idealized liberal legal order—essentially irrelevant—but they say little about how gender actually features in legal operations and practices. Indeed, the idealization of the legal order is part of the problem here as it requires the abstraction of law and the legal subject from any context in which gender is an acknowledged feature. On the question of whether feminism might benefit politically from renewed engagement with liberal values and appeals to universalism, the jury is perhaps still out. However, in terms of understanding the interpenetration of social and legal processes, in terms of getting to grips with the operation of power in legal contexts, and in terms of unpacking the textual particularities of the abstract and universally conceived legal subject in legal discourse—inter alia, bringing gender into view—liberalism continues to offer limited, if any, analytical potential, and indeed is more likely to obscure than illuminate.

3.3 GENDER AS IDEOLOGY OR DISCOURSE

The discussion so far suggests that it may make more sense to understand the operation of gender in law not in terms of an historical trace which still yields occasional and regrettable empirical disparities in legal outcomes, but rather as part of an ideological worldview. Again here, the official position is that law is ideology-free. Law is, or is supposed to be, neutral and impartial, the product of reason and logic not beliefs, dogmas, or opinions. Such rhetoric notwithstanding, even the hardened formalist will concede that law is imbued with moral and political values. It after all is the product of human actions, struggles, and ambitions; as Oliver Wendell Holmes Jr famously observed:

The life of the law has not been logic; it has been experience. The felt necessities of the time, the prevalent moral and political theories, intuitions of public policy, avowed or unconscious, even the prejudices which judges share with their fellow-men, have had a good deal more to do than the syllogism in determining the rules by which men should be governed.[33]

Thus, while not always openly articulated, values and assumptions, intuitions, and even prejudices, are part and parcel of law. Moreover, exposing and unpacking these, challenging their authority as well as their ideological and distributive effects should properly be a focus of legal scholarly endeavour. Nor must it be forgotten that law is a key site of the operation of power; within law power may be conferred, challenged, negotiated, or dispersed, producing winners and losers, inclusions and exclusions, domains of privilege and neglect. There is nothing neutral about these processes or the outcomes they produce.

It is sometimes argued that the values which inhere in law—some of them at least—are a necessary feature of law itself; that is, that certain principles are simply part of what law *is*, rather than some external ideological importation which is up for debate. This is one way in which legal theorists have sought to account for the relationship between law and morality and defend what they see as key legal concepts and ideals.[34] Moreover, within legal and political philosophy, an unspoken line is often drawn between moral and political *values*—which are thought to be accessible through reason as well as necessary and desirable features of social life—and *ideology* which is regarded pejoratively as a corruption of law, an illegitimate usurpation of legal and political space usually for disreputable or

[33] O W Holmes Jr, *The Common Law* (New York: Little, Brown, & Co, 1881), 5.

[34] See eg L Fuller, *The Morality of Law* (New Haven: Yale University Press, 1965). For further discussion of the role of values in law, see §6.5 and §6.6.

fanatical ends. According to this understanding, ideology is a form of deception, entailing the promulgation of false or misleading ideas, often by a ruling class, which deludes oppressed groups into agreeing to the conditions of their own oppression. This notion of ideology as a distortion or manipulation of reality is sometimes found in Marxism, although not all Marxists are wedded to this view and Marx himself deployed the concept of ideology with some ambiguity.[35]

In the analysis here, I use ideology benignly to denote a body of ideas forming the basis of a way of thinking, usually linked in some way to the material conditions which underpin social organization. If we understand ideology in this way, that is, as groupings of ideas, values, and beliefs which produce particular understandings or ways of seeing, it cannot be denied that law is ideologically brimful. The content of law is undeniably expressive—although not necessarily absolutely or unconditionally—of the kind of social organization it supports. Moreover, many of the concepts which we take for granted in our daily lives and which feature prominently in our cognitive armoury—for example, notions of property, contract, and theft—derive their meaning wholly or partly from legal rules and doctrines. Law informs, often quite unconsciously, the way in which we construe and navigate the world around us. It is not just a set of rules or principles which we feel obligated to obey; it is also an interpretative schema which works alongside other founts of sense and value (for example, science, culture, and religion) to influence our perceptions and experiences and give them meaning. Law then is cognitively constitutive of consciousness; it helps to bring into being social (and sexual) subjects and it serves both as a source of knowledge and as a form of knowledge validation.

Understood in this way, 'ideology' is not easily distinguishable from 'discourse', a term popularized by the writings of Michel Foucault[36] and frequently invoked in feminist and other critical analyses of law. In fact, the two terms—ideology

[35] See R Williams, *Keywords: A Vocabulary of Culture and Society* (London: Fontana, 1976), 153–7.

[36] See especially M Foucault, *The Archaeology of Knowledge*, trans A Sheridan (London: Tavistock, 1972).

and discourse—are etymologically related, 'ideology' being derived from combining the Greek terms *ideo* (ideas) and *logia* (discourse or speech). While in common parlance discourse tends to denote speech or language in general, in social and cultural theory, it has a simultaneously narrower and broader meaning: narrower in so far as it signifies not speech in general but sequences or patterns of thought, beliefs, and ideas, which through their repeated deployment create meaningful connections or relations between things; broader in reaching beyond language or texts to capture institutions, practices, and other non-linguistic modes of representation. Effectively discourse is a way of capturing processes of knowledge creation, configuration, and authentication producing what Foucault terms 'regimes of truth'.[37] Because the categories and concepts through which we structure and communicate what we 'know' also have the effect of shaping and containing *how* and *what* we think, powerful and influential discourses like law and medicine, which profess expertise, are strongly self-legitimating, and rely heavily upon claims to truth or objectivity, significantly affect our perceptions of what is 'real'. This is not to say that no reality exists outside discourse—a conclusion which occasionally if erroneously follows this kind of claim—but rather that discourse inevitably frames and mediates our access to the real; we cannot easily or practically disentangle the material world from our experience and apprehension of it.

It follows too that discourse/ideology is imbricated in the production and mediation of relations of power: power and knowledge are closely allied, not just in the sense that those who have access to knowledge therefore have access to power but also in that access to power is of particular significance in determining what counts as knowledge. As Smart has argued, the *power* of law goes beyond the juridical power to compel conduct and directly determine outcomes. Law also exercises power by laying claim to represent a true, objective, or privileged account which has the authority to suppress and

---

[37] See eg M Foucault, *The Birth of Bio-Politics: Lectures at the College de France 1978–1979*, trans G Burchell (Basingstoke: Palgrave MacMillan, 2004).

obscure other points of view.[38] In fact, the contemporary academic preference for 'discourse' over 'ideology' is very much linked to a shift in critical thinking away from a conception of power as top-down and centralized—the prerogative of the sovereign, the state, or the ruling class—to a Foucauldian notion of power as fluid, decentralized, and dispersed among institutions, individuals, and groups.[39] Because ideology is associated with Marxism and power in the former sense, and discourse is viewed as a primary mechanism for operations of power understood in the latter sense, ideology has given way to discourse as the chosen designation for what are effectively patterned forms of representation with truth-conferring potency. In this context, the discursive or ideological power of law flows directly from its ability to present itself as neutral, discrete, and inherently legitimate.

Bringing the focus back to the relation between law and gender, it is often argued that law reflects and purveys gendered ideologies as discursive 'truths'. There are a wealth of examples within the feminist legal literature of the incorporation into law of problematic and contestable gendered assumptions and beliefs. For example, feminists have long maintained that rape law, both in its substance and practical application, is infused with ideas about sexuality which operate to deny women justice if their experiences and accounts do not conform to preconceived (male) notions of appropriate female sexual behaviour.[40] Feminists have also argued that the provocation defence in criminal law, in particular the requirement of 'a sudden and temporary loss of control' as a precondition for the operation of the defence, presupposes, and therefore privileges, the way in which men may respond to the threat of violence or grave insult by reacting in the heat of the moment (as, for example, when a husband, coming upon his wife engaged in sexual intercourse with another man,

---

[38] Smart, *The Power of Law*.

[39] M Foucault, *Discipline and Punish*, A Sheridan trans (London: Penguin, 1991).

[40] The classic account here is C A MacKinnon, 'Feminism, Marxism, Method and State: Towards a Feminist Jurisprudence' (1983) 8 *Signs: Journal of Culture in Women and Society* 635.

erupts in violence). It is increasingly being recognized that women, often for reasons of self-protection and comparative physical vulnerability, are likely to delay reacting to injury or abuse until a time when they feel less threatened (as, for example, when the battered wife attacks her violent husband only when he is asleep or incapacitated). Because provocation is tailored to a type of behaviour with which women are less likely to conform, women have encountered difficulties in invoking the defence. As a consequence, in many jurisdictions the defence has undergone reform.[41] In campaigning for law reform in this kind of context, the feminist object is not just to ensure that law produces more neutral, less gendered outcomes; the concern is also to harness directly the ideological/discursive power of law as a way of interpreting and evaluating human behaviour. In the context of provocation, the aim is at least in part to use law to induce people to think differently about what kind of mitigating factors *ought* to trigger a defence to violence. Similarly, legal reform designed to reframe rape in gender-neutral terms as 'sexual assault' is generally expressive of an ideological aim to change people's understanding of rape, so that instead of regarding it as an extreme expression of sexual (and therefore 'natural') urges, it is seen as violent, criminal behaviour.[42]

The above examples evidence the gendered ideological content of particular laws or areas of law as well as efforts to deploy law expressly for ideological ends. While criminal law is a common focus of attention in this context, feminists have directed this kind of analysis to almost every conceivable area of law and legal policy. Debate about the appropriate legal response to pregnancy in the workplace reveals a gendered conceptualization of workplace participation in labour law. In tort law, Leslie Bender, among others, has explored the gendered

---

[41] See generally D Tyson, *Sex, Culpability, and the Defence of Provocation* (London: Routledge, 2012). In the UK, the defence of provocation was abolished by the Coroners and Justice Act 2009 and replaced with a defence of 'loss of self-control'. Sexual jealousy is expressly excluded as a ground for invoking the new defence (Tyson, 44–8).

[42] P Rush, 'Criminal Law and Reform of Rape' in C McGlynn and V Munro (eds), *Rethinking Rape Law: International and Comparative Perspectives* (Abingdon: Routledge, 2010), 237.

content of civil liability standards. Focusing on the standard of care in negligence (traditionally epitomized by reference to the 'reasonable man'), Bender has argued that negligence law valorizes conduct and attributes typically associated with masculinity. In emphasizing cost-benefit calculation and instrumental rationality as the acknowledged standard by which a defendant's actions are judged, tort law condones a view of the world in which actors can escape responsibility for their injurious conduct by demonstrating that the benefits to them outweigh the costs to the injured. Negligence law also effectively allows tortfeasors to buy their way out of aggressive or harmful behaviour.[43] The argument here is, partly, that legal standards reflect 'male' values and behaviour because law has been crafted by and for men and therefore tends to privilege the way in which men interact with one another. However, a commonly related contention is that as a consequence of this privileging, alternative ways of approaching dispute resolution and more preferable norms for the governance of human conduct in general—norms typically associated with femininity (for example, a standard of care that is actually more caring)—have been overlooked.

At this point, feminist analysis begins to move into rather murky waters as it is not always clear whether what is being claimed is that men are *naturally* calculated and women *naturally* caring, whether these gendered behaviours derive from the social roles men and women typically occupy, whether the alleged correspondence between gender and values/behaviour is absolute or conditional, or indeed, whether the case being made is one which seeks normatively to privilege caring over calculated behaviour as the appropriate standard for tort law. In this context, a text which is both influential and, at the same time, frequently maligned, is Carol Gilligan's *In a Different Voice*[44] which prompted a flurry of articles and considerable

---

[43] L Bender, 'Changing the Values of Tort Law' (1990) 25(4) *Tulsa LJ* 759. For a general overview of feminist critiques of tort law, see J Conaghan, 'Tort Law and Feminist Critique' (2003) 56(1) *Current Legal Problems* 175.

[44] C Gilligan, *In a Different Voice: Psychological Theory and Women's Development* (Cambridge: Harvard University Press, 1980).

debate in feminist legal scholarship in the 1980s. Gilligan engaged in a series of empirical studies of male and female behaviour around moral reasoning and decision-making and suggested a correlation between gender and different ways of thinking through ethical problems. Specifically, she argued that women tended to reason in a different 'voice' or 'register' to men. While men were inclined to invoke abstract principles and a hierarchy (or 'ladder') of rights to resolve dilemmas, women were more likely to think contextually, to eschew a formal, rights-based approach, and to take account of and seek to protect the web of relationships within which a dilemma was located. Although Gilligan was careful to emphasize that her conclusions were based on the data generated by her studies and that their broader application demanded further investigation, it was difficult for feminists (and others) not to succumb to gendered generalizations based on her work, not least because her account resonated strongly with many women's personal experiences, particularly when encountering the study of law. More broadly Gilligan's arguments became the frame for the gendered juxtaposition of two particular ethics: the 'ethic of justice' and the 'ethic of care'. The general thrust of feminist critique was that law deferred too much to the first and not enough to the second.[45]

The engagement of feminist legal scholars with Gilligan's 'ethic of care' usefully draws attention to the different levels at which feminist critiques of law may operate. Sometimes the focus is on excavating the ideological content and operation of particular legal concepts and doctrines. At other times, the analytical gaze is broader, the concern being to establish a more general link between law and gender in the context of such excavations. Gilligan's analysis offers a framework for exploring the claim that the gender dimension in law goes beyond matters of substance and is part of the form that law takes, that gender is implicated in the way law goes about solving legal disputes. At its strongest, this can amount to a

---

[45] For an inclusive theorization of the role of justice and care in legal operations, see R West, *Caring for Justice* (New York: NYU Press, 1997), especially ch 1.

claim that gender is inherent in the idea of law, certainly as understood in modern Western culture. In seeking to understand the extent to which this claim is sustainable it is useful to look at another way in which gender and law have been linked and that is metaphorically or symbolically. In the section that follows, the symbolic or metaphorical deployment of gender in law to link or connect concepts and ideas or establish hierarchies of value is explored.

3.4 GENDER AS SYMBOL OR METAPHOR

Symbol and metaphor are closely connected notions. When we speak of a symbol we generally invoke something which stands in the place of or represents something else, as, for example, when we call upon the image of the female form to depict justice. Similarly, metaphor, etymologically derived from the Greek *meta pherein*—'to carry beyond'—usually entails saying one thing to mean another. It is a linguistic technique which enables us to take our understanding of something beyond its immediate spatial, material, and temporal context and connect or relate it to something else.[46] The physical union of man and woman in sexual intercourse, for example, may be seen as the metaphorical underpinning of the common law notion of coverture, the idea that husband and wife become a unity, a single legal person, on marriage. Thus understood, metaphor is clearly important to processes of conceptualization and abstract thinking. The notion of a category, for example, commonly relies upon the metaphor of container. When we identify 'dog' as belonging to the category 'animal', we are deploying a metaphorical logic of containment which allows us to identify some things as inside and contained by, and other things as outside and excluded from, a particular bounded category.[47]

Legal scholars have long acknowledged the role of metaphor in law and legal reasoning.[48] However, recent developments in

---

[46] J E Murray, 'Understanding Law as Metaphor' (1984) 34 *Journal of Legal Education* 714, 715.

[47] M L Johnson, 'Mind, Metaphor and Law' (2007) 58 *Mercer LR* 845, 857–9.

[48] See eg L Fuller, *Legal Fictions* (Palo Alto: Stanford University Press, 1968), 11–19.

cognitive science emphasizing the significance of embodiment to processes of reasoning and cognition have generated renewed attention towards the operation of metaphor and symbol in law and to processes of cognition and representation more generally.[49] Mark Johnson has observed that 'human law is a many-splendored creation of the human mind'.[50] He argues that law, as much as anything, is the work of the imagination. Metaphors and symbols are part of this imaginative process, providing ready-made images or imaginaries which aid us in conceptualizing, ordering, and navigating legal and philosophical terrain. The image of Justitia is just such an imaginary, as is the idealization of the common law as a medieval lady discussed in Chapter One. These are more obvious examples of the symbolic deployment of gender, and specifically the female form, to communicate particular ideas about law and to valorize aspects of legal operations. There are also close cultural and symbolic links between law and masculinity, supporting the normative privileging of order over disorder, coherence over chaos, reason over emotion and so on. The close association of law with reason provides a particularly good example of the symbolic operation of gender in a legal context, although the nature of the connection here requires some teasing out.

There are of course clear historical and cultural correlations between ideas of reason and masculinity; philosophical and political thought is replete with examples of the tendency to correlate reason with maleness.[51] Such gendered allusions to rationality are also a recognizable aspect of legal culture, 'humorously' captured in Alan Herbert's depiction of women in his parody of the common law: 'There exists a class of beings

---

[49] See generally G Lakoff and M Johnson, *Metaphors We Live By* (Chicago: University of Chicago Press, 1980); G Lakoff and M Johnson, *Philosophy in the Flesh: The Embodied Mind and its Challenge to Western Thought* (New York: Basic Books, 1999) and, in a legal context, S L Winter, *A Clearing in the Forest: Law, Life, and the Mind* (Chicago: University of Chicago, Press, 2001); see also *Mercer Law Review Symposium*, 'Using Metaphors in Legal Analysis and Communications' (2007) 58(3) *Mercer L Rev* 835–992.

[50] Johnson, 'Mind, Metaphor and Law', 845.

[51] See especially G Lloyd, *The Man of Reason: 'Male' and 'Female' in Western Philosophy*, 2nd edn (London: Routledge, 1993).

illogical, impulsive, careless, irresponsible, extravagant, prejudiced
and free for the most part from those worthy and repellent
excellences which distinguish the Reasonable Man'.[52]

What is the nature of the connection being drawn here? Is it
being suggested that women are in fact irrational and men
otherwise? Sometimes, this *is* in fact the claim being made.
Certainly, it is not difficult to find evidence, within and beyond
legal texts, of a belief in actual differences in the intellectual
processes and capacities of men and women. It is a recognizable
aspect of gendered ideology to designate particular attributes
and behaviours as respectively masculine or feminine. Even John
Stuart Mill, a champion of gender equality, speculated about
the differences in men and women's intellectual capacities. The
'general bent' of women's talents, he argues, 'is towards
the practical'. Women are intuitively perceptive; they gravitate
towards what is immediately before them and are far less interested in scientific laws or general principles: 'a woman seldom
runs wild after an abstraction'.[53] Mill goes on to suggest that the
intellectual differences between men and women complement
each other, therefore turning women's apparent deficiencies in
the sphere of reasoning into strengths. He also acknowledges
that until women are free from the yoke of subjection it cannot
confidently be asserted what in fact they are capable of.

At the time Mill was writing (in the second half of the 19th
century), the question of the nature and extent of women's
capacity to reason was of central importance in the context of
arguments for and against female suffrage.[54] A century and a half
later, the debate about whether or not men and women are
equally capable of reason continues, although nowadays it tends
to take the form of scientific contestation about the relative
cognitive capacities of the male and female brain.[55] However,
if we are fully to comprehend the recurrent association of
masculinity with reason (or a particular form of reason) we

---

[52] A P Herbert, *Uncommon Law*, 8th edn (London: Methuen, 1969), 6.
[53] Mill, *Subjection of Women*, 61–3 and generally ch 3.
[54] See further §4.4 and §6.3.
[55] See generally C Fine, *Delusions of Gender: the Real Science behind Sex
Differences* (London: Icon Books, 2010).

must also acknowledge a representational and symbolic dimension. Genevieve Lloyd argues that: 'the metaphor of maleness is deeply embedded in philosophical articulations of ideas and ideals of reason'.[56] Lloyd, among others, has given extended consideration to the cultural association of reason and masculinity in philosophical texts and while it is not my intention at this point to assess the strength of this claim in a philosophical context, I do give some further consideration to the (inter) relation of gender and *legal* reason in Chapter Six. What I want to do here is reflect upon how and why gender and reason might come to be symbolically connected.

At this point we go back to the origins of the term 'gender' and its connotations of 'sort' or 'kind', discussed in Chapter One. Within this context it should come as no surprise that notions of masculinity and femininity often feature as metaphors of difference, and particularly as opposites. As far back as the Pythagorean Table of Opposites, formulated in the 6th century BC and later explained by Aristotle, male and female appear as one of ten oppositional pairs. Strikingly, the Table also includes good/bad, light/dark, finite/infinite, and straight/crooked, arranged in column form and normatively loaded to favour the right side of the column to the left ('right' and 'left' are another included pair). The conceptual dualisms which are so much a feature of Western philosophical thought find their origins in this kind of oppositional pairing which later formed the basis for other important and hierarchically ordered dichotomies such as form/substance, mind/body, and public/private.

This conception of masculinity and femininity as oppositional is so familiar as to seem quite natural. And yet, as we have already seen in Chapter One, certainly in terms of understandings of the physical form, it has not always been the case that men and women have been conceived as opposites. Thomas Laqueur convincingly argues that until the 18th century the predominant (although not exclusive) conception of the female body was as a lesser or deficient version of the male. This yielded what Laqueur describes as a 'one-sex' model, as opposed to a

---

[56] Lloyd, *The 'Man' of Reason*, viii.

'two-sex' model in which sexual difference is conceived in terms of incommensurable opposition.[57] It should be emphasized here that the one-sex model to which Laqueur refers was predominantly understood in terms of the physiological commonality of the sexes. This did not preclude wider understandings of gender predicated on difference, particularly when it came to non-physiological characteristics, for example, intellect or temperament. In general terms, pre-modern understandings of gender were deeply embedded in ideas of status and social order, so that the social inferiority of women to men was simply taken to be natural and given. It is in this way that we can begin to understand what Laqueur describes as 'the corporeal theatrics of a world where at least two genders correspond to one sex'.[58]

While Laqueur suggests that a conception of sex in terms of incommensurable opposition is a particularly striking feature of modern times, the Pythagorean Table of Opposites is illustrative of a tendency throughout history to view gender difference through an oppositional lens. Bringing the discussion back to law, oppositional thinking is undoubtedly a feature of legal thought. Indeed, law is awash with dualities—for example, between criminal/civil, public/private, form/substance, innocence/guilt, good/bad, just/unjust, legal/illegal—all of which serve as features of law's structure and formal ordering. This dichotomous script inevitably encompasses gender difference, not just substantively—that is, in the way in which law in the past has formally distinguished between men and women for purposes of the conferment of rights and obligations—but also metaphorically or symbolically, in its adherence to and deployment of an oppositional aesthetic. The public/private distinction is perhaps the clearest example of this process in operation. As has already been pointed out, this distinction has been a particularly persistent focus of feminist legal scholarship. The thrust of the feminist argument has been that public/private discourse operates in law both to delineate domains of femininity and masculinity (most commonly in terms of family and market) and

---

[57] T Laqueur, *Making Sex: Body and Gender from the Greeks to Freud* (Cambridge: Harvard University Press, 1990).
[58] Laqueur, *Making Sex*, 25.

to set the terms and limits of state engagement, placing the private sphere beyond the reach of state intervention. The point here is not just that the public/private dichotomy in law has traditionally operated ideologically to shore up patriarchal power in the family, but also that the construction of gender as oppositional has facilitated particular conceptual and cultural linkages between gender and other oppositional pairings, including the public/private distinction. When feminist legal scholars argue that legal reasoning is male they are, at least in part, drawing upon these cultural or metaphorical associations— although it must be acknowledged, and as Gilligan's study and the responses to it show, there remains a tendency, evident even in contemporary scientific discourse, to assert more empirically-based links between gender and intellectual capacity.[59]

A striking example of the convergence of law, gender and oppositions in symbolic processes of representation occurs in Hegel's interpretation of Sophocles' *Antigone* which has been the focus of considerable attention by feminist scholars. The story of Antigone is tragic and familiar; it relates the consequences which flow from Antigone's decision to defy a decree issued by her uncle, King Creon, to leave unburied the body of her brother Polynices, who has been killed in combat, on the grounds that he is an enemy of the state. In defying the decree, Antigone excites the King's wrath and is immolated alive notwithstanding that she justifies her actions by invoking a principle of divine law that all men must be properly buried. The tale thus posits a conflict between human law and the divine expressed by Antigone in the following terms:

> It was not Zeus who made that proclamation
> to me, nor was it Justice, who resides
> in the same house with the gods below the earth
> who put in place for men such laws as yours.
> Nor did I think your proclamation so strong
> That you, a mortal, could overrule the laws
> Of the gods that are unwritten and unfailing.

---

[59] Fine, *Delusions of Gender.*

> For these laws live not now or yesterday
> but always.[60]

In *The Phenomenology of Mind*, Hegel uses Antigone's dilemma to explore conflicting conceptions of ethical living. This is part of a broader study by Hegel of the dialectical evolution of forms of reason and consciousness, drawing directly on Antigone's sex both to frame her choice and account for it. Because, as a woman, home and family are at the heart of her being, Antigone places loyalty to her brother above the dictates of the law of the land and acts accordingly. Creon on the other hand represents the ethics of the state or the wider community. Upon him falls the responsibility of instituting political and social order in the aftermath of conflict, and this requires the efficient operation and enforcement of human law.

Within legal texts, Hegel's discussion of *Antigone* is generally invoked to illustrate the potentiality of conflict between natural (or divine) law and human (or positive) law, in which context the gendered associations may seem oddly out of place. However, if we reframe the encounter as a clash between (positive) law and justice, the gendered connotations come more readily to the fore. After all, the personification of justice as female is a persistent motif across history and cultures. Moreover, as is often the outcome of Greek tragedies, those who cross the gods eventually get their come-uppance. Thus, by the end of the play, Creon has paid for his violation of divine law in the loss of his wife and child. Antigone too is dead but in circumstances where her actions appear to be vindicated.

What is striking about Hegel's discussion of *Antigone* is that it does not follow this line at all. Indeed, Hegel's account is generally viewed as a vindication of Creon. Hegel clearly sees Antigone's choice as representing a less developed form of ethical life, centred on home and family. He observes that 'the law of the family is her inherent implicit inward nature, which does not lie open to the daylight of consciousness' and that, as a woman, she is 'director of the home and the preserver of Divine

---

[60] Sophocles, *Antigone (Drama Classics)*, trans R Gibbons and C Segal (Oxford: OUP, 2003), 73.

Law'.[61] It is men, as citizens, Hegel asserts, who possess 'the self-conscious power belonging to the universal life, the life of the social whole'.[62] This is not a wholesale denigration of women's values—Hegel sees divine and human law, represented in the union of man and woman in marriage, as necessarily complementary. However, human law and the sphere of political community clearly represent a more evolved form of rationality and self-consciousness for Hegel which is distinctly male. 'Human law', Hegel observes 'is the manhood of the community' and political citizenship is properly the domain of masculinity which also requires protection from the taint of womanhood. He goes on to state: 'Womankind...perverts the universal property of the state into a possession and ornament for the family. Women in this way turn to ridicule the grave wisdom of maturity'.[63] Women are thus appropriately confined to the family and incapable of full ethical and political citizenship.

It is interesting to speculate about the extent to which Hegel's analysis of *Antigone* represents his views about the attributes, capacities, and appropriate roles of *actual* men and women; no doubt in this respect he was a product of his times. However, this is not the point I wish to make. My purpose rather is to use Hegel's *Antigone* to illustrate the symbolic or metaphorical deployment of gender difference in the context of a philosophical discussion about different forms of law. Of crucial significance here is the construction of masculinity and femininity as oppositional. Equally important is the alignment of that opposition with a series of other dualisms, including community/family (or state/home), public/private, reason/nature or affect, individual/universal, in which one side of the dualism is clearly favoured over another. In this way gender serves to confer meaning and validation to relationships in terms of 'reciprocal

---

[61] G W F Hegel, *The Phenomenology of Mind (Dover Philosophical Classics)*, trans J B Bailey (Dover Publications Inc, 2004), 262–4.
[62] Hegel, *Phenomenology*, 263.
[63] Hegel, *Phenomenology*, 276.

asymmetry'[64] in the broader context of analyses of the social and political order. More generally, the example shows the power of political and legal imaginaries to naturalize difference, shaping and normatively tilting the way in which we see and interpret the world around us. Metaphors are never 'merely' metaphorical. Rather they are an important tool in our linguistic armoury through which we can make otherwise unobserved and unarticulated connections; effectively deployed, they possess enormous rhetorical and discursive power and are a far more common feature of modes of reasoning than is often acknowledged.

3.5 GENDERED OR GENDERING?

In much of the discussion so far, the enquiry has been framed as an exploration of the place of gender in law. However, such a formulation may be too limited; after all, is it not equally important to consider the place of law in gender? Confining the analysis to how gender features in law may present a misleading picture of law as a passive repository of values replicating and reinforcing wider social and cultural arrangements, including gender-based attitudes, practices, and beliefs. This is a conception of law as a reflection and reiteration of an already gendered social world, a mirror of the reality it regulates, supporting and sustaining that reality, including the power relations therein. Reframing the enquiry in terms of how law is implicated in gender accords law a more active role. Law here is not simply a mirror of the real but rather an operative and constitutive feature thereof. In this formulation, law does more than buttress an already gendered social world; it is directly involved in the processes by which gender and gender differences come into being and take effect. It is a conceptualization of law not simply as gendered but as gendering, amounting to a claim that gendered dynamics of power are (at least in part) produced by law rather than simply reflected within or absorbed by it.

---

[64] J B Elshtain, *Public Man, Private Woman: Women in Social and Political Thought* (Princeton: Princeton University Press, 1993), 176.

It is important to emphasize that within the relevant literature, the relationship between law and gender has been conceived both in terms of how gender features in law and how law
is implicated in gender. Moreover, these approaches are rarely
distinguished or placed in opposition. Most scholars rightly
regard the law–gender relationship in terms of an interactive,
two-way process in which law is simultaneously constituting
and constituted by that which it regulates. The approaches also
tend to share an understanding of gender as discursively constructed rather than as naturally occurring, although in theory
one could take the view—and many judges have done so in the
past—that insofar as gender does feature in law it is merely as a
proper reflection of the natural order of things. Such appeals to
nature operate to take gender out of the sphere of legal consideration, to reposition it as a fixed and immutable truth with
which law cannot and should not interfere. It is in this sense, for
example, that Bradley J, in his famous concurring opinion in
Bradwell v Illinois, invoked nature to support his view that
women should be denied access to the legal profession:

The civil law, as well as *nature* herself, has always recognised a wide
difference in the respective spheres and destinies of man and woman....
The *natural* and proper timidity and delicacy which belongs to the
female sex evidently unfits it for many of the occupations of civil life.[65]

Of course this kind of rationale has much less purchase today and
contemporary theories of law and gender are rarely based on
understandings of gender and gender difference as natural
although some feminists have argued that natural differences
between the sexes, for example, with regard to the capacity to
bear children, ought to serve as grounds for differential treatment of men and women under law.[66] In this context, there is
still a tendency to distinguish between gender as an artificial,
constructed category and sex as a natural, biological truth and to
focus on the eradication through law of the former and the
accommodation by law of the latter. Increasingly, however, as

---

[65] 83 US 130 (1873) 141 (emphasis added) and see further §4.4.2.
[66] See eg Wolgast, *Equality and the Rights of Women.*

observed in Chapter One, the viability of the sex/gender distinction thus understood has become difficult to sustain.

In any event, the idea that law plays an active role in the production of gender relations and subjectivities as well as in the broader construction, dissemination, and legitimation of a sexed and gendered social order is very much a theme within contemporary law, gender, and sexuality scholarship. For example, focusing on custody decisions in family law, feminist legal scholars have shown how law produces and valorizes particular notions of motherhood, rewarding 'good' mothers and punishing 'bad' ones according to (hetero) sexist measures of parenting.[67] In this way, legal rules and regimes have disciplinary effects on actual social relations by normatively re-inscribing certain patterns of sexed and gendered social behaviour. Likewise, by favouring the model of the heterosexual nuclear family or by attributing to the battered woman some choices and responses but not others,[68] legal discourse becomes directly implicated in the regulation and governance of sexed and gendered subjects.

One way of putting this is to say that law is a gendering practice, that is, that it acts—alongside and often in collaboration with other institutional discourses—to constrain and enable particular conceptions of gendered identity, behaviour, and selfhood, and to fashion and refashion gendered social forms.[69] This is in contrast, for example, to a liberal notion of law as a neutral instrument which can be deployed for a variety of social and political purposes but is not inherently implicated in any of them. It is also distinguishable from a stance which attributes a strong and consistent masculine bias to law, in which the law-gender relation is conceived solely or predominantly in terms of male domination and female subordination.[70] The notion that

[67] C Smart, 'The Legal and Moral Ordering of Child Custody' (1991) 18 *JLS* 485; S Boyd, *Child Custody Law and Women's Work* (Ontario: OUP, 2003).

[68] See eg M Mahoney, 'Legal Images of Battered Women: Redefining Issues of Separation' (1991) 90 *Michigan L Rev* 1.

[69] D E Chunn and D Lacombe (eds), *Law as a Gendering Practice* (Ontario: OUP, 2000).

[70] For a discussion of domination theories in feminism, see Munro, *Law and Politics at the Perimeter*, ch 4.

law is a gendering practice is a way of capturing the conceptual fluidity and contestability of gender while at the same time drawing attention to law as terrain of some significance in the context of gender struggles. This more flexible depiction allows for the production of gendered regulatory regimes which are oppressive and exploitative but also enables and accommodates tensions and inconsistencies in law's approach. Such an approach prompts a much wider casting of the theoretical net in efforts to account for inequality and injustice; the retreat from a domination model of law paves the way for explorations of the intersection between gender and other factors which contribute to unjust social arrangements and outcomes, including race, class, and sexuality.

The idea of law as a gendering practice also encourages an approach in which law's operations are viewed not in isolation but in conjunction with the operation of other practices (or discursive regimes) such as medicine, science, and so forth. Within such a frame, law is always positioned in a broader context in which the boundaries of the strictly legal are neither clear nor particularly significant. This is a perspective on law in which its internal 'peculiarities', as a self-constituting, self-legitimating rule-bound system are apprehended merely as a function of its operation as a mode of conferring meaning and value and in which a general jurisprudential focus on the nature of law barely makes sense. This is a project in which law is understood quite differently than within the confines of mainstream legal scholarship.

One of the most important intellectual influences in this context is the feminist philosopher Judith Butler. Butler's theory of gender performativity remains a key frame within which the relationship between law and the production of sexed/gendered identities is viewed. Its derivations arguably lie in Foucault's analysis of discourse as a disciplinary technique (which accords law a similarly productive role) although she is also influenced by the work of the linguistic theorist J L Austin. Butler contends that sex/gender is produced by repeated, iterative *performances,* ritualized citations which produce and stabilize gender norms and effects.[71] The basic idea is that how we act determines who we are, rather than who we are determining how we act. Law emerges in this context both as a site in which such performances routinely take place and as an always on-going script. Gender performativity, through law or otherwise, is the process by which gender comes into being and is rendered intelligible. Performativity also offers an account of our apprehension of universals, reframing them as the effects of our practices: by repeated performance, our actions, habits, and beliefs form the basis of our general normative outlook which then assumes a natural and universal quality.[72] In sum, this is a thoroughly and relentlessly constructivist approach to sex/gender differences and identity.

It is not immediately apparent why Butler's theory of gender performativity has attracted such a degree of attention within feminist and queer legal scholarship. *Gender Trouble* was in academic terms a bestseller, capturing perhaps a *zeitgeist* in which the cultural or linguistic turn in critical theory had reached its zenith. Moreover her corporeal focus in *Bodies that Matter* appeared to offer a way out of the theoretical schism apparently presented by a pre-discursive sexed body and wholly constructed gender identity (although in fact it did not).[73] In essence, however, and certainly for purposes of engaging with law, her approach is not so very different from that taken by Dorothy Chunn and Dan Lacombe, who, while clearly influenced by Butler, locate their analysis much more squarely (and accessibly) within the field of feminist legal scholarship. More importantly, it is clear that a concern with the performative dimensions of law as a gendering practice, that is, as a way in which gender as an abstract idea with no fixed content or essence is given concrete substance and practical operative effect

---

[71] J Butler, *Gender Trouble* (NY: Routledge, 1990); J Butler, *Bodies that Matter* (NY: Routledge, 1993).

[72] M Davies, *Asking the Law Question*, 3rd edn (Sydney: Lawbook Co, 2008), 217 and generally ch 8.

[73] See further J Conaghan, 'Reclaiming the Tainted Realm: Feminism, Law and Materialism' in M Davies and V Munro (eds), *A Research Companion to Feminist Legal Theory* (Farnham: Ashgate, 2013).

in and through law, has emerged as perhaps the predominant approach to the law-gender relation within contemporary legal scholarship.

3.6 CONCLUSION

The purpose of this chapter has been to provide a critical overview of the range of ways in which the relationship between law and gender has been theorized to date, set against the backdrop of an official position in which gender is not considered to be a category of theoretical significance in law. In the course of this analysis I have identified and explored a range of departures from this official position. I have also intimated the development of a more complex understanding of the relationship between law and gender over time, in which the focus has gradually moved away from a conception of law as an unequivocal expression of masculine power towards an apprehension of law as implicated in the processes and performances through which gender come into effect, is fashioned and refashioned, contested and re-contested as an aspect of social ordering.

In the context of this analysis, law gradually retreats from centre stage, assuming almost a 'bit part' in the theoretical enterprise: because the issue is framed in terms of the implication of law in gender rather than the implication of gender in law, law ceases to be a central focus. While this undoubtedly yields insights about law and gender, there is a risk that some concerns will become lost from view. In particular, the analytical direction is not one which readily offers an explanation for the continued marginalization of gender in legal scholarship in general and jurisprudence in particular. At this point therefore, the focus of enquiry shifts directly to address this issue. In Chapter One I suggested that in understanding the apparent categorical irrelevance of gender to law, attention must be paid to a number of discursive conventions which support and infuse law as a discipline and place gender in a position of apparent exteriority. In Chapter Four I turn to a deeper exploration of the first of these conventions through which law is encouraged to adhere to a gender-neutral form, supported by a historical narrative which presents legal development in terms of unerring progress towards an ideal notion of general abstract rules and equality before the law.

4

TRANSMISSIONS THROUGH TIME: GENDER, LAW, AND HISTORY

4.1 INTRODUCTION: IN WHICH THE COMMON LAW 'WORKS ITSELF PURE'

... It is suffcicient to rest this case upon the inveterate practice of the centuries that, ever since attorneys as a profession have existed, women have never been admitted to the office, and, in my opinion that shows what the law is and has been ... We have only to determine what the law is, and if there is to be any change from the ancient practice, it is a change which must be effected by Parliament.[1]

When students first embark upon the study of law in English universities, they are quickly made aware of the importance and distinctiveness of the common law tradition. Important because, through colonization, it has become the legal underpinning of so many jurisdictions around the world; distinctive, because, in its particularities, the common law sets the legal systems of the British Isles (with the exception of Scotland) apart from most other European countries, which adhere to a civil law system. In this context, the common law has become equivalent almost to a statement of Britishness with considerable effort devoted to extolling its virtues, often with a view to establishing its superiority over the civilian tradition. The common law has been commended for its bottom-up, custom-based character, for adopting an approach to legal change which is evolutionary not revolutionary, and for an ability to strike the perfect balance between logic and pragmatism. In the 19th century, Sir Frederick Pollock presented it as an object of veneration[2] while in the

---

[1] *Bebb v Law Society* [1914] Ch 286, 297 per Swinfen-Eady LJ.
[2] Sir Frederick Pollock, *The Genius of the Common Law* (NY: Columbia University Press, 1912).

21st century, it has been recently extolled by Lord Justice Laws for having an 'inherent moral force'.[3]

David Sugarman has argued that the common law is also politically coloured, in particular by a commitment to the protection of individual freedoms.[4] In contrast to a positive rights approach, characteristic of jurisdictions with written constitutions, the common law, particularly in its original English incarnation, is thought to be quintessentially laissez-faire, countenancing the free pursuit of individual interests unless good reason compels legal intervention. Within this normative frame, doctrinal elaborations of contract, tort, and property law are understood as neutral and facilitative, merely providing background support for the free pursuit of individual transactions minimally constrained by law. Legal scholars adopting a law-and-economics approach have often claimed that the common law best expresses market operations and ideals.[5]

Against such benign and often affectionate depictions, Albie Sachs and Joan Wilson have painted a picture in which the common law features as partisan and deeply conservative.[6] In a pioneering study of sexism in law, Sachs and Wilson chart the course of a series of late 19th and early 20th century cases in which women invoked law to secure access to education, the professions, the franchise, and public office, grimly noting that in every single case heard by the English and Scottish judiciary

---

[3] Lord Justice Laws, 'Our Lady of the Common Law', lecture delivered to the Incorporated Council of Law Reporting on 1 March 2012 and downloaded on 28 May 2012 from <www.londonllb.com/2012/ . . . /our-lady-of-common-law-iclr-lecture.ht>.

[4] D Sugarman, 'Legal Theory, the Common Law Mind, and the Making of the Textbook Tradition' in W Twining (ed), *Legal Theory and the Common Law* (Oxford: Basil Blackwell, 1986), 27.

[5] See eg P Rubin, 'Why is the common law efficient?' (1977) 6 *J Legal Studies* 51; G Priest, 'The Common Law Process and the Selection of Efficient Rules' (1977) 6 *J Legal Studies* 65. For a critique of the idea that the common law provides a neutral background framework for individual transactions, see D Kennedy, 'The Stakes of Law or Hale and Foucault!' (1991) 15 *Legal Studies Forum* 327.

[6] A Sachs and J Hoff Wilson, *Sexism and the Law: A Study of Male Beliefs and Judicial Bias* (Oxford: Martin Robertson, 1978).

the decision went against the women litigants.[7] While a variety of reasons were prayed in aid by the courts, ranging from the technicalities of particular statutes to alleged 'differences in the mental and physical constitutions of the two sexes',[8] by far the most commonly invoked justification for denying these claims was that the common law had not hitherto recognized them. The quotation opening this chapter, taken from a case in which the outstanding Ms Bebb lost her claim to be admitted to the Law Society,[9] shows how the courts often retreated to the crudest articulations of past practice as a reason for retaining the status quo, drawing a bright and seemingly uncrossable line between what the legal position *is* and what it *ought* to be, should Parliament deign to intervene. In this way, as Sachs and Wilson observe, 'the English common law ... so often extolled as being the embodiment of human freedom in fact provided the main intellectual justification for the avowed and formal subordination of women'.[10]

In the event, the British Parliament *did* intervene, passing the Sex Disqualification Removal Act 1919 along with the Representation of the People Act 1918 (extending the vote to women over 30).[11] Some years later in *Edwards v Attorney-General*, the Privy Council had little difficulty in holding that the word 'person' in s 24 of the British North America Act 1867 (pertaining to eligibility to sit in the Senate or Upper House of the Parliament of Canada) included members of both sexes. After a lengthy trawl of the relevant authorities, the Lord Chancellor, Lord Sankey, considered the relevance of past practice in the following terms:

The fact that no woman had served or has claimed to serve such an office is not of great weight when it is remembered that custom would

---

[7] Sachs and Wilson, *Sexism and the Law*, 34.

[8] *Jex-Blake v University of Edinburgh Senatus* (1873) 11 M 784, 791 per Neaves LJ.

[9] *Bebb v Law Society*. On the fate of Miss Bebb herself, see R Auchmuty, 'Whatever Happened to Miss Bebb? *Bebb v the Law Society* and Women's Legal History' (2011) 31 *Legal Studies* 199.

[10] Sachs and Wilson, *Sexism and the Law*, 41.

[11] The vote was eventually extended to men and women on equal terms by the Representation of the People Act 1928.

have prevented the claim being made, or the point being contested. Customs are apt to develop into traditions which are stronger than law and remain unchallenged long after the reason for them has disappeared. The appeal to history, therefore . . . is not conclusive.[12]

In distinguishing law and custom, Lord Sankey displays a degree of analytical perspicacity sadly lacking in those members of the bench who had considered hitherto the question of women's membership of the class of legal persons. Granted the relation between law and custom is a complicated one, particularly in the context of the common law: it is not reducible to a simple line-drawing exercise but nor can it be correct to collapse law into custom as the judges in the persons cases appear to have done.[13] More generally, the persons cases illustrate not just how the common law can be effectively deployed to uphold the political interests of, in this case, the male legal establishment, but also the potency of the past in relation to legal struggles taking place in the present. As *Best v Fox*[14] demonstrates, the past provides a useful buffer behind which the judiciary can make decisions as much determined by their personal and political preferences as by legal doctrine. At the same time, *R v R*[15] suggests that the past can also be conveniently discarded when judicial preference and/or practical and political exigency so demand.

This chapter explores the relationship between law and gender by probing the role and significance of history, temporality, and the past. The examples above demonstrate how past ideas and practices are routinely 'transmitted through time'[16] in the course of legal operations. Law bears the mark of history not just as a consequence of the formal application of the doctrine of precedent but also in a general deference to tradition and past practice which is characteristic of, indeed underpins, common law thought. This has enabled an often conservatively-minded judiciary to protect the legal and political status quo from

---

[12] *Edwards v Attorney-General for Canada* [1930] AC 124 (PC), 128.

[13] For an analysis of the relation between common law and custom, see A W B Simpson, 'The Common Law and Legal Theory' in Twining, *Legal Theory and the Common Law*, 8.

[14] [1952] AC 716.   [15] [1992] 1 AC 599.

[16] Simpson, 'The Common Law and Legal Theory', 20.

challenge in a wide range of contexts.[17] However, temporality also operates more subtly in law and in ways which pertain particularly to gender. Specifically, I would suggest that time is implicated in the erasure of gender from legal exposition and analysis. This occurs in two related ways. First, temporal narration situates the deeply patriarchal legal past as the 'before' of law; as no more than a tatty historical legal remnant which occasionally needs tidying up. For example, when the British Government announced plans in 2011 to amend the rules of succession to allow daughters of the incumbent monarch an equal right to the British Crown, the initiative was cast in terms of addressing a legal anomaly which had somehow survived past expurgation, occasioning little comment or substantial reflection.[18] Likewise, in *R v R*, the judges approached the marital exemption as a distasteful leftover which no one had yet bothered to clear away. What is remarkable—and yet too often unremarked—about these kinds of situations is that they evidence the extraordinary tenacity of a still deeply gendered legal and political system, a tenacity which goes unheeded as the legal broom sweeps briskly over the patriarchal cobwebs of the past. *R v R*, for example, was decided after extensive consultation, policy review, and parliamentary debate in the preceding decade had revealed no clear consensus on the question: in other words, the ideas and beliefs underpinning the marital exemption clearly had some currency even at the time of its formal demise.[19] Removing the doctrinal debris of a legally instituted gendered hierarchical order does not necessarily get rid of deeply ingrained social and cultural attitudes which law has long endorsed and which continue to infuse the criminal justice process, albeit in more covert, less accessible forms.[20] Put simply, the

---

[17] See here the classic study of J A G Griffith, *The Politics of the Judiciary*, 5th edn (London: Fontana, 2010).

[18] N Watt, 'Royal succession gender equality approved by Commonwealth' *The Guardian* (London, 28 October 2011) <http://www.guardian.co.uk/uk/2011/oct/28/royal-succession-gender-equality-approved> accessed 20 August 2012.

[19] See further §2.3.2.

[20] In a review of marital rape cases post *R v R*, Sue Lees argues that marital rape is still not regarded as 'real rape' by the judiciary: 'Marital Rape and Marital

relationship between law and its patriarchal past is not reducible to clearly delineable 'before' and 'after' historical ascriptions. There is a second and related way in which time contributes to the expulsion of gender from the contours of legal discourse. Because gender as a category of relevance appears for the most part to reside in the legal past, and because law in the present continues unimpeded and in substantially the same form, it is easy to conclude that gender is not a significant feature of law's nature and operations. The gender-neutralization of law appears to have occasioned no fundamental disturbance in the legal fabric, reinforcing the view that gender has never been more than an incidental aspect of a legal past with limited purchase on the present. Adherence to the rhetoric of the Rule of Law only serves to compound the view that it is in the nature of law to render gender irrelevant. Time works here to present the law–gender relation teleologically, as a progressive process in which law 'works itself pure'[21] of error and misjudgement. History yields a narrative of gradual erosion in which gender is steadily expunged from the forms and categories of law, and by the same sleight of historical hand, attention is diverted away from the operation of gender in law other than in formal, categorical terms. Within the logic of the frame which encases the official story of law and gender, gender emerges as of little contemporary conceptual and theoretical significance but only because the framing of the problem of gender in historical terms shapes our expectations and directs our understanding in ways which ensure that we find gender only when we look for it in the prescribed form and according to the conventional account.[22]

These arguments about the role of temporality in situating gender in law are elaborated and explored in the analysis which follows. However, it may first be useful briefly to consider some

Murder' in J Hamner and C Itzen (eds), *Home Truths about Domestic Violence* (London: Routledge, 2001), 57.

[21] The idea of law 'working itself pure' comes from R Gordon, 'Critical Legal Histories' (1984) 36 *Stanford L Rev* 57, 65 (see further §4.2).

[22] For discussion of the errors that flow from excessive adherence to the 'logic of the frame', see P Schlag, *The Enchantment of Reason* (Durham, NC: Duke University Press, 1998), 1–14.

general observations and concerns raised in the context of legal historical study.

4.2 LAW AND HISTORY: AN UNSATISFACTORY COMPOUND?

In *The Common Law*, Oliver Wendell Holmes Jr stresses the importance of looking at law through the lens of history:

> The law embodies the story of a nation's development through many centuries and it cannot be dealt with as if it contained only the axioms of a book of mathematics. In order to know what it is, we must know what it has been and what it tends to become.[23]

In this passage, Holmes is seeking to counter the tendency then prevailing in Anglo-American jurisprudence to view law in scientific terms; hence his emphasis, not just on law as a source of history, but also on history as a source of law. To the modern reader this may seem a trite and obvious point. After all, the common law is nothing if not a historical creation, a doctrinal expression of congealed historical acts which reach back in common law mythology to a 'time immemorial'. However, behind the apparent banality of Holmes' remarks lies a relationship infinitely more complex. As the 19th-century English jurist and historian Sir Frederic Maitland observes, the 'compound' of law and history is oddly unsatisfactory: 'The lawyer must be orthodox otherwise he is no lawyer; an orthodox history seems to me to be a contradiction in terms . . . if we try to make history the handmaid of dogma, she will soon cease to be history'.[24]

Maitland is suggesting that history and law are two very different activities exhibiting distinct and somewhat conflicting approaches to the past. In law, the decisions, practices, and ideas of previous generations of juristic actors are framed within (what he terms as) a 'logic of authority'[25] in which conformity to the

---

[23] O Wendell Holmes Jr, *The Common Law* (Boston: Little, Brown, & Co, 1881), 1.

[24] F W Maitland, *Why the history of English law is not written: an inaugural lecture delivered in the arts school at Cambridge on 13th October, 1888* (London: C J Clay & Sons, Cambridge University Press, 1888), 14–15.

[25] Maitland, *Why the history of English law is not written*, 14.

past is understood as an agreed feature of legal rationality, a reason for proceeding in a particular way in the legal present. By contrast, history tends to be governed by a 'logic of evidence'[26] in which the object is to interrogate the past on its own terms, to seek out and discover what happened *then*, not how it applies *now*. While endorsing the value of legal history as an enterprise, Maitland cautions against 'mixing up' these two, almost contradictory, logics. His words are a wise and salutary warning to anyone seeking to traverse the tricky terrain of legal historical study: at what point are you doing history and at what point are you doing law? To what purpose or end is the past being put?

Jonathan Rose offers a threefold typology of different approaches to legal history which he labels 'classical', 'liberal', and 'critical'.[27] The classical tradition, according to Rose, originates with Maitland and is concerned with charting the intellectual history of law understood primarily but not exclusively in terms of legal doctrine and the ideas and norms which infuse its development. Such an approach to legal history is sometimes characterized as 'internal'[28] although, as Rose points out, internal legal sources cannot be understood in a vacuum and some attention to the external context (particularly with regard to legislation) is generally necessary. More than anything, classical legal history is concerned with analysing legal change in terms of specifically legal ideas, conceptualizations, and conventions.

Liberal legal history, Rose contends, derives from the political values associated with the liberal tradition, in particular respect for individual freedom and equality of opportunity.[29] Rose associates liberal legal history with legal realism although it also encompasses socio-legal perspectives, for example, law-in-context or law-in-society approaches—what is sometimes described

---

[26] Maitland, *Why the history of English law is not written*, 14.

[27] J Rose, 'Studying the Past: the Nature and Development of Legal History as an Academic Discipline' (2010) 31 *Journal of Legal History* 101, 116–20.

[28] D Ibbetson, 'Historical Research in Law' in P Case and M Tushnet, *Oxford Handbook of Legal Studies* (Oxford: OUP, 2003), 863, 870–1.

[29] Rose, 'Studying the Past', 119.

as 'external' legal history.[30] According to Rose, 'liberal legal history's dominant characteristic is the integration of law with social and economic institutions and ideas'.[31] This includes interdisciplinary analyses of social development in which law features as well as more legally focused social and political histories. As Rose observes, much of the legal historical work on race and gender takes this form. It is an approach in which law is not necessarily the direct object of analysis but is a function of some other, generally normative or political enquiry, for example, into the operation of racism, sexism, or social inequality. In many ways classical and liberal legal history complement one another in that they share a common underlying (liberal) political vision. However, in emphasizing the interaction of the legal and the social, liberal legal history tends to subvert the idea of legal autonomy which is a characteristic of classicism. Therefore, liberal legal history is more likely to be allied with critical legal history, the third category in Rose's typology.

According to Rose, critical legal history is a fairly recent invention; Rose links it with the work of American legal scholars, Robert Gordon and Morton Horwitz, and, more generally, with the American Critical Legal Studies Movement (CLS) which emerged in the 1970s. In many ways critical legal history switches the analytical lens back to legal doctrine albeit presenting a very different picture from the classicists. CLS contests the presentation of legal doctrine as stable and coherent, emphasizing uncertainty and incoherence as features of doctrinal development. The focus is on discontinuity rather than continuity in the application of legal principles and rules yielding legal outcomes which are contingent and indeterminate; the idea is to disrupt any notion that law evolves in a natural, preordained, normatively or conceptually coherent manner. Above all, critical legal history emphasizes the ideological function of law and the way in which it is implicated in relations of power and inequality. In summary, the critical legal historian is concerned with unsettling doctrinal orthodoxies and offering more subversive interpretations of the role and operation of law and the nature of legal development.

---

[30] Ibbetson, 'Historical Research in Law'.
[31] Rose, 'Studying the Past', 120.

In 1984, Robert Gordon published a lengthy and influential article entitled 'Critical Legal Histories' as part of a symposium on CLS in the *Stanford Law Review* in which he puts forward the following view:

> Over the last 150 years or so, enlightened American legal opinion has adhered with remarkable fidelity to ... a single set of notions about historical change and the relation of law to such change. Stated baldly, these notions are that the natural and proper evolution of a society (or at least of a 'progressive' society, to use Maine's qualification) is towards the type of liberal capitalism seen in the advanced Western nations ... and that the natural and proper function of a legal system is to facilitate such an evolution.[32]

According to Gordon, legal scholarship and particularly legal historical scholarship was premised (implicitly or explicitly) on an 'evolutionary functionalist' approach to law. Underpinning this approach were a number of (he argues) contestable assumptions. These included: first, a conception of law and society as separate legal categories albeit causally related; second, the idea that society has particular needs and that legal development is best understood in terms of responding to those needs; third, a view of law as naturally and normally adaptive and adapting to social change; and, finally and consequentially, an assumption that law is on 'an objective, determined, progressive, social evolutionary path'[33] towards advancement.

As Gordon acknowledges, evolutionary functionalism along with its concomitant assumptions is no more than an ideal-type.[34] He is certainly not alleging rigid and unwavering adherence to such a model by all legal historians. Nor should it be assumed that association with one kind of legal history rather than another (whether invoking Rose's typology or otherwise) is a necessary indicator of the degree of adherence: the trained or experienced legal historian should already be alert to the risk of proceeding on the basis of unfounded assumptions and unarticulated suppositions. However, by making use of ideal-type

---

[32] Gordon, 'Critical Legal Histories', 59.
[33] Gordon, 'Critical Legal Histories', 63.
[34] Gordon, 'Critical Legal Histories', 59.

analysis, Gordon, like Rose, is able to draw attention to processes by which unconscious importations *can* and often do slip into and shape legal historical study, encouraging readings of the past which are already normatively and ideologically loaded. For example (and continuing to draw upon Gordon's analysis), a view of legal development in terms of responsiveness to social need—as if 'need' is self-evidently and incontestably identifiable—may obfuscate the legal privileging of some social interests over others, cloaking operations of power which generate inequalities. Moreover, to understand legal 'development' (itself a normatively loaded word) solely or even predominantly as *functional* is likely to divert attention away from other, non-functional (or dysfunctional) aspects of legal change and the complexities and contradictions which often accompany legal reform processes.

Gordon's model of evolutionary functionalism is also useful in illuminating aspects of legal historical approaches to gender, particularly in the context of accounts of women's struggle to secure equality in law. I will now explore this resonance more directly.

4.3 A DARWINIAN LEGAL NARRATIVE

I was an ENGLISH WIFE, and for me there was no possibility for redress. The answer was always the same . . . The LAW can do nothing for you.[35]

Caroline Norton (1808–1877) is generally credited with playing a significant part in improving the legal position of married women in 19th-century England. A granddaughter of the playwright, Richard Brinsley Sheridan, as well as a poet and novelist in her own right, Caroline had the misfortune to wed an inadequate and abusive man, George Norton, and later to be embroiled in a scandalous criminal conversation suit arising from allegations by her husband that she had conducted an adulterous

---

[35] C Norton, 'A Letter to the Queen on Lord Chancellor Cranworth's Marriage and Divorce Bill' in P Hollis (ed), *Women in Public: The Women's Movement 1850–1900* (London: George Allen & Unwin, 1979), 181.

affair with Lord Melbourne. Caroline also lived much of her life deprived of her children's company while economically and legally tied to Norton even regarding access to her own earnings. Although Norton's suit against Melbourne failed,[36] implicitly exonerating Caroline, her social reputation never recovered from the indignity of a trial in which, by virtue of her married state, she could neither offer evidence nor defend herself publicly. Under the legal doctrine of coverture, Caroline's legal personality became absorbed in her husband's upon marriage. Indeed, the practical consequence of Norton's failure to prove adultery meant that Caroline remained legally tied to her husband until his death in 1875, two years before her own.

Mary Poovey observes that Caroline's life story is 'a veritable case study in the wrongs that a married woman could suffer in the first half of the nineteenth century'.[37] At every step Caroline found herself stymied by a legal web coiled so tightly around her that escape seemed impossible. By ceding her legal and physical personhood to her husband on marriage, Caroline lost virtually all rights to physical and sexual integrity, control of personal property, and access to and enjoyment of her children. While the passing of the Infant Custody Act 1839 (directly prompted by her plight) accorded mothers limited rights of access to very young children, divorce remained a practical impossibility for Caroline even after the Matrimonial Causes Act 1857, for which she campaigned.

And yet while her own life was marred by tragedy and misfortune, Caroline Norton's name has become closely linked with a particular account of the changing legal status of women during the course of the 19th century. This is a period in which law is seen to move inexorably forward, slowly but surely casting off the medieval shackles of a status-based social and

---

[36] *George Norton v William Lamb, Viscount Melbourne* (unreported) heard before a Middlesex special jury in the Court of Common Pleas on 22 June 1836. For a compelling account of Norton's life including the circumstances surrounding the trial, see D Atkinson, *The Criminal Conversation of Mrs Norton* (London: Random House, 2012).

[37] M Poovey, 'Covered but not Bound: Caroline Norton and the 1857 Matrimonial Causes Act' (1988) 14 *Feminist Studies* 467, 469.

legal order to embrace and extol a brave new world of equality under law. Such a process of progressive transition is expounded most famously by Henry Summer Maine. In his classic 19th-century legal anthropological study, *Ancient Law*, Maine broke new jurisprudential ground in emphasizing the importance of socio-historical study to contemporary understandings of legal concepts. At the heart of Maine's argument is the claim that 'the movement of progressive societies has hitherto been a move-ment from *Status to Contract*'.[38] Highlighting the patriarchal basis of 'primitive' societies in which the family was the core social unit, and power (*patria potestas*) was vested solely in the father/ husband, Maine chronicles a shift away from this early social and legal preoccupation with the family or group towards recogni-tion of the social and legal pre-eminence of individual. Loosen-ing the patriarchal bonds governing the status of women, for example, the gradual abandonment of the Roman law concept of perpetual female tutelage, are identified by Maine as part of this broader process of socio-legal evolution. More importantly, it is within such a Darwinian frame of natural legal selection that the modern story of gender and law, symbolized and humanized by Caroline Norton's sorry plight, is generally located.

It cannot be denied that the second half of the 19th century was a time of intense feminist engagement with law not just in England but in the United States, France, and other European countries.[39] For many, this is the moment in which the mod-ern feminist movement was born—the term 'feminism' is widely believed to have originated in France in the late 19th century.[40] At the same time, the presentation of the struggle which marks this period as a simple modernist tale of social and

---

[38] H Maine, *Ancient Law* (London: JM Dent & Sons, 1917), 101.

[39] For a thoughtful study of the feminist 'turn' to law during this period, see M Drakopoulou, 'Feminism and the Siren Call of Law' (2007) 18 *Law and Critique* 331.

[40] On the origins of feminism as a term, see K Offen, 'Feminism' in P Stearns (ed), *Encyclopedia of Social History* (Garland, 1994), 272. Those involved in women's rights campaigns during the period discussed here would not necessar-ily have been familiar with the term, 'feminist' or describe themselves as feminists. I use the term non-historically to encompass the activities of those seeking to advance women's interests, regardless of self-identification.

legal enlightenment is as inaccurate as it is misleading. It is inaccurate because close historical study yields a more complex picture of conflict and contestation in which the goals were far from agreed and the outcomes far from assured. It is misleading because it tends to encourage or to be prompted by retrospective misreadings of the past. Toby Milsom observes that 'the largest difficulty in legal history is precisely that we look at past evidence in the light of later assumptions, including our own assumptions about the nature and working of law itself'.[41] This penchant towards retrospectivity is particularly pronounced in instrumentalist accounts of legal change in which the past is viewed as part of the problem to be solved and as a resource from which lessons for the future may be learned.

Legal actors, politicians, and even feminists are implicated in the production of teleologically determinist accounts of legal development. Judges in particular are apt to see legal change as a natural developmental process of steady forward movement, and they frequently locate gender issues within this narrative frame. The chronicle which underpins the reasoning in *R v R*,[42] and even more so, *S v HM Advocate*[43] (upon which the courts in *R v R* rely), for example, is highly redolent of such teleological judicial contemplation. A fresh illustration of this judicial mindset is *Midland Bank v Green (No 3)*,[44] a Court of Appeal decision from 1981 which has the distinction of finally consigning the common law doctrine of marital unity to the annals of history. The case involved a suit against a husband and wife for civil conspiracy in which it was contended that the doctrine of marital unity precluded commission of conspiracy on the grounds that the conspiring parties constituted one person in law. The Court unequivocally rejected this suggestion, pronouncing the doctrine of marital unity legally dead and buried except in so far as judicially or legislatively retained. The reasoning the judges deploy is notable in illustrating the

---

[41] S F C Milsom, *A Natural History of the Common Law* (New York: Columbia University Press, 2003), xvi.

[42] *R v R* [1992] 1 AC 599.

[43] (1989) SLT 469.

[44] *Midland Bank Trust Co Ltd and another v Green (No 3)* [1981] 3 All ER 744.

various ways in which temporality may be invoked to support judicially-instigated legal change. Fox LJ, for example, relies directly upon the passage of time to support his conclusion that the marital unity doctrine is now obsolete. Drawing on the imagery of travel, he commends counsel for taking the Court through 'seven centuries of authorities', presenting the rejection of the doctrine as the end of a legal 'journey'.[45] In Fox LJ's imagination, legal development is a kind of expedition in which there is a legal point of origin and a final destination along with intermittent signposts (in the form of cases and commentaries) to aid navigation along the way.

For Lord Denning, then Master of the Rolls, time is relevant to verifying what is real and what is not. Focusing directly on the fictional status of the marital unity doctrine, Denning presents the failure of law to correspond to social reality as conclusively demonstrating the unsoundness of unity principle: 'It was a fiction then. It is a fiction now. . . . It has been so much eroded and cut down in law, it has long ceased to be true in fact'.[46] In contrast to the pretence of marital unity enshrined in 'medieval' law, Lord Denning insists that a husband and wife—'in law and in fact'—are two persons not one.[47] He then proceeds to articulate a thoroughly modern understanding of conjugality in which the parties are cast as 'equal partners in a joint enterprise'.[48] In so doing, the Master of the Rolls purports to pronounce not just upon the legal character of modern marriage; he is also asserting equality *as matter of fact*, as a social truth about the married state to which law must respond.

The third judge, Sir George Baker, conjures up a farrago of images to support his claim that law is purposeful and responsive to social need. He contends that 'the law is a living thing; it adapts and develops to fulfil the needs of living people. . . . Like clothes it should be made to fit people. It must never be strangled by the dead hand of long discarded custom, belief,

---

[45] *Midland Bank v Green (No 3)*, 749, per Fox LJ.
[46] *Midland Bank v Green (No 3)*, 748, per Denning MR.
[47] *Midland Bank v Green (No 3)*, 748, per Denning MR.
[48] *Midland Bank v Green (No 3)*, 748, per Denning MR.

doctrine or principle'.[49] What is striking about these remarks is
that they almost perfectly express Gordon's idea of evolutionary
functionalism, invoking a conception of law as naturally and
necessarily adaptable to changing social conditions. Moreover,
in associating the past with *death* and the present with *life*, Sir
George presents the demise of the doctrine of marital unity as a
wholly natural process, as the work of time and nature not
judicial fief.

Sir George then turns to the idea of enlightenment through
reason for further support:

To extend this rule or exemption to the tort of conspiracy because of
the legal fiction of ancient times that husband and wife being one
person could not agree or combine with each other would to my
mind be akin to basing a judgment on the proposition that the Earth is
flat, because many believed that centuries ago. We now know that the
Earth is not flat. We now know that husband and wife in the eyes of
the law and in fact are equal.[50]

Gender equality, Sir George contends, is as *real* as the earth is
round and old ideas about the nature of the marriage have as
much current purchase as the belief that the earth is flat. Just as
new scientific knowledge has displaced old scientific fallacies,
modern ideas about gender have freed marriage from the fetters
of ancient and discredited beliefs. In other words, law, like
science, gravitates naturally and progressively towards truth.

Midland Bank v Green (No 3) provides a clear illustration of the
close association of time with notions of truth and reality in legal
discourse. Temporality allows judges to elevate their personal
views and values to the status of factual and legal truths so that
the knowledge they claim to have about contemporary marriage
is assumed to be correct, notwithstanding the absence of any
reference to external evidence. It is not of course that the
characterization of marriage as an equal partnership is necessarily
objectionable; it is the status of that characterization which is at
issue. What the court offers as 'fact' is no more than normative
aspiration in disguise, a disguise rendered all the more effective

---

[49] *Midland Bank v Green (No 3)*, 751, per Sir George Baker.
[50] *Midland Bank v Green (No 3)*, 751, per Sir George Baker.

by being located within a narrative frame of past and present, before and after, then and now. At the time the case was decided, the judicial characterization of marriage as an 'equal partnership' was likely far from a reality for many couples; even today there are continuing gendered asymmetries in marriage with regard to household spending, domestic labour, and other matters. What emerges from *Midland Bank v Green (No 3)* is how deeply law and, in particular, the courts, are implicated in the construction and validation of marriage as a formal institution—an institution which is crucially determinative of gender relations in our society. Indeed, the ability to offer a narrative about the nature of marriage—'in law and in fact'—powerful enough to trump competing narratives in its claim to authenticity accords judges almost unparalleled power to influence legal policy around sex and gender issues, as recent debate about the desirability of same-sex marriage in the UK demonstrates.[51]

Narratives of legal progress are not the peculiar prerogative of judges. The assumption that as we move forward we leave the past behind, combined with a tendency to read history retrospectively, gauging the activities and achievements of earlier times against the norms and standards exercising a grip upon the present, is an all too common feature of feminist theorizing. Feminist scholars frequently assert, for example, that contemporary feminist analysis significantly *advances* feminist theorizing by moving *beyond* the gender-essentialism of earlier generations.[52] Not only does this kind of claim often overstate or misrepresent the 'errors' of past feminist scholars, it encourages readings of bodies of scholarship which were the product of particular times, energies, and concerns against the times, energies, and concerns of later generations. Within this narrative frame, the struggles of historical actors are almost always deemed to have fallen short of the goals and objectives which contemporary scholars attribute to their activities; the present cannot fail but to overcome the limitations of the past.

[51] See further §5.3.1. On law as a discourse of truth, see C Smart, *Feminism and the Power of Law* (London: Routledge, 1989).
[52] See generally C Hemmings, *Why Stories Matter: the Political Grammar of Feminist Theory* (Durham, NC: Duke University Press, 2011).

Mary Lyndon Shanley, in her account of feminist law reform efforts in Victorian England, frequently gauges the success and failure of feminist initiatives in terms of the extent to which they moved women closer to a state of equality with men. This is notwithstanding that, by Shanley's own account, many Victorian feminists were openly disdainful of the idea of gender equality and acted with diverse and often conflicting aims in their engagements with law.[53] In her exploration of the married women's property reforms of the late 19th century, Rosemary Auchmuty seeks to counter this approach by suggesting that the reforms in question were not about gender equality at all but were motivated primarily by a concern to protect vulnerable women from abuse at the hands of unscrupulous men.[54] Certainly, there was much more going on around this set of reforms than a simple demand for formal legal equality and indeed, as Shanley herself points out, the cumulative effect of the Acts was not to grant married women the same legal status as their husbands or even *sole feme* ('single woman') status but rather to enact a kind of statutory marriage settlement based upon the rules already developed in equity to protect propertied women on entry into marriage.[55] This enabled Dicey, as Shanley goes on to acknowledge, to cite the married women's property reforms as an example of 'judicial legislation', by which he means legislation enacted by Parliament but deriving much of its form and content from previously developed judicial doctrine.[56] This is an approach to law-making of which Dicey heartily approves on the grounds that it better maintains the logic and symmetry of law, promotes legal certainty, and, by virtue of having already been tried out, is more likely to stand the test of time.[57] In this way too, Dicey is able to posit the married women's property

---

[53] M L Shanley, *Feminism, Marriage, and the Law in Victorian England, 1850–1895* (Princeton: Princeton University Press, 1999), 17–18, 65–6, 124–30.

[54] R Auchmuty, 'The Married Women's Property Acts: Equality was not the Issue' in R Hunter (ed), *Rethinking Equality Projects in Law: Feminist Challenges* (Oxford: Hart, 2008), 13.

[55] Shanley, *Feminism, Marriage, and the Law*, 127–8.

[56] A V Dicey, *Lectures on the Relation between Law and Public Opinion in England during the Nineteenth Century* (London: MacMillan & Co Ltd, 1930), 361–98.

[57] Dicey, *Law and Public Opinion*, 361–70.

reforms as 'natural' legal developments which the judiciary had already anticipated and effectively 'enacted' through equity. For Dicey the primary benefit of parliamentary intervention is in extending the advantages of equity—previously the exclusive purview of expensive lawyers—to ordinary people.

If we look carefully at how 19th-century feminists framed their demands, what becomes apparent is their concern to eliminate legal disabilities which placed married women in a position of unacceptable dependence and vulnerability in relation to their husbands.[58] This is not necessarily the same thing as demanding legal equality. Interestingly, etymologically, the term 'equality'—derived from the French *equalite* and Latin *aequalis*—is closely associated with mathematical conceptions of uniformity and sameness.[59] While it cannot be doubted that by the 19th century, equality operated in political and philosophical discourse other than as a mathematical measure—indeed, as a result of the social and political upheavals of the 17th century and the rise of natural rights arguments in the 18th century, equality had become widely associated in political discourse with ideas of common humanity—understandings of gender in the late 19th century were more likely to be underpinned by notions of difference than sameness. Even John Stuart Mill, while advocating, 'a principle of perfect equality'[60] between men and women, openly acknowledged natural differences between the sexes already reflected in the gender division of labour: '... the common arrangement by which the man earns the income and the woman superintends the domestic expenditure seems to me in general the most suitable division of labour between the two persons'.[61]

What exercised Mill, and feminists more generally, was women's *subjection* by law, the fact that, because of their sex, they endured legal disadvantages which (it was argued) defied rational justification and offended the principle of individual

---

[58] Auchmuty, 'The Married Women's Property Acts'.

[59] M Beard, *Women as Force in History* (NY: Macmillan, 1946), 147.

[60] J S Mill, *The Subjection of Women*, edited by S M Okin (Indianapolis: Hackett Publishing Inc, 1988), 1.

[61] Mill, *Subjection of Women*, 50.

freedom. This was not seen as incompatible with the view that considerable differences nevertheless existed between the sexes. It is interesting that in making the case for women's suffrage, feminist campaigner, Barbara Bodichon, makes no direct appeal to equality.[62] Instead she points to the inconsistency of law in treating women as responsible citizens for some purposes and not others. She also proffers what we would recognize today as a pluralist argument, the thrust of which is expressive of a concern that the interests of women as a class will be overlooked if they are not represented in some way in the political process. Bodichon goes on to suggest that extending the franchise to women would enhance patriotism and public spirit by encouraging women to look beyond the immediate practicalities of family life and to gain a wider understanding of political and community matters. Perhaps most significantly, Bodichon's arguments in favour of suffrage are confined to 'single ladies and widows' who are not as weighed down by domestic duties as wives. She observes that 'women of the class we are thinking about have as a rule more time for thought than men'.[63]

From a contemporary perspective, Bodichon's willingness to compromise on the issue of the female franchise seems unsatisfactory. At best, it is likely to be interpreted as strategic, that is, as a tactical step in the longer term struggle for gender equality. However this is not necessarily how the matter was viewed by women (or men) of the day. As Shanley points out, feminists at the time were deeply divided on the issue of how far the female franchise should extend.[64] The Victorian era is notorious for its veneration of home and family supported by a gendered ideology of 'separate spheres' in which husband and wife were thought to perform distinct but complementary roles.[65] Many of those who actively campaigned for marriage law reform shared an understanding of gender relations in terms of complementarity of roles.

[62] B Bodichon, *Reasons for and Against the Enfranchisement of Women* (London: McCorquodale & Co, 1872).

[63] Bodichon, *Reasons for and Against*, 10. Bodichon also sought suffrage only for women of a certain class, ie those who met the various property holding requirements. At that time full universal male suffrage was still some years away.

[64] Shanley, *Feminism, Marriage, and the Law*, 109–14.

[65] Shanley, *Feminism, Marriage, and the Law*, 3–8.

Indeed, their argument was that women would better perform the tasks nature had assigned to them if they enjoyed protection from domestic abuse and received the respect of their husbands. Almost a century before, Mary Wollstonecraft had declaimed: 'Make women rational creatures and free citizens and they will quickly become good wives and mothers'.[66] Like her Victorian successors, Wollstonecraft's primary concern was to secure women's freedom from subjection; this she saw more as a matter of justice than equality.[67] On the rare occasion when her thoughts did drift in the direction of gender equality, she simultaneously conceded the foolishness of such ruminations:

A wild wish has just flown from my heart to my head, and I will not stifle it though it may excite a horse-laugh. I do earnestly wish to see the distinction of sex confounded in society, unless where love animates the behaviour.[68]

Wollstonecraft also saw women's liberation from subjection as less a question of law and more a matter of women's access to education. By the 19th century, however, women appeared more conscious of the extent to which law supported their formal subjugation to their husbands through the doctrine of coverture and associated legal restrictions on their capacity and status. Therefore, feminist attention shifted to legal terrain.[69] The retrospective (re)framing of that shift as driven primarily by equality considerations does not adequately or accurately capture the nature of feminist engagement with law at the time which, as has been observed, was characterized by far less unanimity in terms of the problems to be tackled or the goals to be achieved.

---

[66] M Wollstonecraft, *Vindication of the Rights of Women* (Dover Publications Inc, 1995, originally published 1792), 184.

[67] In a letter of dedication to Talleyrand-Perigord, which prefaced the main text, Wollstonecraft famously concluded by 'loudly demand[ing] JUSTICE for one half of the human race', *Vindication*, 4.

[68] Wollstonecraft, *Vindication*, 57.

[69] Drakopoulou, 'Feminism and the Siren Call of Law'. In a separate article, Drakopoulou highlights the relative lack of engagement with law in 18th century women's writing: M Drakopoulou, 'Women's Resolutions of Lawes Reconsidered: Epistemic Shifts and the Emergence of the Feminist Legal Discourse' (2000) 11 *Law and Critique* 47.

One of the ways in which the conventional legal story is given further credence is through the classification and ordering of feminist history in terms of 'waves'. The metaphor of waves is widely deployed in gender and feminist studies as a way of classifying and serializing various stages in recent history both temporally and thematically. For example, 'first wave feminism' is generally associated with the efforts of late 19th and early 20th century feminists to secure the same (equal) rights and privileges as men, particularly with regard to suffrage and entry into the professions. 'Second wave feminism' signals the activities and beliefs of the mid to late 20th century Women's Liberation Movement, temporally located in the 1960s through to the 1980s. Finally, 'third wave feminism' is increasingly deployed to capture a shift in feminist thinking, from at least the 1990s onwards, away from an isolated focus on gender towards broader, more inclusive engagement with issues of sexuality and diversity. Third wave feminism is also sometimes character-ized as 'postfeminism', often pejoratively by feminists unhappy with the direction that feminist thought has taken. Third wave feminism has been castigated for encouraging feminists to aban-don the category 'woman' as a core analytical category and for shifting the focus away from a concern with gender-based, material disadvantage towards a preoccupation with cultural, linguistic, and representational issues.

The waves typology presented above is far from written in stone. Some feminists locate the first wave earlier or later and some deny the existence or legitimacy of a third wave alto-gether. For others, feminist waves are better understood con-ceptually and thematically rather than merely temporally, for example, in terms of a shift from formal to substantive equality and/or from equality to intersectionality. Alternatively, the metaphor may be deployed to signal particular political and theoretical moves, for example from a focus on the state to engagement with the individual subject or from scrutiny of the public to interrogation of the private sphere. Moreover, as is true of the conceptual composition of feminism more gener-ally, the waves metaphor maps most closely onto feminist theory and activism in a Western, predominantly Anglo-American, middle-class context.

The 'periodization' of feminist thought and activities is undoubtedly a tidy way to order and present development and change within feminism over a broad time frame. However, the use of such temporal indicators to situate theoretical and conceptual positions is not without problems. In particular, it can lead to the neglect of evidence suggestive of a contrary or more complex picture of the period under scrutiny. Periodization functions as a form of teleology, discouraging exploration of historical complexity and downplaying the presence of tensions and contradictions in historical accounts. Periodization also fosters a tendency to contrast and oppose as a way of constructing boundaries. For periodization to be meaningful there must be a beginning and an end to a period, followed by the beginning of something new again. Periodization demands juxtaposition.

The result is often to yield random and potentially misleading temporal demarcations through which historical events are subsequently interpreted. Lengthy time periods are collapsed into single instances or struggles, producing bland and reductionist explanations of historical actions and events. Some time periods are ignored altogether: the periodization of feminist history into waves, for example, tends to jump from the putative end of the first wave when female suffrage was achieved in the 1920s to the beginning of the second wave with the birth of the civil rights movement in the 1960s. The inter-war period and immediately thereafter is generally deemed to be a time in which feminists achieved little of significance. Yet, closer historical inspection reveals this to be far from the case.[70]

Of course these problems of periodization are not confined to feminist history but apply to any history, including legal history, which purports to adopt a periodization approach.[71] I draw attention to them here because they help to throw light on

---

[70] See eg A Logan, *Feminism and Criminal Justice: A Historical Perspective* (London: Palgrave MacMillan, 2008), focusing particularly on the years 1920–1970, and challenging the idea that the period represented an 'intermission' between first and second wave feminism.

[71] For a discussion of these problems, see P Fitzpatrick, 'Imperial Ends' in J Nichols and A Swiffen (eds), The *Ends of History: Questioning the Stakes of Historical Reason* (London: Routledge, 2012), 44.

the complex interplay of theoretical and temporal discourses contributing to the configuration of gender as a category of no great relevance or significance in law, other than in terms of a past with fleeting purchase on the present.

4.4 UNPACKING THE SIGNIFICANCE OF EQUALITY IN THE FEMINIST TURN TO LAW

The discussion so far reveals ambivalence about equality as a feminist goal even during a period commonly associated with early gender equality struggles. It also suggests a tendency in feminist legal discourse to reframe the past in terms of progress towards equality and, by so doing, to overstate the importance attached to equality by contemporaneous historical actors. How then *does* equality fit in? And what is its significance in terms of understanding the relationship between gender and law? My argument here is that the idea of equality has played a crucial role in rendering gender an improper category of law. By the same token, the feminist turn to law, which over time and repeated iteration became reconceived in equality terms, is thereby implicated in the expulsion of gender from legal discourse. I am not suggesting that equality is not a fine goal for feminists to pursue; nor am I denying that it has featured historically in feminist strategy and activism. What I am saying is that part of the cost of invoking law as a progressive discourse to advance women's interests is that it set late-Victorian feminists upon a course in which their actions, arguments, and analyses assumed the form of an equality project. Moreover, the nature of that project became determined by a particular legal understanding of equality premised upon ignoring rather than acknowledging gender.

4.4.1 GENDER EQUALITY AND THE RULE OF LAW

At the heart of all this is the idea of juridical equality enshrined in the Rule of Law. One of the enduring puzzles of feminist historical enquiry is how the inequality of the sexes appeared to co-exist quite comfortably with the principle of equality before the law. By what 'patriarchal trick'[72] was it possible to deny women the full bundle of rights and duties associated with legal personhood while simultaneously extolling the virtues of legal equality? In his late 19th-century exposition of the principles of the Rule of Law in English constitutionalism, Dicey proudly proclaims that in England the principle of legal equality 'has been pushed to its utmost limit'.[73] Yet, Dicey was widely acknowledged to be an anti-suffragist, his objections extending not only to votes for women but also to the universal male franchise.[74] Maitland, writing around the same time, is a little more circumspect about the status and scope of equality as a moral and political principle. However, like Dicey, he is quick to endorse formal legal equality, observing: 'Equality has never been so universally accepted an ideal of politics as Liberty. Still, it would on all hands be admitted that "equality before the law" is good'.[75]

The notion of equality before the law has a long history reaching back to the principles which governed Athenian democracy in Ancient Greece[76] although its modern origins derive from the political philosophical ideas associated with natural rights and social contract theories. John Locke asserts that in a state of nature men enjoy perfect freedom and equality, subject to natural laws requiring that they preserve themselves and refrain from harming others.[77] In agreeing to give up some of their natural freedoms to form an effective social and political

---

[72] S A Gavigan, 'Petit Treason in Eighteenth Century England: Women's Inequality before the Law' (1989) 3 *Canadian Journal of Women and Law* 335, 339.

[73] A V Dicey, *Introduction to the Study of the Law of the Constitution*, 6th edn (London: Macmillan & Co, 1902), 189.

[74] A V Dicey, *Letters to a Friend on Votes for Women* (London: Murray, 1909).

[75] F W Maitland, 'A Historical Sketch of Liberty and Equality as Ideals of English Political Philosophy from the time of Hobbes to the Time of Coleridge' in H A L Fisher (ed), *The Collected Papers of Frederic William Maitland: Vol 1* (Cambridge: Cambridge University Press, 1911), 121.

[76] B Tamanaha, *On the Rule of Law: History, Politics, Theory* (Cambridge: Cambridge University Press, 2004), ch 1.

[77] J Locke, *Second Treatise of Government*, edited by C B MacPherson (Hackett Publishing Co, 1980, originally published 1690), ch 2, §§4–8. See also discussion of Locke in Tamanaha, *On the Rule of Law*, ch 4.

order, men submit themselves to government through 'settled, standing laws'[78] which are 'common to everyone of that society'[79] thus enabling all persons equally to plan their affairs within the constraints of generally applicable laws. Rousseau also advocates equality under law as a necessary corollary of consensual governance, observing that:

> The social compact establishes such an equality among citizens, that all lay themselves under the same obligations, and ought all to enjoy the same privileges. Thus from the very nature of this compact, every act of sovereignty . . . is equally obligatory on, or favourable too, all the citizens without distinction.[80]

According to English social historians, equality under law was not just the province of philosophical tracts. It was also of considerable rhetorical importance in helping to legitimate class rule in 18th-century England. Douglas Hay suggests that the power of criminal law lay not just in the terror instilled by a highly punitive legal framework which included a vast number of capital offences, but also in the authority law commanded, an authority which, Hay argues, relied upon a belief by the general population in the essential integrity and impartiality of law.[81] Hay highlights the symbolic importance of the trial and execution of Lord Ferrars in 1760 for the murder of his steward in conveying a powerful message to the masses that no one, not even a great lord, was beyond the reach of British justice. E P Thompson also emphasizes the ideological significance of equality before the law in supporting and legitimating the exercise of class power in 18th-century Britain.[82] According to Thompson, to do the job of legitimation, law had to appear to possess some degree of institutional autonomy and to deliver on its promise of justice and fairness. The appearance of neutrality

---

[78] Locke, *Second Treatise of Government*, ch 2, §137.

[79] Locke, *Second Treatise of Government*, ch 2, §23.

[80] J-J Rousseau, *A Treatise on the Social Compact: or the Principles of Politic Law*, Book 2 (1762), II:4.

[81] D Hay, 'Property Authority and Criminal Law' in Hay et al (eds), *Albion's Fatal Tree: Crime and Society in Eighteenth Century England* (London: Random House, 1975), 17.

[82] E P Thompson, *Whigs and Hunters* (London: Penguin Books, 1975).

was therefore crucial to the effectiveness of law as an instrument of class rule. As Thompson observes:

> It is inherent in the special character of law as a body of rules and procedures that it shall apply logical criteria with reference to standards of universality and equity . . . if the law is evidently partial or unjust it will mask nothing, legitimize nothing.[83]

Of course Hay and Thompson both acknowledge that the legal reality was quite different. While criminal provisions might take the form of general applicable rules, many were tailored to ensuring that the interests of the rich and propertied were protected against encroachment from the poor and landless. Gaming laws, for example, were subject to property and income qualifications, so that the criminality of hunting depended not upon the nature of the act itself but upon the depth of the actor's pocket.[84] In addition, women, or certainly married women, did not stand in the same position as men with respect to the application of criminal law. Violence committed by a husband upon the person of a wife was for the most part non-actionable, either because it was lawfully in accordance with his right to beat her[85] or because the rules of evidence prohibited spouses from testifying for or against each other. As we have seen, a husband could not be guilty of raping his wife. However, he could be guilty of her murder (if it were proved) in which case he could be executed by hanging. If a wife killed her husband, on the other hand, she committed the crime of *petit treason* (a term expressive of a husband's sovereignty over his wife) and was subject to a special penalty, namely to be burned alive. Blackstone explains the penalty discrepancy between men and women as derived from a concern to preserve female modesty.[86]

---

[83] Thompson, *Whigs and Hunters*, 263.

[84] D Hay, 'Poaching and the Game Laws on Cannock Chase' in Hay et al, *Albion's Fatal Tree*, 189.

[85] *R v Jackson* [1891] I QB 671 famously rejected the alleged right at common law of a husband to beat his wife (known as the doctrine of reasonable chastisement) as well as his power to confine her. See further M Doggett, *Marriage, Wife-beating and the Law in Victorian England* (London: Weidenfeld & Nicolson, 1992).

[86] *Blackstone's Commentaries on the Law of England*, 15th edn (London: A Strahan, 1809), Vol 4, 92. The differential penalty for *petit treason* and murder

Finally, crimes committed by a wife in her husband's presence could be attributed to him based on a presumption of marital coercion. Indeed it seems likely that this defence helped to obscure the true extent of female criminality historically.[87]

More generally, the legal fabric of 18th-century Britain was deeply invested in sustaining distinctions between different classes of people according to birth, social status, property, wealth, and so on. This emerges very clearly in Blackstone's *Commentaries*. In the first volume which is devoted to 'the rights of persons', Blackstone systematically distinguishes between different categories of citizens, from the king right down to the lowest kind of servant. While acknowledging a generic class of 'persons', Blackstone draws a distinction between the *absolute* rights 'such as would belong to . . . persons merely in a state of nature and which every man is entitled to enjoy' and *relative* 'rights and duties which pertain to individuals as members of society . . . standing in various relations to each other'.[88] Blackstone concedes the importance of absolute rights but he also suggests that they are 'few and simple' in comparison to relative rights which are 'far more numerous and complicated'.[89]

Blackstone is not explicit about whether or not women possess absolute rights. Throughout the text he does of course refer almost exclusively to 'men', Englishmen', and so forth, as was the convention of the time. As Mary Beard points outs, the deployment of the masculine both collectively to denote persons in general and specifically to denote men as opposed to women is far from helpful historically.[90] Indeed, this linguistic convention bears significant responsibility for the absence of women from historical accounts in which silences about gender

was abolished in the late 18th century but *petit treason* itself was not abolished until 1828. See generally, Gavigan, 'Petit Treason in Eighteenth Century England'.

[87] The presumption was finally abolished in 1925 and replaced by a statutory defence which required establishing a husband's coercion in fact. On the position of married women in criminal law, see further Doggett, *Marriage, Wife-Beating and the Law*, 45–58.

[88] Blackstone, *Commentaries*, Vol 1, 123.

[89] Blackstone, *Commentaries*, Vol 1, 124.

[90] Beard, *Women as Force in History*, 47–51.

cannot be 'read' with any confidence. Nor is Blackstone's association of absolute rights with a state of nature particularly
helpful as social contract theorists diverged in their accounts
of women in this regard, Locke suggesting that men's physical
superiority determined women's subjection even in a state of
nature, Hobbes taking the view that women and men were
equal in their natural state but that women agreed to their
subjection as part of the social contract.[91] Blackstone's identification of private property as an absolute right prompts a
reading of the text which at the very least excludes married
women. Certainly the rights as a package—which include a
right to bear arms—resonate strongly with masculine interests
and priorities.

Blackstone furnishes no separate or distinct category for
women under the law. Women are variously affiliated within
other formal categories, though many of these exclude women
as a matter of fact if not law, for example, the clergy, members of
Parliament, the military, and so forth. One clear categorical
distinction Blackstone draws is between *feme sole* and *feme couvert*,
that is, between single and married women and much of
Chapter 15 of the first volume of *The Commentaries* is taken up
with an account of the 'benign' disabilities that women incur on
marriage because, as Blackstone concludes: 'So great a favourite
is the female sex of the laws of England'.[92] The king's consort
occupies the unique position of retaining her *sole feme* status after
matrimony. In explaining this anomaly, Blackstone cites Coke's
view that the queen is permitted to act on her own behalf in
transactions with others so that the king, whose responsibilities to
the realm are many, is not 'troubled and disquieted on account of
his wife's domestic affairs'.[93] The queen's special status serves as
yet another example of the complex schemes of classification
which governed legal status in Blackstone's England.

A century later, when artist, writer, and feminist activist, Barbara
Leigh Smith Bodichon, published an account of women's status

[91] For a discussion of the diverging views of Locke and Hobbes on this point,
see C Pateman, *The Sexual Contract* (London: Polity Press, 1988), ch 3.

[92] Blackstone, *Commentaries*, Vol 1, ch XV, 445.

[93] Blackstone, *Commentaries*, Vol 1, ch IV, 218.

under law[94] the picture she presented did not deviate significantly from that of Blackstone. *A Brief Summary*, which appeared in 1854, was far from the first 'modern' attempt to expound women's legal status and position. In 1632, an anonymous author, 'T.E.', had published *The Lawes Resolution of Womens Rights or The Lawes Provision for Women*[95] addressing the legal situation of women under categories which reflected the various stages of their lives as they progressed from maiden, wife, to widow. Moreover, in 1777 another unknown author, whom many identify as Lady Elizabeth Chudleigh, penned *The Laws Respecting Women as they Regard Their Natural Rights,* in which she listed the 'interests and duties' of women as 'daughters, wives, wards, widows, heiresses, spinsters, legatees, sisters, executrixes'.[96] In addition, by the 19th century, treatises on the legal relation of husband and wife (or *baron* and *feme* to use the more arcane legal terminology of the time) were becoming almost commonplace.[97]

Bodichon's text is nonetheless significant because it was widely disseminated and drew considerable comment. Appearing at a time when Caroline Norton's marital woes were once again catching the public eye, *A Brief Summary* was undoubtedly instrumental in bringing the issue of women's legal status to the fore in mid-19th century England. The text also had the advantage of being relatively accessible; it was not a daunting legal digest but rather a relatively short document in the form of a pamphlet and, as the title indicates, in plain and fairly uncompromising language.

Like Blackstone, Bodichon distinguishes between the legal position of single and married women, emphasizing that in the former case, women enjoy many but not all the same rights and responsibilities as men. She also devotes separate attention to

[94] B L S Bodichon, *A Brief Summary in Plain Language of the Most Important Laws Concerning Women together with a few Observations thereon* (London: J Chapman, 1854).

[95] T E, *The Lawes Resolution of Womens Rights or The Lawes Provision for Women* (London: John More, 1632).

[96] Anon, *The Laws Respecting Women as they Regard Their Natural Rights* (London: Joseph Johnson, 1777).

[97] A number of these texts are usefully listed in Doggett, *Marriage, Wife-Beating, and the Law*, 182–92.

widows and to 'women in other relationships' (for example, as agents, trustees, or executrixes). The legal picture she sketches is one in which unmarried women are in a broadly similar position to adult men subject to 'special' laws which preclude them from voting, holding public office, and so on. Bodichon comments that 'the professions of law and medicine, whether or not closed by law, are closed in fact'.[98] As we have seen, later efforts to test this position in law confirmed Bodichon's bleak surmisal as to the legality of women access to the professions.

The main focus of Bodichon's tract is the legal situation of married women in which she spells out the implications of coverture in blunt and unambiguous terms:

A man and wife are one person in law; the wife loses all her rights as a single woman and her existence is, as it were, entirely absorbed in that of her husband. He is civilly responsible for her wrongful acts . . . and she lives under his protection and cover.[99]

In contrast to Blackstone, Bodichon's exposition is not accompanied by any attempt to present the wife as a 'favourite' of English law. Thus, she emphasizes that women 'lose' their rights and legal personality on marriage, that a husband may assign or dispose of a wife's personal property 'at his pleasure', and that a husband is under no formal obligation under common law to support his wife (although Bodichon acknowledges the possibility of equity intervening in such contexts). She also states (with one suspects deliberate provocation) that 'a woman's body belongs to her husband: she is in his custody, and he can enforce his right by a writ of *habeas corpus*'.[100] Auchmuty argues that it is the very starkness of Bodichon's prose, the list-like quality and lack of obvious rhetorical embellishment, which renders it such a powerful indictment of law.[101]

As has been observed, Bodichon's presentation adopts a form of classification in which rights and duties are assigned to the

---

[98] Bodichon, *Brief Summary*, 3.
[99] Bodichon, *Brief Summary*, 6.
[100] Bodichon, *Brief Summary*, 6. In a later edition, Bodichon qualifies this by commenting that 'in practice this is greatly modified' (1869, 3rd edn).
[101] Auchmuty, 'The Married Women's Property Acts', 35.

various statuses women acquire through their relationships with others. This is in line with the legal conventions of the time. Bodichon offers no generic conception of women's status under law nor, in the observations that follow her exposition, does she explicitly advocate women's legal equality. Rather she frames her objections in *laizzez-faire* terms, equating progress with the absence of legal regulation and the corresponding promotion of individual freedom: 'Women, more than any other members of the community' she observes 'suffer from over-legislation'.[102] It is not immediately obvious then that Bodichon viewed the legal treatment of sexes as creating an unacceptable double standard in law. In a later text she does point to the inconsistency of treating women as full persons in law for some purposes but not others.[103] Mill is also exercised at times about legal consistency although his general concern too is a liberal one, namely that the differential legal treatment of the sexes violates the principle that persons should be equally free, unrestrained by government, to pursue their own affairs.[104]

What Bodichon's account reveals is the continued adherence in 19th-century legal writing to status-based ordering schemes. The Blackstonian discursive style, which, as we have seen, was deeply imbued by a worldview premised upon status and hierarchy, was very much a feature of legal exposition even in the heyday of laissez-faire liberalism. In his classic study of Blackstone's treatment of the contract of employment, Otto Kahn-Freund observes that even in the late 18th century, the categories Blackstone deployed to distinguish different kinds of labour relationship were out of keeping with the fast-changing economic and social realities of industrialization.[105] And yet remarkably, the law of master and servant, which placed employers and worker in a position of hierarchical asymmetry with respect to their contractual rights and duties, was for most of the 19th century actually strengthened and put to greater use

---

[102] Bodichon, *Brief Summary*, 13.
[103] Bodichon, *Reasons for and Against*.
[104] Mill, *Subjection*, see in particular, ch 1.
[105] O Kahn-Freund, 'Blackstone's Neglected Child: The Contract of Employment' (1977) 93 *LQR* 508.

notwithstanding that it constituted a clear violation of the principle of freedom of contract.[106] Similarly, the 19th century witnessed the introduction of legislation restricting the hours which women and children could work in factories and other industrial occupations.[107] While the differential treatment of men and women in law in terms of their capacity freely to contract with employers met with liberal objections at the time, gender-specific protective legislation in Britain in fact remained in force until the late 20th century.[108] Duncan Kennedy suggests that the structure of Blackstone's Commentaries, and in particular his distinction between absolute and relative rights, locates his account historically at the cusp of changes in the form of social and legal ordering from medievalism to modernism.[109] It seems clear that a century later, law continued to exhibit these schizophrenic tendencies, not only because of the enormous influence Blackstone exerted over the form and stylization of legal doctrinal exposition[110] but also because it continued to suit the interests of those in power to depart from ideas of legal equality as and when the circumstances required.

A remarkable decision in the early 1890s illustrates the extent to which the courts were prepared to go to compromising the integrity and intelligibility of law to achieve the result which

[106] S Deakin and G Morris, *Labour Law*, 6th edn (Oxford: Hart Publishing, 2012), 21–3.

[107] The first example of gender-specific protective legislation in employment is the Mines Regulation Act 1842 prohibiting the employment of women and children underground. Over the course of the 19th century, the scope of protection gradually spread to other industries, in particular factory work. See generally S Walby, *Patriarchy at Work: Patriarchal and Capitalist Relations in Employment 1800–1984* (London: Polity Press, 1986), ch 5.

[108] Walby, *Patriarchy at Work*, 122. Legislative provisions governing women's work in factories and other industrial occupations were finally abolished in the UK in 1986 (Sex Discrimination Act 1986, s 7).

[109] D Kennedy, 'The Structure of Blackstone's Commentaries' (1979) 28 *Buffalo L Rev* 205, 286.

[110] K M Parker, 'Historicising Blackstone's Commentaries on the Laws of England: Difference and Sameness in Historical Time' in A Fernandez and M Dubber (eds) *Law Books in Action: Essays on the Anglo-American Legal Treatise* (Oxford: Hart, 2012), 22, although note Parker emphasizes that Blackstone's long-term influence was probably greater in the United States than in England.

best cohered with their worldview. In *De Souza v Cobden*[111] a woman stood for and was elected to London County Council, holding her post for a year before her eligibility was challenged. She was then prosecuted and fined under s 41 of the Municipal Corporations Act 1882 for acting in a corporate office without being qualified. Miss De Souza appealed but, unsurprisingly, the Court of Appeal upheld her conviction. In doing so, they readily affirmed that she was disqualified at common law from standing in a county council election, a position which had already been determined in *Beresford Hope v Lady Sandhurst*[112] two years previously. The argument put by the plaintiff that if, by virtue of her sex, she was not a 'person' eligible to stand in an election for purposes of the Local Government Act 1888 then surely she could not also be a 'person' for purposes of s 41 of the 1882 Act, was roundly rejected by the court who had no difficulty in holding that the plaintiff could be a person in law for some purposes and not others. At no point in the decision does the principle of equality before the law make an appearance; neither the plaintiff nor the court seeks to pray it in aid. The Master of the Rolls robustly affirms that 'by the common law of England women are not in general deemed capable of exercising public functions'[113] although he does not agree that this precludes them from committing a criminal act if they attempt to do so. Lord Justice Fry ponders the validity of the plaintiff's election particularly after the elapse of time and the existence of a provision in the 1882 Act which states that an election which goes unchallenged after twelve months must be deemed valid.[114] He asks: 'Is the election of woman, for instance, like that of a dead man, or that of an inanimate thing which cannot be elected?' to which he concludes that the election was indeed invalid as a woman is 'disqualified by nature' from being elected to the council.[115] The contemporary reader of this tiny slice of history is left with the almost impossible challenge of getting inside the head of a judge who would equate the legal status of a woman to that of a corpse or an inanimate object.

---

[111] (1891) 1 QB 687.   [112] (1889) 23 QBD 79.

[113] *De Souza v Cobden*, 691 per L Esher MR.

[114] Municipal Corporations Act, 1882, s 73.   [115] *De Souza v Cobden*, 692.

When we consider that Dicey was writing his constitutional treatise boasting that the principle of legal equality had been pushed in England to its veritable limit at around the same time, one cannot but wonder what notion of legal equality inhabited the juristic mind. In fact when we probe beneath the rhetorical surface of legal equality in the 19th century we should not be surprised to find more than one conception in play. On the one hand, legal equality might be understood narrowly simply to mean that the law, *whatever its terms may be*, is applied as prescribed, without interference or manipulation to affect the result in particular cases. This is the idea of equality before the law embraced by the ancient Athenians.[116] It is also the kind of equality which Hay and Thompson identify as underpinning 18th-century criminal justice and which is not inconsistent with the formulation of legal rules governing the rights and duties of different categories of citizens. It is an idea of equality essentially concerned with imposing legal restraints upon the exercise of power. At first glance, Dicey's conception seems to go further than this, as he argues that legal equality is the second principle of the Rule of Law in the English constitution, the first being precisely the inability of government to exercise arbitrary power over its citizens in the absence of validly enacted laws. Legal equality, Dicey elaborates, is 'the universal subjection of all classes to one law'.[117] However, when we read on we find that Dicey is primarily concerned with ensuring that public officials are held responsible for their acts in the same way as private individuals: 'the "rule of law" in this sense excludes the idea of any exemption of officials or others from the duty of obedience to the law which governs other citizens or from the jurisdiction of the ordinary tribunals'.[118] Thus understood, Dicey's second principle of the Rule of Law seems to be little more than a reformulation of the first.

An alternative more expansive understanding of legal equality nevertheless had currency during this period although its actual purchase in law is open to serious question. This is the principle

---

[116] Tamanaha, *On the Rule of Law*, 7.
[117] Dicey, *Law of the Constitution*, 189.
[118] Dicey, *Law of the Constitution*, 198.

of liberal equality, expressive of the idea everyone is entitled to be treated under law in the same way, that is, equally. This notion of equality plainly rejects the logic of status in favour of freedom of contract and other market-oriented ideas of citizenship. Mill's objections to the legal disabilities imposed on married women are strongly underpinned by an understanding of equality in these terms, an understanding which in turn is closely allied to his general philosophical endorsement of liberty. The dissenting judgment of Justice Harlan of the United States Supreme Court in the notorious *Plessy v Ferguson* decision[119] is similarly resonant of such a liberal outlook. *Plessy* involved a challenge to a state law requiring the segregation by race of passengers in railway carriages. By a majority the Court held that the provision of separate but equal accommodation for 'white' and 'coloured' passengers (to use the terminology the judges deployed at the time) did not violate the principle of equal protection under the Fourteenth Amendment. Speaking for the Court, Brown J opined that the Amendment 'in the nature of things . . . could not have been intended to abolish distinctions based upon color'.[120] He simply could not contemplate that legal distinctions between different classes, particularly those which were *naturally* derived, violated the principle of legal equality. Harlan J disagreed, arguing that with regard to civil rights all citizens were indeed entitled to be treated in the same way: 'Our Constitution is color-blind, and neither knows nor tolerates classes among citizens'.[121] In supporting his position Harlan J adopted a classic laissez-faire position to the role of the state. The Louisiana statute, he argued, interfered with the personal freedom of citizens by effectively preventing people of different colour from choosing to sit in the same carriage.[122] Harlan J's opinion thus evidences a clear link between a notion of legal equality based on sameness of treatment and the acceptance of liberal ideas with regard to the proper sphere and functioning of the state.

William Lucy, in a recent philosophical interrogation of the idea of legal equality, draws a useful distinction between equality

[119] 163 US 537 (1896).   [120] *Plessy v Ferguson*, 544.
[121] *Plessy v Ferguson*, 599.   [122] *Plessy v Ferguson*, 577.

before the law and equality *under* the law, or between what he describes as the 'presumptive identity' component and the 'uniformity of standards' component of juridical equality.[123] Equality before the law, he argues, is associable with the presumptive identity component, the idea that those who stand before the law are presumed for all relevant purposes to be the same or identical. The uniformity of standards component or equality under the law, Lucy argues, is concerned not with the identity of addressees but rather with the equal application of whatever standards the law has enacted. As Lucy puts it 'the former [i.e., presumptive identity component] illuminates the assumed similarity of those whom the law judges, the latter [uniformity of standards component] the similarity of the standards by which they are judged'.[124]

It seems clear that during the 18th and 19th century, the uniformity of standards component of juridical equality was generally accepted: standards duly enacted were expected to be uniformly applied. In this sense, English law did indeed purport to embrace the principle of equality *under* the law. However, it is difficult to conceive Blackstone's detailed exposition of differentiated legal statuses in terms of the presumptive identity of the law's addressees. Similarly, when the Court of Appeal in *De Souza*, after casually invoking the authority of the common law to establish women's incapacity to stand for election, proceeded to determine that women may be deemed legal persons for some purposes but not others, it is hard to reconcile this mind-set with the principle of equality *before* the law.

At the same time, the logic of liberalism aligned with theories of natural rights exercised a pull which moved political and legal thought more firmly in the direction of a conception of juridical equality which relied upon the presumptive identity of addressees. This conception is expressed most fully in Mill's call for perfect equality between the sexes and in his insistence that 'the law should be no respecter of persons, but should treat all alike,

[123] W Lucy, 'Equality Under and Before the Law' (2011) 61 *University of Toronto L J* 411.
[124] Lucy, 'Equality Under and Before the Law', 416.

save where dissimilarity of treatment is required by positive reasons, either of justice or of policy'.[125]

What we plainly see in 19th-century political and legal discourse is a struggle for ascendancy between these two notions of legal equality. However, even by the late 19th century, as *De Souza* and the persons cases suggest, the presumptive identity conception was rarely in evidence in legal discourse, particularly when questions of gender arose. The idea that men and women were in any and every sense relevant to law *identical* would have been anathematic to most judges, indeed, would have been viewed as quite unnatural. Nor could it be said that judges were alone in regarding men and women in terms of natural differences. During the late 18th and 19th century, new understandings of science and nature were combining with cultural and political ideas increasingly to produce a conception of the sexes in which men and women were viewed not in terms of their similarities but rather in terms of fundamental incommensurability. There is a strange irony therefore in the fact that just as law was beginning to contemplate ideas of legal equality in terms of the presumptive identity of citizens, understandings of gender became increasingly preoccupied with sexual difference.

4.4.2 SEX, LAW, AND NATURE

We have seen that in matters of gender, nature has been a frequently invoked theme in legal and political discourse. Dicey contends that 'the real strength (and it is great) of the whole conservative argument against the demand of votes for women lies in the fact that this line of reasoning, on the face thereof, conforms to the nature of things'.[126] The Court in *De Souza* readily concluded that nature disqualifies women from standing in elections. John Stuart Mill also concedes the role that nature has played in shaping the gendered social order when he explains women's historical subordination to men in terms of their natural physical weakness.[127]

---

[125] Mill, *Subjection*, 2.
[126] Dicey, *Law of the Constitution*, 8th edn (1915), lxvi.
[127] Mill, *Subjection*, ch 1.

Two narratives of the natural emerge in explanations of sex and gender. The first posits the relationship between men and women in terms of broad commonality, in which women are conceived as similar to but lesser versions of men. Such a view of the gendered order is inevitably hierarchically inflected in men's favour. The second conception views the sexes through the lens of natural difference. Although difference may, and often has, provided a reason for men's dominance over women, the idea that men and women are fundamentally distinct does not necessarily imply a tiered view of gender arrangements. Certainly, from a feminist point of view, it is better to be *different* from men than to be a substandard model of the *same*.

An emphasis on women's natural inferiority to men, not just physical but also intellectual and moral, can be traced back to Aristotle.[128] Moreover, the Judeo-Christian belief that Eve was created from Adam's rib perfectly symbolizes the idea that women are derivative of men. During the Middle Ages, Christianity was actively involved in the promulgation of a belief in women's lesser worth and, as we have seen, the common law also embodied the idea that women lacked full capacity to act in their own interests. Although some scholars have argued that the construction of women as the 'subject sex' in the writing of Blackstone, Hale and others overstated the extent to which law in fact colluded in women's subjugation—for example Mary Ritter Beard highlights Blackstone's failure to give a proper account of the mitigating effects of equity in expounding the legal situation of married women[129]—there seems little doubt of the dominance of the cultural belief in women's natural inferiority right up to the 19th century, and the idea continued to have currency. Caroline Norton, for example, publicly states her belief in women's natural subservience to men:

---

[128]   Aristotle expresses his views on women's inferiority inter alia in *Generation of Animals*, *Nichomachean Ethics*, and *Politics*. See generally M L Homack, 'Feminism and Aristotle's Rational Ideal' in L M Antony and C Witt (eds), *A Mind of One's Own: Feminist Essays on Reason and Objectivity* (Boulder, Col: Westview Press, 1993), 1.

[129]   Beard, *Women as Force in History*.

The natural position of a woman is inferiority to a man. Amen!
I believe it sincerely as part of my religion and accept it as a matter
proved to my reason. I never pretended to the wild and ridiculous
doctrine of equality.[130]

If we look at legal texts, however, particularly from the second
half of the 19th century, we see the idea of nature increasingly
deployed not to establish women's inferiority but rather to
highlight their difference. Lord Neave, for example, is at pains
to stress that his reasons for denying Sophia Jex-Blake and her
companions the right to enter medical school are not based on
any assumption of women's inferiority, observing that: 'The
powers and susceptibilities of women are as noble as those of
men; but they are thought to be different...'.[131] Likewise, in
the American decision of *Bradwell v Illinois*, Bradley J justifies his
refusal to permit Myra Bradwell to enter the bar by asserting that
'The civil law, as well as nature herself, has always recognised a
wide difference in the respective spheres and destinies of men and
women'.[132] Bradley J is appealing here to a notion of separate
spheres and to an understanding of gender difference in terms of
complementarity of roles. The idea that a women's natural place
was in the home while men's was in the world was a frequently
invoked trope in Victorian times in the context of debate about
women's access to education and the professions.[133]

References to nature carry particular significance in the context of law because natural law was for so long the primary
theoretical lens through which the content and legitimacy of
law was viewed and assessed, and indeed natural law theorists
such as Aquinas were quite unequivocal in viewing the subordination of women by men to be naturally ordained.[134]
Although by the 18th century the scholarly grip of natural law

[130] Norton, 'A Letter to the Queen', 183. Norton goes on to argue that as
her husband's 'inferior' she should at least have the same rights and protections as
his other inferiors, for example, his servants.
[131] *Jex-Blake v University of Edinburgh*, 792.
[132] 83 US 130 (1873) 141.
[133] For a contemporaneous critique of separate spheres ideology, see E Davies,
The Higher Education of Women (London: Alexander Strahan, 1866), ch 2.
[134] T Aquinas, *Summa Theologiae*, especially Q92, Art 1.

theory had begun to weaken and, by the 19th century, it faced increasing challenge from early legal positivism, the view that law should conform to nature, as decreed by God the Creator or otherwise, continued to be a strongly entrenched cultural belief which was rarely challenged. Indeed, the 17th and 18th century natural rights arguments gained their political strength precisely because the idea that law and state ought to conform to nature was such a widely held belief. Some advocates of women's rights, for example Wollstonecraft, sought to counter the potency of nature-based arguments by emphasizing that women's intellectual inferiority was social and culturally rooted.[135] Likewise John Stuart Mill is at pains to dismiss the many beliefs held about women's natural capacity and disposition: 'what is now called the nature of women is an eminently artificial thing—the result of forced repression in some directions, unnatural stimulation in others'.[136]

In relation to ideas of nature and the sexes it is useful to consider again Thomas Laqueur's work on historical conceptions of sex because arguably it helps to shed light on the way in which gender was conceived in law, particularly in the premodern period.[137] Focusing on physiological conceptions of the human body over time, Laqueur contends that until the 18th century the female body was generally viewed as a lesser version of the male. In other words, instead of viewing the sexes as anatomically 'opposite', male and female bodies were predominantly viewed through a lens of physiological commonality in which the male body represented canonical perfection. Laqueur locates this 'one-sex' model of the human body as originating in the work of Galen in the 2nd century AD, contrasting it with the 'two-sex model' with which we are familiar today.

Laqueur is not suggesting that sex was exclusively viewed in this way and is at pains to document deviations from the one-sex model. Nor is he denying the historical prevalence of ideas of gender in oppositional terms. Indeed, we saw in Chapter Three that an understanding of gender difference in terms of opposition

---

[135] Wollstonecraft, *Vindication*.   [136] Mill, *Subjection*, 22.
[137] T Laqueur, *Making Sex: Body and Gender from the Greeks to Freud* (Cambridge, Ma: Harvard University Press, 1990).

can be traced back to the Pythagorean Table of Opposites. What Laqueur *is* saying is that until the 18th century, differences between men and women were understood less in terms of biological make-up and more in terms of a natural social order. It needs to be stressed that the idea of nature in play here is not the modern understanding in which nature tends to be associated with biology and the 'natural world'. In a context in which birth overwhelmingly determined one's place and future prospects, pre-modern ideas of nature evoked a causal understanding in which the world and one's place within it were believed to be subject to the direction of some natural inherent force. To view differences in status as already preordained was a way of making sense of one's experience; and this is undoubtedly the prism through which gender-based social rank was viewed. In other words, the gendered order resting upon the one-sex model envisaged a kind of 'cosmic hierarchy' in which 'the boundaries between male and female are of degree not kind'.[138]

How does all this relate to law? First Laqueur's account does help to make some sense of the position of women in pre-modern law. The status of *sole feme* in Blackstone, for example—in which a single woman enjoys many but not all of the same rights as men—is consistent with a view of women as lesser versions of men. Moreover, the idea that women are absorbed in the personality of their husbands on marriage makes a strange kind of sense of the fiction of marital unity. It seems easier to accept the idea that husband and wife become one if woman is merely derivative of man in the first place. Similarly, Blackstone's world of many different kinds of legal status in which no discrete category attaches to woman, and gender is differentially positioned depending upon the relational form becomes far more intelligible for, under the one-sex model, the category 'woman' would have had no independent ontological foundation.[139]

Laqueur's analysis also throws light on the legal view that a woman who becomes pregnant following rape willing participated in the sexual act. This is a defence which in the

---

[138] Laqueur, *Making Sex*, 25.   [139] Laqueur, *Making Sex*, 142.

17th century Hale referred to as dubious but which was nevertheless invoked to counter allegations of rape.[140] Because men and women's bodies were believed to be similar and because it was known that, physiologically, the male orgasm was required for conception, it was assumed that in order for conception to occur a woman also had to achieve orgasm, that is, both the man and the woman had to eject 'seed' to reproduce.[141] According to this understanding, pregnancy was plainly contra-indicative of rape. Interestingly, in the summer of 2012, a US congressman, Todd Akin, was reported to have remarked that in a case of 'legitimate rape' (certainly a category which needs a good deal of unpacking) pregnancy is very rare as 'the female body has a way to try to shut the whole thing down'.[142] This suggests that old ideas about female physiology still garner support from some quarters.

The notion that women are lesser men thus fits well with the kind of patriarchal society reflected in common law tradition. Nor is there a need to justify women's cumulatively disadvantaged position under law. Once, however, we begin to see women not as inferior models of male canonical perfection but rather as fundamentally and incommensurably different, patriarchy requires justification other than on grounds of women's alleged inferiority. It is in this context that social contract and more particularly natural rights theories posed a real challenge to the traditional patriarchal order. The development of a discourse of equality, however limited and imperfect, along with the collapse of traditional justifications for the social order based on ideas of natural authority demanded an account of women's subordination which was not predicated on women's inadequacy. As Mary Astell so pertinently remarks in 1700: 'if all men are free, how is it that all women are in chains?'[143]

---

[140] M Hale, *Historia Placitoruma Coranae: Vol I* (first published 1736, Sollom Emlyn 1800), 631 ('*The History of the Pleas of the Crown*').

[141] See generally Laqueur, *Making Sex*, 161–2.

[142] 'Todd Akin "legitimate rape" remark rebuked by Romney and others', *The Guardian* (London, 20 August 2012) <http://www.guardian.co.uk/world/2012/aug/20/todd-akin-legitimate-rape-romney>.

[143] M Astell, *Some Reflections upon Marriage Occasioned by the Duke and Duchess of Mazarine's Case; Which is also Considered* (John Nutt, 1700), 107.

At this point, women's bodies come more clearly into view. It is not insignificant that social contract theorists such as Hobbes and Locke endeavoured to account for women's social position by reference to their physiology, in Locke's case by reference to their lesser physical strength and in Hobbe's in terms of their vulnerability as child-bearers. By the 19th century, Laqueur argues, science and politics had conspired to promote a new two-sex model of biological incommensurability in which increasingly differences in men and women's capabilities, role, and general situations were explained somatically. This was a period in which women's wombs were seen as the root cause of many female disorders, mental and physical, and differences in men and women's bodies were thought to require different approaches to their education. In 1874, the psychiatrist, Henry Maudsley grimly remarks upon the consequences of mixed classes in American education:

It is asserted (by doctors) that the number of female graduates of schools and colleges who have been permanently disabled . . . by improper methods of study, and by a disregard of the reproductive apparatus and its functions, is so great as to excite the gravest alarm.[144]

Inevitably these ideas fed into legal arguments concerning women's access to the professions, where women's physical weakness was presented as rendering her ill-equipped for the rigours of professional training.[145]

It is also striking that the emergence of the doctrine of separate spheres coincided with the triumph of the two-sex model. According to Laqueur, the idea that men and women occupy separate spheres, performing complementary roles in social organization, was an ideological response to the challenge posed by egalitarianism.[146] The collapse of a belief in natural social hierarchies, including gender, required the articulation of other reasons for keeping women in their place and, in this way, women's natural differences from men became a legal reason to

---

[144] H Maudsley, 'Sex in Mind and Education' (1874) 15 *Fortnightly Review* 466.
[145] See eg *Jex-Blake v Edinburgh* per Lord Neaves; *Bradwell v Illinois* per Barker J.
[146] Laqueur, *Making Sex*, 195.

exclude them from public office and the professions. Of course the difference argument can cut both ways. Feminists such as Millicent Fawcett and Emily Davies argued that the distinctiveness of women's viewpoint and experience added particular value to the public sphere. Barbara Bodichon maintained that the absence of women's public representation would mean that their interests and concerns would be systematically overlooked by male policy-makers.

The emergence of the two-sex model inevitably impacted upon understandings of gender and law. The one-sex model was part of a world view in which hierarchies, whether gender-based or otherwise, required no independent justification other than they were in accord with the nature of things. When understandings of nature changed, so that men and women were viewed not in hierarchical relation to one another but as opposites, the alliance of law and nature was able to continue through the adoption of a discourse of sexual difference. At the same time, circumstances were conspiring to render difference a problematic platform for women's advancement. Increasingly, the logic of liberalism was pushing feminist discourse in a direction in which achieving their goals depended upon asserting their sameness with men, their presumptive identicality as the law's addressees. In campaigning for the vote, for access to public office, and the professions, feminists were confronted with a swathe of arguments premised upon their difference and which, taken as a whole, contributed to the discursive construction of a new gendered order in which women's disadvantages were seen to flow from the non-negotiable facts of their physiology.[147] To counter this required the suppression of difference and with it, the suppression of gender. It required an approach to law in which personhood could encompass women as well as men and in which sex, therefore, was irrelevant; and it demanded uniformity of application in this regard. The conceptual fudge of *De Souza* in which women were sometimes persons and sometimes not, did no service to women or indeed to law.

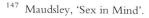

[147] Maudsley, 'Sex in Mind'.

4.5 CONCLUSION

In explaining the presumptive identity component of the idea of equality before the law William Lucy remarks: 'Make no mistake: regarding all addressees of the law as fundamentally the same both under and before the law entails excluding or ignoring a great deal of information about the character, context and conduct of those addressees'.[148] By securing equality before the law, feminists effectively sanctioned the expulsion of gender from the formal parameters of legal discourse, colluding in the idea that law was a neutral and autonomous space in which sex had no place. History however reveals a very different picture, in which law has long been complicit in the construction and maintenance of a gendered social order based on status and hierarchy. While aspects of that history continue to manifest in contemporary legal discourse, the general assumption is that law has all but expunged its patriarchal past.

What however if that assumption is not sustainable? Many feminists have argued, for example, that law is not as invested in a unitary notion of legal personhood as is commonly thought. Does gender still lurk within the discursive contours of law's person? What too if law is not the neutral and autonomous space from which gender may be appropriately excluded but rather a terrain in which, as in *Midland Bank* and *R v R*, gender struggles and debates continue to take place. How can and should law account for this? In the next chapter, I begin to look more closely at jurisprudential conceptions of law in an effort to answer these questions.

[148] Lucy, 'Equality under and before the Law', 442.

5

GENDER AND THE JURISPRUDENTIAL IMAGINATION

5.1 INTRODUCTION: A JURISPRUDENTIAL QUESTION

I want my marriage, and same-sex marriages more generally, to be recognised in Britain . . . because I want to be able to refer to Celia as my wife and have that immediately and unproblematically understood as meaning that she is my life-partner with all the connotations and social consequences that using the term 'wife' or 'husband' has for a heterosexual couple. . . .[1]

What is a wife? What kind of question is this? Is it a factual or a normative question? Is it a legal question and, if so, how does the law go about answering it? Early in this century, just prior to the implementation of the Civil Partnership Act 2004, which conferred a form of legal recognition upon same-sex partnerships, Sue Wilkinson applied to have her marriage to Celia Kitzinger—previously lawfully conducted in Canada—recognized as such in the UK. The case was heard in the High Court by Sir Mark Potter P who declined to find in the petitioner's favour, holding unequivocally that neither the principles of private international law nor human rights arguments sufficed to support a claim which would have resulted in the legal recognition of the marriage of a same-sex couple under UK law. In the course of his judgment Potter P calls upon the existence of a shared social understanding of marriage as 'a formal relationship between a man and a woman, primarily (though not exclusively) with the aim of producing and rearing children'.[2] He also expresses his approval of the enactment of the Civil Partnership Act 2004, endorsing the account offered by the Lord Chancellor (making a

---

[1] *Wilkinson v Kitzinger (No 2)* [2007] 1 FCR 183, 187, per Sir Mark Potter P quoting from the witness statement of the petitioner.
[2] *Wilkinson v Kitzinger (No 2)*, 217.

third party intervention in the case) that the Act was not a discriminatory measure but designed to 'redress a perceived inequality of treatment of long term monogamous same-sex relationships'.[3]

The judicial reasoning in *Wilkinson v Kitzinger* is suitably extensive, the legal argument reassuringly technical. Nevertheless, from the outset of Potter P's judgment one is left in little doubt about the outcome of the petitioner's claim. This is not because no compelling legal arguments can be made in her favour. In a simulated judgment, feminist academic, Rosie Harding, highlights the doctrinal strengths of the petitioner's claim, producing a careful and measured decision which, while agreeing with Potter P on a number of legal points, ultimately finds in Ms Wilkinson's favour.[4] In the end, the difference between the two judgments comes down to a disagreement about whether the differential legal treatment of same-sex couples with respect to marriage is a legitimate aim supported by measures which are reasonable and proportionate. Whether it *is* legitimate for the state to accord protection to traditional ideas of marriage is certainly a morally debatable question, but in what sense is it a legal question?

In her statement Sue Wilkinson contends that the symbolic affirmation of heterosexuality conferred by existing law inflicts a concrete and tangible harm upon same-sex couples:

[The] symbolic status of marriage as a fundamental social institution is, in many ways, as important as its formal legal status. It provides for social recognition of key relationships, and to have our relationship denied that symbolic status devalues it relative to the relationships of heterosexual couples.[5]

Potter P, while acknowledging that the petitioner has experienced feelings of 'hurt, humiliation, frustration, and outrage' because of the legal situation nevertheless expresses doubt about

---

[3] *Wilkinson v Kitzinger (No 2)*, 197.
[4] R Harding, 'Wilkinson v Kitzinger' in R Hunter, C McGlynn, and E Rackley (eds), *Feminist Judgments: from Theory to Practice* (Oxford: Hart Publishing, 2010), 430–42. See also the accompanying 'Commentary' by Karon Monaghan, who acted as the petitioner's counsel, 425–9.
[5] *Wilkinson v Kitzinger (No 2)*, 187.

whether those feelings are likely to be widely shared by other same-sex couples.[6] The judge clearly struggles here—as, one might speculate, do others—to see in the dual carriageway of marriage and civil partnership any real wrong to gay and lesbian couples. His inability to see the petitioner's harm as anything other than a subjectively experienced hurt which does not correspond with the objective reality of the relevant legal arrangements has eerie echoes of *Plessy v Ferguson* in which Brown J decries as fallacious the claim that racial segregation in railways carriages imposes a 'badge of inferiority' upon non-whites, observing: 'If this be so, it is not by reason of anything found in the act, but solely because the colored race chooses to put that construction upon it'.[7] In *Plessy* as in *Wilkinson*, what the judge sees and feels is objectively the case but what the petitioner experiences is subjective and legally discountable.

One cannot help but feel discomfited about this kind of reasoning. It does not seem satisfactory, nor indeed does the general way that the law goes about deciding that Celia Kitzinger is not the wife of Sue Wilkinson. Why should a particular moral view about marriage infuse the legal process and govern the legal outcome? Why do the feelings and experiences of the judge trump those of the petitioner? How can such an important matter turn on a particular and individual view of what is reasonable and proportionate? Moreover, although the question implicitly posed by the petitioner's statement has been answered, are we any the wiser about what kind of question it is or about the nature and validity of the process by which the judge has reached his answer? Do we know for sure that the answer he reached is correct? How can we be confident that justice has been done?

To answer these questions is of course the job of jurisprudence. If it can do nothing else, jurisprudence can tell us what is and what is not a legal question and how properly to go about answering questions posed in legal form. Surely too it can tell us something about how to gauge the justice of the outcome or at least throw some light upon how law and morality are configured for purposes of resolving the kind of dilemma which

---

[6] *Wilkinson v Kitzinger (No 2)*, 216.

[7] *Plessy v Ferguson* 163 US 537 (1896), 551.

Wilkinson v Kitzinger presents. Maybe jurisprudence can offer a
theory which makes us feel less uncomfortable about the fact
that the judge appears to have made a straight value choice
between traditional marriage and formal equality in which the
former has (once again) prevailed: is this perhaps an example of
'law as integrity'[8] in action?

Also, can jurisprudence tell us anything about the gender
dimension in *Wilkinson*? Imagine that we substitute gender for
race so that Potter P upholds a situation where two people can
only marry if they are of the same race or colour. We would all
be outraged. We would consider the decision deeply, fundamentally wrong regardless of its legal correctness. This is not to
suggest that many of us do not also find the decision in *Wilkinson
v Kitzinger* deeply and fundamentally wrong. However, it is
probably fair to say that were this a case of race, there would
be a far greater level of public outrage and far less disagreement
about what constitutes a just outcome. Does this matter? What,
if anything, is the difference between sex and race here? Can
jurisprudence provide us with an answer? Where does gender
feature in the jurisprudential imagination? These questions and
the potency of jurisprudence to provide answers form the focus
of this chapter.

5.2 THE PROVINCE OF JURISPRUDENCE (LOOSELY AND HIGHLY PROVISIONALLY) DETERMINED

The term 'jurisprudence', etymologically understood as 'knowledge of law' (from the French *jurisprudence*) or 'science of law'
(from the Latin *iurisprudentia*), is much contested in contemporary legal thought. Its precise meaning and use varies culturally,
spatially, and temporally, so that in some contexts it may refer to
theories *about* law while in others it is understood as a type or
source of law.[9] Some legal scholars view jurisprudence as a

---

[8] R Dworkin, *Law's Empire* (Cambridge, Ma: Harvard University Press, 1986).
[9] See eg H F Jolowicz, *Lectures on Jurisprudence* (London: Athlone Press, 1963),
1–5; and generally A H Campbell, 'A Note on the Word "Jurisprudence" ' (1942)
58 *LQR* 334.

politically loaded term which it is better to avoid. Others, including on occasion feminists, have consciously appropriated the term, generally with a view to transforming jurisprudential ideas from within. In recent years, it has probably become more fashionable to talk in terms of 'legal theory' or 'philosophy of law' although the latter, being aligned to a particular discipline, is inevitably more narrowly focused and methodologically contained. Once we move into the terrain of 'legal theory', the field of engagement is far wider and the analytical focus much less constrained by the preoccupations and concerns which are traditionally associated with philosophy of law or jurisprudence. At the same time those traditional preoccupations and concerns undoubtedly remain of significance and indeed, notwithstanding the changing contours of the discipline of jurisprudence/legal theory, there continues to be a broad consensus about what constitutes the core of the jurisprudential canon.[10] The textbook presentation of jurisprudential ideas in historical chronology encourages such conformity by framing theoretical development in terms generally set by the scholastic enquiry of previous generations. The retention of 'jurisprudence' as a descriptor of legal theory often also signals a commitment to a more traditional agenda although some scholars advocate as expansive an understanding of jurisprudence as possible. For William Twining, for example, jurisprudence is simply 'the theoretical part of law as a discipline'.[11]

Most people will agree that at the heart of jurisprudential endeavour are questions about the nature of law and its relation to social arrangements and practices. However, beyond that commonality, there is a great deal of variation in purpose and approach. Many legal theorists draw a distinction between 'general' and 'particular' jurisprudence, the former addressing questions about the general nature of law, the latter engaging in analysis of particular legal concepts and ideas, for example,

---

[10] H Barnett, 'The Province of Jurisprudence Determined—Again!' (1995) 15 *Legal Studies* 88.

[11] W Twining, *General Jurisprudence: Understanding Law from a Global Perspective* (Cambridge: Cambridge University Press, 2009), 5.

rights, duties, property, contract, and so forth.[12] Formally, general and particular jurisprudence are thought to be of equal scholastic value. In practice, however, there appears a propensity within the discipline to regard general jurisprudential theorization as the pinnacle of scholarly achievement. This is notwithstanding significant challenge to the idea of a general jurisprudence as well as considerable debate about the necessary level of generality to which to aspire.[13] Pursuing 'the law question' remains the ultimate jurisprudential project.

Another common line of demarcation in jurisprudential discourse is between explanatory/descriptive and evaluative/normative legal theory.[14] Hart's *The Concept of Law*, for example, purports to be descriptive, Hart emphasizing that he is 'concerned with the clarification of the general framework of legal thought, rather than with the criticism of law or legal policy'.[15] This distinction between descriptive and normative analysis, or in Hume's terms between making 'is' and 'ought' claims,[16] is central to legal positivism, the particular branch of jurisprudence with which Hart is associated. This is illustrated with particular clarity in John Austin's famous pronouncement that 'the existence of law is one thing; its merit or demerit another'.[17] According to this understanding there is a clear distinction between giving an account of what is or is not law and making an evaluative judgement based on some external standard, moral or political, about law or about particular laws. While often styled as the 'separation thesis', to indicate a strict demarcation of legal and moral terrain, this is a rather misleading

---

[12] W Twining, 'General and Particular Jurisprudence' in S Guest (ed), *Positivism Today* (London: Dartmouth, 1996), 119.

[13] B Tamanaha, *A General Jurisprudence of Law and Society* (Oxford: OUP, 2001).

[14] J Dickson, 'Methodology in Jurisprudence: A Critical Survey' (2004) 10 *Legal Theory* 117. See also Hart's 'Postscript' to the 2nd edition of H L A Hart, *The Concept of Law*, edited by P Bulloch and J Raz (Oxford: Clarendon Press, 1994).

[15] H L A Hart, *The Concept of Law* (Oxford: Clarendon Press, 1961), v.

[16] D Hume, *A Treatise of Human Nature: Being an Attempt to introduce the Experimental Method of Reasoning into Moral Subjects* (Penguin Classics, 1985, originally published 1739), 521.

[17] J Austin, *The Province of Jurisprudence Determined* (London: J Murray, 1832), 278.

sobriquet as legal positivism does not necessarily deny the presence in law of, inter alia, moral values. Rather the stance is one in which the morality or immorality of the law in question is immaterial to the determination of whether or not it is valid (unless of course moral compliance is a recognized criterion by which the norms of a particular legal system are authenticated). The crucial point is that the identification of the criteria which determine what is or is not law and the explication of the system of norms which these criteria collectively produce is, or at least can be, a neutral, non-evaluative exercise. This is not to say that evaluative analysis is not jurisprudentially valuable, simply that it is important to recognize the distinctiveness of descriptive and normative modes of engagement. William Lucy, for example, in his jurisprudential analysis of the concept of juridical equality, considered in Chapter Four, identifies his project as comprising both descriptive and normative aspects: it is descriptive in purporting to offer an account of juridical equality which, Lucy claims, captures the way in which the concept is understood and used in a wide variety of legal contexts; and it is normative in propounding a particular version of juridical equality which Lucy considers to be most inclusive and therefore desirable.[18]

Whether or not the distinction between descriptive and normative theorizing is as sustainable as legal positivism would have us believe is open to debate. Few would deny that even a 'descriptive' project entails making choices about objects, scope, limitations, and priorities, choices which are hardly made in a value vacuum. Recognizing this, some legal scholars from within the positivist tradition have sought to distinguish between the kinds of evaluative judgements which are a necessary accompaniment to any explanatory analysis of law and evaluations of a moral or political nature which seek to justify and defend law or legal arrangements by presenting them in the best possible light.[19] The former but not the latter, it is argued,

---

[18] W Lucy, 'Equality under and before the Law' (2011) 61 *University of Toronto Law Journal* 411.

[19] Dickson, 'Methodology in Jurisprudence', 142; see generally J Dickson, *Evaluation and Legal Theory* (Oxford: Hart, 2001), where she elaborates on her 'evaluative-but-not-morally evaluative' view of legal theory.

remain within the purview of description or explanation. On the other hand, critical legal scholars tend to reject the descriptive/normative distinction as fallacious and as covertly facilitating what are in fact justificatory forms of evaluation. It has been suggested, for example, that *The Concept of Law* is normatively loaded in offering an account which privileges state-based law over customary or international legal systems.[20] It has also been said that Hart's designation of some kinds of legal arrangements as 'primitive'[21] relies upon the articulation of a conception of law which is ideologically expressive of Western legal norms. This has led to more general accusations of jurisprudential parochialism and ethnocentricity. In order to counter these tendencies, Twining, among others, insists there is pressing need to expand the jurisprudential canon to take better account of approaches and perspectives which reach beyond Western insularity and get to grips with the jurisprudential implications of globalization.[22]

Read carefully, I suspect that Hart can be acquitted of at least some of the more egregious allegations levelled at him by his critics. There is a tendency in legal theoretical circles to overstate the extent to which Hart seeks to make grand claims with infinite application. In fact Hart is very cautious about stressing the limitations of the project undertaken in *The Concept of Law* (although, granted, the ambitious title might be thought to confound the caution he otherwise displays). At the same time, there can be little doubt that Hart's account of law is value-laden; it is imbued by ideas and informed by perceptions, which are reflective of the concerns and preoccupations of the time and place in which he happened to be situated and within which he was required to navigate in order to produce a jurisprudential account. Brian Tamanaha astutely observes that

---

[20] See eg R Cotterrell, 'Transnational Communities and the Concept of Law' (2008) 21 *Ratio Juris* 1; W Twining, 'Have Concepts, Will Travel: Analytical Jurisprudence in a Global Context' (2005) 1(1) *International Journal of Law in Context* 5. This kind of critique also raises questions about the extent to which Hart's analysis can claim to be general.

[21] P Fitzpatrick, *The Mythology of Modern Law* (London: Routledge, 1992).

[22] Twining, *General Jurisprudence*; see also Tamanaha, *A General Jurisprudence of Law and Society*.

Hart's articulation of law is in many ways a historical expression of the triumph of the nation state.[23] Roscoe Pound makes a similar point about the historicity of Austin's conception of law as the command of the sovereign, which emerged during a period of increasing legislative activity. Pound goes on to emphasize the temporal and spatial dimension of all theoretical attempts to explain the nature of law: 'The theory [of law] necessarily reflects the institution it was designed to rationalize, even though stated universally. It is an attempt to state the law or the legal institution of time and place in universal terms'.[24]

There is then nothing neutral about Hart's analysis. The idea that knowledge is always situated, and that, therefore, what counts as knowledge is necessarily morally, culturally, and indeed politically charged, sits uncomfortably alongside any attempt to offer a description which is not in some sense already normatively imbued. The object of enquiry—in Hart's case, the concept of law—takes its shape within the 'logic of the frame' (to deploy once again Schlag's useful idiom[25]) that Hart has constructed. This is one reason why the longstanding debate between Hart and Dworkin which has so absorbed the jurisprudential community over the last thirty or so years is ultimately irresolvable.[26] The two protagonists construct their object of enquiry quite differently. Recognizing this, and in part prompted by Hart's own analysis of his differences with Dworkin,[27] published posthumously, jurisprudential scholars have taken 'a methodological turn'[28] so that there is now much greater awareness and acknowledgement of differences in jurisprudential approach as

---

[23] Tamanaha, A General Jurisprudence of Law and Society, 170.

[24] R Pound, An Introduction to the Philosophy of Law (New Haven: Yale University Press, 1922), 30.

[25] P Schlag, The Enchantment of Reason (Durham: Duke University Press, 1998), 3.

[26] B Leiter, 'Beyond the Hart/Dworkin Debate: the Methodology Problem in Jurisprudence' (2003) 48 American Journal of Jurisprudence 17. See also Dickson, 'Methodology in Jurisprudence'.

[27] Hart, 'Postscript'.

[28] L Green, 'General Jurisprudence: A 25th Anniversary Essay' (2005) 25 OJLS 565, 575.

well as increasing sensitivity to the role such differences play in shaping the terms (and outcomes) of the discourse.

Many legal scholars are receptive to the diverse cohabitation of different kinds of theory—moral, political, normative, explanatory, social scientific, or philosophically based—residing peaceably under a broad jurisprudential roof. According to Michael Giudice, diversity signals a welcome end to imperialism in jurisprudence, expressed in the pursuit of a single theoretical framework for law which will trump all others.[29] Giudice cites Kelsen's articulation of a 'pure theory of law' as an example of such imperialism because it professes to offer an exclusive approach to understanding law free of the taint of 'alien [ie non-legal] elements'.[30] While Giudice welcomes diversity he also warns against theoretical fragmentation and stresses the need for some degree of continuity of aim focused around achieving 'the broadest possible understanding of law'.[31] Other theorists are more sceptical about whether 'methodological hygiene' will produce the kind of theoretical convergence to which Giudice aspires.[32]

The expansion of the field to encompass greater theoretical plurality is further evidence that jurisprudence is far from insulated from wider intellectual trends and developments. The situational character of jurisprudential enquiry in general and the influence of recent social and cultural theory on legal thought in particular is spelled out in Margaret Davies' compelling account of the contemporary 'dissolution' of legal theory in a miasma of postmodernist indeterminacy,[33] but one only has to look at textbook presentations of jurisprudence over the last century to identify trends and emphases in jurisprudence over different periods, signalling the situational specificity of jurisprudential

---

[29] M Giudice, 'Ways of Understanding Diversity among Theories of Law' (2005) 24 *Law and Philosophy* 509.

[30] Giudice, 'Ways of Understanding Diversity' 509, citing H Kelsen, *Pure Theory of Law*, 2nd edn (Berkeley, CA: University of California Press, 1970), 1.

[31] Giudice, 'Ways of Understanding Diversity', 542.

[32] Green, 'General Jurisprudence: A 25th Anniversary Essay', 577–8.

[33] M Davies, *Asking the Law Question*, 3rd edn (Sydney: Lawbook Co, 2007). See especially ch 8.

enquiry and the significance of contextual influences. When William Guthrie Salmond, for example, first published his text on jurisprudence at the turn of the 20th century, matters of general jurisprudence were accorded fairly limited space; the bulk of attention was devoted to analysis of significant legal concepts, that is, to particular jurisprudence.[34] By the time the 12th edition was published in 1966 (obviously not authored by Salmond), questions about the general nature of law had assumed far greater significance (and space), although analysis of legal concepts and engagement with legal sources (such as precedent or legislation) continued to fall under the jurisprudential mantle.[35] Jolowicz's *Lectures on Jurisprudence*, published posthumously in 1963, exhibit a broad similarity in structure and content to mid-century editions of Salmond although, interestingly, Jolowicz gives considerably greater attention than Salmond to sociological theories of law.[36]

Dennis Lloyd's *Introduction to Jurisprudence*, first published in 1959 just before the appearance of Hart's *The Concept of Law*, and currently among the most commonly prescribed jurisprudential texts in the UK, reflects contemporary trends in presenting the field in terms of a succession of different general theories about law, more or less chronologically ordered, but including, in addition to what one would expect from the traditional canon, chapters on critical legal studies, feminist jurisprudence, critical race theory, and postmodernist jurisprudence.[37] All of these theoretical approaches engage with general ideas about law or explore the relation between law in general and something else, whether race, gender, class, society, morality, or politics. Particular jurisprudence has all but disappeared certainly from Lloyd's text, making way for infinite difference in kinds of general jurisprudence. Variations, sometimes idiosyncratic, of

---

[34] W G Salmond, *Jurisprudence or the Theory of Law* (London: Stevens & Haynes, 1902).

[35] P J Fitzgerald, *Salmond on Jurisprudence*, 12th edn (London: Sweet & Maxwell, 1966).

[36] Jolowicz, *Lectures on Jurisprudence*.

[37] M Freeman, *Lloyd's Introduction to Jurisprudence*, 8th edn (London: Sweet & Maxwell, 2008).

this approach are in evidence in other texts[38] and the appearance of jurisprudential 'nutshells' and 'core facts' has tended to cement a conception of the field in which different labels attach to different theories of or about law which the student is encouraged to digest chronologically and in strict succession. There have been remarkably few attempts to remap the field, for example, by departing from the 'labels' approach to focus on themes, concepts, and ideas,[39] although there have emerged a number of 'alternative' jurisprudential texts (of which Davies' is a prime example) which approach the tradition canon with a critical eye.[40]

To be fair to textbook writers, students, and indeed teachers, of jurisprudence, are rarely sympathetic to disciplinary innovation and prefer the safe parameters of the conventional approach. Nevertheless, a brief (and admittedly unsystematic) survey of the field as it is currently displayed in jurisprudential textbooks, does suggest that fears of theoretical fragmentation may not be without merit. Whether such fragmentation constitutes a problem for the discipline is another matter. For purposes of the analysis here, the difficulty with what I will call 'the labels approach' to jurisprudence is that it allows, indeed encourages, the pursuit of parallel projects with little incentive or compulsion to engage in the exchange of ideas or promote theoretical cross-fertilization. Consider, for example, feminist legal theory which now makes a fairly regular appearance as a separate topic in jurisprudential texts. While this suggests that feminism has attained a certain level of intellectual respectability,

---

[38] See eg R Wacks, *An Introduction to Legal Theory*, 2nd edn (Oxford: OUP, 2009); J G Riddall, *Jurisprudence*, 2nd edn (Oxford: OUP, 1999); W Morrison, *Jurisprudence: From the Greeks to Postmodernism* (London: Routledge-Cavendish, 1995).

[39] For an example of innovation in approach, see S Veitch, E Christodoulis, and L Farmer, *Jurisprudence: Themes and Concepts*, 2nd edn (London: Routledge, 2012) in which the text is divided into three parts—Law and Politics, Legal Reasoning, and Law and Modernity—and a genuine attempt is made to resituate jurisprudential ideas thematically.

[40] Davies, *Asking the Law Question*; see also C Douzinas and A Gearey, *Critical Jurisprudence* (Oxford: Hart Publishing, 2005).

it has not encouraged the integration of gender perspectives into mainstream jurisprudential analysis. Nor has it prompted consideration (other than by feminists) of the gender dimensions of central jurisprudential concerns, for example, the relation between law and morality or the character and content of legal reasoning, both areas where, it might be speculated, a gender perspective might bear considerable fruit.

Has understanding of what asking the law question entails significantly changed as a consequence of the jurisprudential embrace of feminist legal theory? Yes and no. It cannot be denied that a range of factors, including the emergence of feminism, critical race theory, and jurisprudential re-engagement with social scientific studies and interdisciplinarity more generally, are all contributing to the reshaping of jurisprudential terrain and the revision and/or reformulation of central jurisprudential aims and problems. The methodological turn, the growing aversion to theoretical imperialism, and extensive reconsideration of what a general jurisprudence might entail[41] are all evidence of the impact and influence of theoretical perspectives such as feminism which emphasize difference, are sceptical about universalizing projects, and attend to the unarticulated values and assumptions which underpin legal discursive structures. All this is good but it doesn't get us any closer to situating gender in jurisprudence other than as another topic on the syllabus. Moreover, the trend away from particular jurisprudential enquiry, and the emergence of a new imperative to strive towards even greater levels of generality in relation to the law question, makes it even less likely that gender will make an appearance in the jurisprudential heartland. How then are we to get jurisprudence and gender on the same page (literally as well as figuratively) and, in any case, why should we bother? In the analysis which follows I hope, if not to answer these questions, at least to show why they matter.

---

[41] Twining, *General Jurisprudence*; Tamanaha, *A General Jurisprudence of Law and Society*.

5.3 GENDER AND JURISPRUDENCE: PARTICULAR ENCOUNTERS

It has already been noted that gender rarely features in legal scholarship other than in feminist legal theory or theories of gender, sexuality, and law. While other theoretical approaches may occasionally refer to it (usually as part of a passing reference to 'gender, race, and class' as a collectivity), sex/gender does not generally emerge as a category of legal significance other than in theoretical engagements in which it is deliberately foregrounded. Unless we expressly look for it, in other words, gender is unlikely to be found. Again this seems counter-intuitive. After all, gender is deeply implicated in relations of power, and power is a crucial feature of law. Gender is a central category of social ordering and law is supposed to function to maintain social order. In addition, if, as is often asserted, law reflects social reality, should we not expect gender to figure as a more prominent feature of that reality? Gender norms and divisions are hardly an insignificant dimension of social life. Finally, what significance should we attach to the fact that the history of law is very much a history of male privilege and female exclusion? Jurisprudence hardly emerged in conditions of gender-neutrality and if we accept that it is as affected by its circumstances and situation as any other intellectual enterprise, then, like it or not, gender, or more specifically maleness, has got to be lurking in there somewhere. Could it be that the significance of gender in legal thought is not that we can see it, but that we cannot?

5.3.1 A JURISPRUDENTIAL ANALYSIS OF SEX, MARRIAGE, AND THE COMMON LAW

In pondering gender's lack of conspicuous presence in legal theory, I want to take a look at a rare and recent effort by a legal theorist in the jurisprudential mainstream to engage with questions of sex and gender. Leslie Green is the Professor of the Philosophy of Law at the University of Oxford and undoubtedly among the most prominent scholars working within the analytical jurisprudential tradition today. His work encompasses both general and particular jurisprudential enquiry, spans a healthy range of jurisprudential topics and themes, and includes both descriptive and normative theoretical engagements. Among his most recent publications is an article advocating the legal adoption of 'sex-neutral marriage', that is, a conception of marriage which is neutral as to the sex of the parties and indeed as to whether sexual or procreational purposes should be a necessary feature.[42] The article forms part of a growing body of legal scholarship which lends support for the legal recognition of same-sex marriage but it is of particular significance for current purposes in providing a rare glimpse into how sex/gender is conceived in the analytical jurisprudential mind.

Let us begin with an outline of the substantive argument which Green propounds, situated within the broader field of jurisprudential endeavour. Green's project falls within the category of *particular* jurisprudence, that is, jurisprudential analysis which engages with a particular legal concept, classification, categorical structure or, in this case, legal relation. By focusing upon marriage, Green brings into the realm of particular jurisprudence the category 'sex': in fact, sex is the central analytical concept which he deploys. Moreover, in seeking to offer a sound theoretical justification for the legal recognition of same-sex marriage, Green can also be said to be engaged in a form of *normative* or *justificatory* jurisprudence although, as we shall see, there is also a sense in which he is making descriptive claims about the nature of marriage as an existing legal relation which tally with his prescriptive recommendations. In fact, Green's article is a fine example of that jurisprudential gem to which I have previously alluded, the argument from immanence, that is, an argument which proceeds upon the basis that whatever is being legally contended for is already there.[43]

How does it work? Green begins by pointing out that in a very technical sense it could be argued that 'sex-restricted marriage', that is, marriage which requires that parties be of the opposite sex, does not discriminate against people on grounds of sexual orientation. This is because gays and lesbians are as free to marry as heterosexuals so long of course as they comply with the

[42] L Green, 'Sex-Neutral Marriage' (2011) 64 *Current Legal Problems* 1.
[43] See further §1.4.

sex-restriction requirement the law imposes. To put in another way, homosexuality per se is no formal disqualification from entering into the married state: a marriage between a gay man and a lesbian woman, for example, would be perfectly consistent with the sex-restriction requirement.

From this conclusion Green deduces that sex—meaning the sexual act—and, by inference, sexual orientation, are actually of little consequence in marriage law: 'The fact that the capacity to marry is already and everywhere neutral with respect to sexual orientation shows how little interest the law takes in sex within marriage. *This is as it should be*'.[44] Green goes on to point to other aspects of conventional legal marriage which support the view that sex is of little importance in law. In particular, he highlights the fact that consummation has generally not served as necessary precondition of civil marriage although it may be a ground for voiding a marriage already contracted. Similarly, incapacity to reproduce on the part of one party may provide a ground upon which either party can rely for purposes of annulling a marriage already contracted. However, this generally requires the initiation of a legal process, until the resolution of which the marriage will continue to be valid.[45]

The central and generally essential feature of marriage as a legal relation, Green argues, is not coitus but consent: marriage is a contract, a status entered into by exercise of a 'voluntary power'.[46] It cannot come into being unless that power is exercised by both parties who, in turn, possess the legal capacity (by virtue of age, soundness of mind, and so forth) to do so. Even the Romans, Green continues, viewed consent to be the crucial constituting feature of the marital relation; hence the Digest proclaims '*nuptias non concubitus sed consensus facit*'.[47] Green goes on to conclude that since the sexual act has never

---

[44] Green, 'Sex-Neutral Marriage', 3 (emphasis added).

[45] Of course the details here vary historically and jurisdictionally so much so that Green comes close at times to constructing an 'ideal type' of marriage as a legal relation which transcends time and space.

[46] Green, 'Sex-Neutral Marriage', 10.

[47] By my crude translation: 'it is not copulation but consent which makes a marriage' 30, Ulp 1 36 ad Sabinum, quoted by Green, 'Sex-Neutral Marriage', 16.

been an essential condition of marriage and since homosexuals are as free as heterosexuals to enter into the married state, the sex-restrictive characteristic of conventional marriage is simply not consistent with a legal conceptualization which has long adopted a position of studied indifference to the sexual dimensions of nuptiality. It follows that sex-neutral or same-sex marriage actually better coheres with marriage as a legal institution. What Green has been arguing for—same-sex marriage—is (in the sense that it is conceptually and logically the better position) already there.

On the surface this is a brilliant argument from immanence. Moreover, because I agree with Green that the law *ought* to recognize same-sex marriage, I am disinclined to pick over the fabric of his case in search of rips or flaws. And yet, if I am to explore the place and significance of gender in law—and in jurisprudential discourse—this is too good an opportunity to miss. In any case, Green's conclusion about the *insignificance* of sex as a core feature of marriage seems so far out of line with the picture of marriage we have encountered up to now as to demand examination. In particular, the fact that until 1990, marriage in England and Wales conferred upon men a legal licence to rape their wives sits uneasily alongside Green's assertion of the essential sexlessness of marriage as a legal institution. To be fair, Green makes reference to the marital rape exemption at various points in his analysis and always with disapproval but, curiously, he sees the exemption as supportive of his position that the law regards sex as unimportant. This is never quite explained by Green. However, it appears to be because the kind of sex which the common law accepted as satisfying the requirement of consummation was minimal—the merest penetration of the vagina by the penis would suffice. Moreover, there was no need for either party to experience pleasure, let alone achieve orgasm, for consummation to occur; the requirement could indeed be 'brutally satisfied by an act that was in all but name rape'.[48] This tells us more about what Green thinks of as sex than it communicates about the common law. The

[48] Green, 'Sex-Neutral Marriage', 21.

implication appears to be that because the kind of sex which the common law sanctioned in marriage could be unpleasant (particularly for women), it wasn't really sex at all. The point is tangential to Green's main argument so I do not wish to make much of it, but his spare and elusive references to marital rape at the very least occasion pause for puzzlement.

In any event, Green is only able to reach his conclusion that sex is an unimportant dimension of marriage, legally conceived, by paring that concept down to its bare bones and extracting it from the broader social, legal, and historical framework in which it is situated. Let us not forget that from the legal relation of marriage many rights traditionally flowed, including sexual rights. We have already noted the marital rape exemption but consider also the domestic torts, discussed in Chapter Two, which equipped husbands with an armoury of legal actions to counter the advances of other men trespassing on their sexual domain. Consider too that if a wife left her husband he could apply to the courts for restitution of his conjugal rights. It was only in *R v Jackson* in 1891 that the Court of Appeal finally ruled that the award of a decree of restitution of conjugal rights did not confer upon a husband a right to physically capture and confine his wife.[49]

When we step back and look at marriage in its historical context, we do not see a picture of legal indifference to sexual matters. Rather we see a framework of rules which guaranteed a husband's access—and exclusive access—to the physical person of his wife. This in turn allowed a husband to be confident that any progeny of the marriage were his in fact as well as in law. Within this context, for example, the gender asymmetrical nature of 19th-century divorce law makes perfect sense. While a husband could secure a divorce based on his wife's adultery

---

[49] *R v Jackson* (1891) 1 QB 671. In fact the right to restitution of conjugal rights, which originated from the Ecclesiastical courts, was available to either husband or wife and encompassed conjugal rights in the general sense and not just rights to sexual access. In practice it enabled deserted wives to seek financial support from their husbands. For our purposes the formal sexual symmetry of the right does not detract from its significance as one of a number of remedies buttressing the sexual rights of husbands. The right was finally abolished in England and Wales by the Matrimonial Proceedings and Property Act 1970, s 20.

alone, a wife seeking divorce had to prove much more egregious behaviour on the part of her husband.[50] The sexual double standard reflected a social and legal order in which men's control over women's sexuality was not only seen as natural but also integral to family-based property and financial arrangements. Of course, most of the legal framework supporting a patriarchal conception of marriage has since been dismantled; the law looks far less interested in ensuring a husband's sexual access to his wife than it once did. However, to assert as Green as done that the legal conception of traditional marriage as embodied in law was never really concerned about sex other than to require that the two participating parties were male and female,[51] is to ignore the historical existence of a complex legal structure supporting marriage which was *all about sex*, understood as a hierarchical order based upon male domination and female subjection.

It is also by extracting the marriage from its context and repositioning it as an abstract concept which can be analysed in isolation that allows Green to make much of the fact that the common law did not require consummation as a validating condition of marriage. The extent to which this *is* a fact historically requires, I would surmise, considerably more exploration. Green distinguishes between the common law position in relation to consummation as stated by Blackstone and the requirements of Roman Catholicism, suggesting that consummation has generally been of more religious than secular interest. However, historically, church and state, ecclesiastic and civil law, have not always been as easy to disentangle as Green's analysis might suggest, particularly when it comes to determining the validity of a marriage. During much of the early modern period, the model of law was pluralist in that common and ecclesiastic law co-existed as normative systems, both of which fell within the prevailing understanding of what constituted 'the law'. In any event, even if consummation did not generally function as a

<hr />

[50] Under the Matrimonial Causes Act 1857 which for the first time allowed the possibly of divorce without a Private Act of Parliament, a wife had to establish, in addition to adultery, incest, bigamy, cruelty, or two years desertion. She could also divorce the husband for rape, sodomy, and bestiality (s 27).

[51] Green, 'Sex-Neutral Marriage', 5.

validating precondition for marriage, it certainly functioned as such after the marriage had taken place. Blackstone, while confirming Green's position on consummation as a condition of the formation of the marital relation, also cites a statute from the time of Henry VIII as authority for the proposition that consummation 'with bodily knowledge and fruit of children' thereafter rendered a marriage indissoluble. Blackstone also points out that while a pre-contract (that is, an agreement to marry at a future date) was by the same statute declared no longer to pose an impediment to marrying another, it would do so if the pre-contracting couple had consummated the relationship as this would give rise to a marriage *de facto* by canon law.[52]

The mere fact that consummation was not a requirement for the formation of the contract of marriage does not allow one to leap to the conclusion that it was of no legal importance; indeed ancient legal texts prove otherwise. John Barton cites an example from Sanchez' *Disputationes de Matrimonio*, published at the turn of the 17th century in which the Spanish Jesuit scholar ponders the position of a woman, recently married, who wished to leave her husband and enter religion but before she could do so, her husband had sexual intercourse with her by force. Sanchez concludes that as the marriage is now consummated, violence notwithstanding, it is indissoluble, but he is clearly troubled by the conclusion that the husband thereby benefits of his own wrong.[53] That Sanchez is operating within the parameters of canon law is neither here nor there: the two systems of canon and common law borrowed heavily from each other, particularly in relation to family matters.

 Where Green has a point is when he emphasizes the reluctance of the courts to probe too deeply into the intimate details of the marital relationship. We have seen evidence of this already in *Best v Fox*,[54] discussed in Chapter Two. And as Green points out, the law does not require people to prove their heterosexual orientation before entering into marriage, nor

---

[52]   W Blackstone *Commentaries on the Law of England in Four Volumes*, 15th edn (London: A Strahan, 1809), Vol 1, 435.

[53]   J L Barton, 'The Story of Marital Rape' (1992) 108 *LQR* 260, 260.

[54]   *Best v Fox* [1952] AC 716.

does it probe into questions of sexual or reproductive capacity as a precondition of marriage.[55] If marriage is really about reproduction, Green asks, why is there no age ceiling preventing women past child-bearing age from getting married? Why are the courts so reluctant to specify the details of what is required for consummation?[56] Green goes on to argue that the courts only started to get specific about the sexual and reproductive purposes of marriage when the legal demand for recognition of same-sex and transgender marriages emerged.[57] Again, historically this would require further exploration. However, assuming for the moment that it is true, what does it tell us about the significance of sex in the law of marriage? First, it tells us that legal understandings of marriage are not stable but fluid, not abstract but contextually embedded. It also tells us that marriage as an institution is deeply political and that its status as a legal relation does not insulate it from political and ideological trends. The courts' general reluctance to get into the messy details of a couple's sexual lives was and is, as much as anything, the product of a liberal ideology tilting legal discourse away from close state scrutiny of 'private' matters. This of course has never stopped the law from intervening to regulate sexual behaviour where it has considered this appropriate. Indeed, as we know, until the mid-20th century, English law showed few scruples about prohibiting homosexuality. The private sphere was reserved for sexual conduct of which the law approved: the reluctance to enquire too closely into the intimate details of married life, the legal disinclination to impose specific norms of sexual behaviour (as, for example, not raping your wife) came down in the end to the legal enshrinement of a belief in and commitment to sustaining the existing hierarchical (hetero)sexual order.

Eventually of course the ideology of liberalism caught up with itself. It is no coincidence that in making the case for legalizing homosexuality, the Wolfenden Report relied heavily on the principle of state restraint in relation to matters of private

---

[55] Green, 'Sex-Neutral Marriage', 12.
[56] Green, 'Sex-Neutral Marriage', 15–16.
[57] Green, 'Sex-Neutral Marriage', 18.

morality.[58] Nor is it surprising that in the policy debate preceding the abolition of the marital rape exemption in England and Wales privacy arguments were frequently invoked in support of the exemption. However, the boundaries of public and private, like the boundaries of marriage, are far from fixed and the sphere of legally acceptable sexual conduct has varied accordingly. A number of jurisdictions have already taken steps to reconstitute marriage in terms which allow for same-sex unions. As a legal institution, marriage is currently 'under construction'. Whether the step is taken in the UK depends not on the extent to which same-sex marriage coheres with an abstractly conceived idea of marriage, repackaged as a social and legal fact, but on the outcome of a political battle about what is sexually and morally acceptable in contemporary British society.

5.3.2 SEX AND GENDER AS LEGAL CATEGORIES

I have dwelt at length upon my points of disagreement with Green because they serve to draw out what I see as the methodological limitations which characterize some kinds of jurisprudential analysis. These include: the abstraction of legal concepts from the framework in which they operate and the tendency to treat them as having a fairly fixed content over time and space; the unarticulated normative prioritization of some features (here the formative aspects of the marriage contract) over others (the conditions of continuance), evidencing the presence of evaluative choices which problematize any claim to be rendering a descriptive or value-neutral account; the overlooking, or at least unexplained disregard, of contra-indicative evidence (as, for example, a more thorough exploration of the legal significance of consummation might have yielded). These criticisms apply not just to Green's characterization of marriage but also to his conceptualization of sex and gender. Early in the article, Green draws a clear distinction between the two concepts along the conventional lines outlined in

---

[58] The Wolfenden Committee, *Report on Homosexual Offences and Prostitution* Cmd 247 (London: HMSO, 1957).

Chapter One. Sex, according to Green, is a way of classifying people and depends upon a cluster of biological indicia (which may render the classification process difficult or indeterminate in some cases). Gender on the other hand corresponds with 'the behaviour, attitudes and social roles that, in a particular society, are conventionally considered appropriate to a given sex. Gender is as socially constructed as it gets, and in this way it differs from sex'.[59] Green acknowledges the existence of arguments suggesting that sex is also subject to processes of social construction but dismisses them quite cavalierly as 'radical-sounding', 'way out on the fringes', and 'ill-considered'.[60] Why? According to Green, such arguments are incoherent because unless sex is to some extent objective and fixed, we have no stable reference point for identifying gender norms and no measure for determining gender conformity or non-conformity: it makes no sense to suggest that a man who wears a dress is violating gender norms unless we already know that he is *a man*. It is true of course that sex, biologically understood, is often the referent for gender-based evaluations and judgments. It is also true, as Green points out, that bodies are not 'formless' and indeed vary anatomically along lines which we generally interpret according to prevailing understandings of sexual difference. However, to argue that sex is subject to processes of social construction is not to suggest that bodies are 'formless' or that material differences between bodies do not exist. Rather, it is to emphasize that the significance we attach to the materiality of bodies is socially and culturally imbued. For example, and as discussed in Chapter Four, because medieval anatomists viewed the vagina as an inverted penis, they drew from this various conclusions about the nature of sex (one sex not two) and women's bodies (a second-rate, defective version of the paradigm male model).[61] Women's 'natural' inferiority to men followed easily from the 'objective' reality of their physical deficiencies. However as men and women's bodies began to be understood differently, in

---

[59] Green, 'Sex-Neutral Marriage', 4.

[60] Green, 'Sex-Neutral Marriage', 4.

[61] T Laqueur, *Making Sex: Body and Gender from the Greeks to Freud* (Cambridge, Ma: Harvard University Press, 1985).

terms of incommensurability rather than correspondence, so too did ideas about gender undergo change so that women became viewed less as inferior to men and more as different from them (although sometimes difference also served as a ground for asserting women's inferiority). The point is that bodies are one thing, the meaning and significance we attach to them another. It is in this sense that it is wrong to assert that our understandings of sex (as opposed to gender) are not also socially and culturally imbued.

One way of bringing out this point is to look at how sex and gender have been expressly conceptualized in law. We have seen already that sex and gender rarely function as formal legal categories. Indeed, the terms hardly crop up in legal discourse at all, even as social categories or descriptors in cases such as *Best v Fox* or *R v R* where we might expect to encounter them. Of the two, 'sex' is more likely to be called upon to do legal work than 'gender', in part because, as observed in Chapter One, gender as an indicator of sexual characteristics or behaviour was not commonly deployed until relatively recently. In British law, sex tends to be the default term, as, for example, in the Sex Discrimination Act 1975, the provisions of which are now encompassed in the Equality Act 2010 but with 'sex' continuing to serve as the prohibited ground of discrimination.[62] Gender only seems to feature explicitly in UK law in connection with measures supporting the rights of transsexuals as, for example, in the Gender Recognition Act 2004 which facilitates the legal recognition of an 'adopted' sexual identity through the issuing of a Gender Recognition Certificate. Similarly, in British anti-discrimination law, the protection of transsexuals is captured by the concept of 'gender-reassignment'.[63]

It is not clear how these legal usages of 'sex' and 'gender' map onto the distinction in theoretical discourse between sex as biology and gender as social construction. In strictly legal terms, the tendency appears to be to reserve the term 'sex' for (perceived) biological difference. Thus, for example, in the cases preceding the Gender Recognition Act 2004 in which transsexual claimants

---

[62] Equality Act 2010, s 11.   [63] Equality Act 2010, s 7.

sought legal recognition for their new sexual identities, the courts adhered tenaciously to a conception of sex in terms of biological indicia in denying such claims.[64] At the same time, in other legal contexts, 'sex' has been construed more broadly and in ways which encompass the psycho-social factors we attribute to gender. Under sex discrimination law, for example, the UK courts have gone well beyond the narrow definition of sex as biology to include within the scope of protection acts of discrimination which are not strictly sex-based (where sex is understood as biology) but are underpinned by social beliefs and assumptions about sexual difference that are plainly socially constructed: for example, the belief that women with young children will be less reliable employees,[65] or the assumption that when a married couple are making career decisions, the wife will necessarily defer to her husband's interests rather than the other way round.[66]

In fact because British anti-discrimination law was for so long confined to only two protected grounds—sex and race[67]—'sex' was called upon to a lot more legal work than was likely initially envisaged at the time the Sex Discrimination Act 1975 was passed. An early legal decision[68] holding that discrimination against a woman on grounds of pregnancy was not sex-based because it could not be said that she was treated less favourably than a similarly situated man (men not being capable of pregnancy) was later rejected in favour of an approach which upheld pregnancy discrimination as sex-based notwithstanding the lack of a male comparator.[69] By taking this approach the courts (under the direction of the European Court of Justice) were recognizing that problematic social assumptions about the

---

[64] *Corbett v Corbett* [1970] 2 All ER 33; *Bellinger v Bellinger* [2003] UKHL 21.

[65] *Hurley v Mustoe* [1981] IRLR 208.

[66] *Horsey v Dyfed CC* [1982] IRLR 395.

[67] Sex Discrimination Act 1975; Race Relations Act 1976. Anti-discrimination protection was extended to disability in the Disability Discrimination Act 1995. In the early 2000s, mainly as a result of changes in the law of the European Union, the grounds of discrimination were further expanded to include religion, sexual orientation and age. See now Equality Act 2010.

[68] *Turley v Allders Stores Ltd* [1980] ICR 66.

[69] See *Webb v EMO Cargo* (No 1) [1992] 2 All ER 43; *Webb v EMO Cargo* [1994] IRLR 482 (ECJ); and *Webb v EMO Cargo (No 2)* [1995] IRLR 645.

suitability or otherwise of women's participation in paid work were directly linked to perceptions of biological differences between the sexes. For the same reason, the courts rejected any distinction between employer decisions based on the fact of pregnancy per se and decisions based on the social and financial consequences of the pregnancy for the employer's enterprise: to refuse to hire a pregnant woman because her pregnancy would create additional costs and administrative inconvenience, for example, was held to be a decision which is nevertheless sex-based.[70]

A similar difficulty arose with fitting acts of sexual harassment into the rubric of sex-based discrimination. In *Strathclyde Regional Council v Porcelli*,[71] a woman was harassed by two male co-workers who subjected her to a campaign of abuse in the form of sexually insulting remarks and behaviour. The perpetrators argued that their treatment of Ms Porcelli was not sex-based because they acted out of personal dislike rather than objecting to the fact that she was a woman. Reasoning that the two co-workers would have treated a man they disliked equally badly, the industrial tribunal rejected Ms Porcelli's claim of sex discrimination. However, on appeal, this decision was reversed, the Scottish Court of Session eventually holding that because the *form* of the treatment meted out to Ms Porcelli was sexual in nature and this in turn was determined by the fact that Ms Porcelli was a woman not a man, the harassment *was* sex-based and Ms Porcelli's claim was upheld. As the Lord President remarks, the sexual nature of the harassment was 'a particular kind of weapon based upon the sex of the victim'.[72]

In all of these cases it could be argued that something more was at issue than the mere biological fact of the claimant's sex. In *Hurley, Horsey, Dekker, Webb*, and *Porcelli*, the claimant's sex was not the per se focus of objection; rather it was something additional—pregnancy, motherhood, financial and administrative inconvenience or sheer personal animosity—which, *in combination with her sex*, triggered the discriminatory action. In each case the strategy of the defendant was to try to confine the reach

---

[70] *Dekker v VJV Centrum* 177/88 (1991) IRLR 27 (ECJ).
[71] [1986] IRLR 135.   [72] *Porcelli*, 137.

of sex as a protected ground to exclude the circumstances before the court. The claimants, on the other hand, faced the challenge of pushing the boundaries of sex-based protection sufficiently wide to encompass their claims. These attempts to 'stretch' the conceptual reach of sex to render it a more inclusive category eventually confronted their limits in the late 1990s in litigation to include within the remit of sex-based protection discrimination on grounds of sexual orientation.

In *Grant v South-West Trains Ltd*,[73] a lesbian employee applied for travel concessions for her partner in line with an employment policy which offered certain concessions to the 'spouse and dependants' of employees, including non-married partners 'of the opposite sex'. When Ms Grant's application was denied, she lodged a claim for sex discrimination, contending that had she been a man, her application would have been granted. The logic of this argument relied upon asserting that had Ms Grant been a man in a relationship with the same woman (or indeed any woman), she would have been granted the concession; the employer's refusal to do so therefore was based on her sex. The British industrial tribunal referred the case to the European Court of Justice for a preliminary ruling, asking whether it was contrary to European equality law to deny concessions to an employee with a same-sex partner where they were available in the case of opposite-sex partners. The tribunal also asked the Court to determine directly whether discrimination based on 'sex' encompassed discrimination based on an employee's sexual orientation. The Court held that the employer's treatment of Ms Grant was not sex-based. The reason for denying travel concessions to her partner was because Ms Grant was not cohabiting with someone of the opposite sex. A male employee cohabiting with another male would have been treated in the same way. The Court also held that discrimination on grounds of sexual orientation did not fall under the mantle of sex-based discrimination. The argument that it did depended on drawing such a close connection between sex-based discrimination and discrimination on grounds of sexual orientation as to render

---

[73] [1998] ECR I-621.

them virtually impossible to disentangle. Accordingly, Ms Grant had emphasized that differences in treatment based on sexual orientation generally derive from prejudices about how persons of a particular sex ought to behave: lesbians, for example, violate gender-based social norms by being attracted to women rather than to men. It followed that lesbians were discriminated against because they did not behave as women ought to behave; the root of prejudice against gays and lesbians was sex-based. This is all true. However, it did not prevent the Court from rejecting Ms Grant's argument. The decision left legal commentators feeling rather muddled because two years prior to *Grant*, the Court had accepted a not dissimilar argument made on behalf of transsexuals. *P v S and Cornwall*[74] involved the dismissal of a male employee because he proposed to undergo gender re-assignment. The Court held that this treatment was sex-based first, because the principle of equality between the sexes under-lying European equality law was a fundamental human right that extended to transsexuals, and secondly, because the appli-cant was treated less favourably than persons of his former sex. Either approach would have worked for Ms Grant.

Thanks to legislative developments recognizing sexual orien-tation as a separate protected ground in European equality law, all this is now history. However, while it is surely better all round to recognize sexual orientation as a separate legal category rather than to try and squeeze it into the framework of sex, it is worth reflecting upon how courts have been able to disaggre-gate sexual orientation from sex when the former is only mean-ingful by reference to the latter, suggesting a considerable degree of normative and conceptual intimacy. In *Grant*, the Court severed the tie by bringing into play a comparison between same-sex and opposite-sex couples rather than, as Ms Grant contended, between the applicant and a member of the opposite sex. Anyone familiar with discrimination law will be aware that the judicial choice of comparators is often crucial to the deter-mination of legal outcome. Because 'sex' here is located within a legal framework in which establishing a wrong depends upon a

---

[74] *P v S and Cornwall* [1996] IRLR 347.

process of comparison—claimants must show that they have been treated *less favourably* than someone of the opposite sex—the scope and meaning of 'sex' as a category of law has developed through a process of interaction with the logic of comparison. To put it another way, fully to understand how and why sex as a category developed as it did in discrimination law requires an 'on site' investigation, that is, an analysis of the category as it operates within the broader legal and policy framework of which it is a part.

More importantly, such investigation reveals that within legal discourse 'sex' is neither as fixed nor as biologically rooted as, for example, Green's analysis might suggest. What this analysis of anti-discrimination case law demonstrates is that law operates as a site of contestation over what sex means, with, at different times and in different contexts, biology triumphing over social construction and vice versa. Certainly, it cannot be contended that sex discrimination law is confined strictly to discrimination based on biological factors alone. In this sense then, the distinction between sex and gender proffered by Green is not sustained. In fact, sex emerges from discrimination law as a rather unstable category and certainly one which is far harder to pin down than is first imagined. One could argue that in a narrow sense, sex discrimination law relies upon some notion of biology in requiring an actual or hypothetical comparison between a biological male and female. However this is to ignore the extra work which the concept of sex does in bringing within the ambit of equality protection the kind of gender-based disadvantage which flows from socially embedded norms and practices.[75]

In summary, this brief exploration of the deployment of sex and gender as formal legal categories in UK law reveals: first, that the sex/gender distinction as put forward by Green is not really sustainable; secondly, that meanings of sex and gender in law (particularly sex) change over time, with 'sex' often been called up to encompass what Green and others would understand as 'gender'; and thirdly, that legal concepts, including sex/gender

---

[75] Indirect discrimination, the prohibition of provisions, criteria, and practices, which while gender-neutral on their face, nevertheless produce gender-disparate effects which cannot be justified, is yet a further example of the interplay of sex, gender, and disadvantage (Equality Act 2010, s 19).

have to be understood and analysed within the broader legal and normative framework within which they operate. To pluck concepts out of legal discourse and consider them in isolation produces an analysis which is coherent but only within the logic of the frame which the analyst has constructed; it tells us little or nothing about how the concept operates in its legal context or what processes are brought into play to confer meaning and shape conceptual development over time and space.

5.4 TOWARDS A GENERAL JURISPRUDENCE EN*GENDERED*

One reason for engaging in a critical analysis of Green's arguments is to cast serious doubt upon the value and efficacy of analysing legal concepts wholly abstracted from the contexts in which they operate. Moreover, although my critique is directed at the *particular* jurisprudential project Green is pursuing, arguably, it might also be applied to general jurisprudence. Indeed, it might be said that the whole idea of a general jurisprudence calls for a level of abstraction from context that is likely to render the analytical end result hardly worth the effort. This may be so. At the same time, I am not unsympathetic to the view expressed by Tamanaha, Giudice, and others that there is something to be gained from aspiring to as comprehensive an understanding of law as possible. To express reservations about seemingly arbitrary and selective processes of theoretical abstraction is not necessarily to advocate the reduction all theoretical activity to the level of localized, contingent encounters. Moreover, the aspiration to relate and connect seemingly disparate phenomena within a broader, more encompassing conceptual framework that renders those phenomena more intelligible is not necessarily to be discouraged. There is merit then in pursuing some kind of general jurisprudential project.

But what exactly should that project entail? For some scholars general jurisprudence requires conceptualizations of law at higher and higher levels of abstraction and generality in order to encompass the many manifestations of the legal which a global focus in particular has revealed. For others, it involves questioning the tendency to conceive law as a distinct and self-contained realm which can be analysed in relative isolation from its social origins, operations, and purposes. This separation of law from non-law continues to infuse general jurisprudential endeavours, certainly in their legal positivist manifestations. The spatial conceptualization of law as a closed and bounded terrain is also a characteristic feature of legal reasoning. Lon Fuller once humorously observed: 'Thomas Reed Powell used to say that if you can think of something that is related to something else without thinking about the thing to which it is related, then you have the legal mind'.[76] While a quick look at how law operates in practice is more than enough to reveal that no bright and crossable line lies between law and everything else, the idea that law lives in splendid isolation, discoverable 'free of any foreign elements'[77] is a persistent myth which is repeatedly reiterated in processes of constructing, organizing, and validating legal knowledge. Modern jurisprudence may have jettisoned theoretical imperialism but arguably it has not really given up on the idea of a philosophically and/or scientifically *pure* theory of law.

At the same time, the starting point for a general jurisprudence in which gender is apprehensible must be to challenge this notion that law is best understood separately from everything else. A conception of law as a discrete and bounded category, the properties of which can be abstractly identified and elaborated, is a conception in which gender, at least in form, has already been written out. It has been previously noted that Hart's concept of law is now regarded as far more limited by its temporal and spatial origins than Hart and many others recognized at the time. The historical specificity of jurisprudential ideas is only thinly disguised by their presentation as ahistorical and universally applicable. That gender is not a category of significance within the context of historically specific jurisprudential accounts does not tell us that gender is irrelevant to general jurisprudence; it does tell us that it has been deemed to be so, consciously or unconsciously, by those who produced

---

[76] L Fuller, *The Morality of Law*, revised edn (New Haven: Yale University Press, 1977), 4.

[77] Kelsen, *Pure Theory of Law*, 1.

such accounts and considered them meaningful. Does it matter in this context that the history of jurisprudence is a history in which women, for the most part, have not been allowed to participate? Should we expect the nature and direction of jurisprudential enquiry to change significantly now that women have secured a firm place in the legal academy? It is interesting that notwithstanding the greater proportion of women in legal academia, jurisprudence, particularly in its more traditional manifestations, continues to be a predominantly male-dominated field. Should this be treated as a factor of significance?

In *The Phenomenal Woman*, feminist philosopher, Christine Battersby asks 'what happens if we model personal and individual identity in terms of the female? . . . What would have to change if we were to take seriously the notion that a "person" could normally, at least always potentially, become two?'.[78] In posing this question, Battersby is engaged in a kind of metaphysical re-imagining in which the female subject position is posited as the paradigm model of the self in philosophical thought. Battersby's purpose here is to expose the gendered dimensions of the apparently gender-neutral subject position of Western philosophical discourse, a subject position which *cannot* normally become two and is generally presumed to be a separate, autonomous being. Battersby goes on to elaborate the various ways in which, she imagines, theoretical premises and priorities might differ if they were predicated upon a female subject, in particular, by taking into proper philosophical account the fact that selves are born and begin life inextricably connected to another. Moreover, by virtue of this fact, dependency and interconnection, rather than autonomy and separation, are the normal state of being. In this metaphysical universe, there is no sharp division between 'self' and 'other' because the self is already infused by otherness. The significance of natality is that 'the other' always emerges out of an 'embodied self'.[79] For the same reason, the Cartesian construction of the mind as disembodied necessarily gives way to an understanding of mind as always already embodied.[80]

---

[78] C Battersby, *The Phenomenal Woman* (London: Polity Press, 1998), 2.
[79] Battersby, *The Phenomenal Woman*, 8.
[80] On the mind/body distinction, see further §6.3.

Battersby's imaginary suggests that the categories and concepts through which we see and interpret the world and our (gendered) perceptions and experiences of that world are cognitively connected and, more particularly, that the common sense, gender-neutral outlook of philosophical discourse rests upon an unarticulated male subject position. The philosophical self is male *precisely because* he is devoid of all traces of femininity. In the same way, the legal person—conceived as an independent, autonomous, fully grown, formally equal, and wholly self-reliant individual in pursuit of his own interests—is male, not because men are more likely to correspond to this model of personhood than women (which is an empirical question), but because the very invocation of the idea of gender difference renders the legal person problematic. In other words, the kind of claim entailed here is not so much descriptive as normative. In both contexts—philosophical and legal—gender is called into play to disrupt settled understandings and to nudge concepts and ideas towards new, arguably more inclusive meanings. The issue then is not so much whether Hart would have produced a different concept of law if he had been capable of becoming pregnant. Rather it is what can gender difference tell us (if anything) about the concept of law?

In the chapter which follows I will return to this theme, probing more closely the relation between how we experience the world, including our embodied experiences, and how we make sense of that world. For the remainder of this chapter, however, I want to return to the question of how the project of general jurisprudence might be reconceived so as to render it more receptive to gender and other 'alternative' perspectives which, by virtue of their range and diversity (if for no other reason) offer greater possibilities for achieving 'as broad as possible an understanding of law'.

5.4.1 TAMANAHA'S GENERAL JURISPRUDENCE OF LAW AND SOCIETY

Brian Tamanaha argues that the terms of general jurisprudence as conceived by legal positivists are misconceived. He suggests that instead of focusing on the identification of a 'corpus of common legal concepts' which can be said to express the essence of law regardless of social or cultural context, general jurisprudence should concentrate on the relationship between law and society because it is in the nature of that relationship that one finds the framework which best accounts for what we apprehend as law.[81] Tamanaha emphasizes that what counts as law varies in time and space; moreover, this is the most significant conclusion to emerge from debate about the alleged parochialism and ethnocentricity of legal positivist efforts 'to provide a theory of law which is both general and descriptive'.[82]

Tamanaha's advocacy of a shift in focus from law in splendid isolation to law and/in society has much to recommend it, including from a general jurisprudential point of view. Hart himself acknowledged that law is, first and foremost, a social artifact which performs social functions and much criticism has been directed at him for failing adequately to spell out the full implications of recognizing the social character of law.[83] Moreover, the fact that both Hart and Kelsen rely upon a non-legal norm—in Hart's case the 'rule of recognition' and in Kelsen's, the *grundnorm* (basic norm)—as the ultimate test of the validity of all other norms in the legal system, is frequently cited as evidence of the failure of legal positivism to present an account of law as a distinct and bounded sphere which can be explained independently of the contexts in which it operates.[84] Furthermore, sociology of law reveals a relation between forms of law and particular kinds of social organization. Max Weber, for example, accounts for developments in legal form in terms of a series of ideal types which correspond to different kinds of social arrangements;[85] Henry Sumner Maine, as we have seen in Chapter Four, makes not dissimilar arguments in his account of the social evolution of law.[86] Finally, and from a gender perspective,

[81] Tamanaha, *A General Jurisprudence of Law and Society*, xvi.

[82] Hart, *The Concept of Law*, 239.

[83] See eg M Krygier, 'The Concept of Law and Social Theory' (1982) 2 *OJLS* 155.

[84] See eg M Davies, *Delimiting the Law* (London: Pluto Press, 1996), 24–9.

[85] M Rheinstein (ed), *Max Weber on Law in Economy and Society* (Cambridge, Ma: Harvard University Press, 1966).

[86] H S Maine, *Ancient Law* (JM Dent & Sons, 1917).

Tamanaha's stance has obvious appeal. We have seen both in Green's analysis above and from previous chapters that the tendency in legal discourse is to treat sex/gender as a biological and/or social fact which exists beyond the boundaries of law, is occasionally the object of law's applications, but is not, in any meaningful sense, legally inscribed. Surely then a focus on the law and society relationship rather than law as an isolated category is more likely to draw out the social/legal significance of gender. Put simply, if gender is not a category of significance in law it is certainly so in social organization.

If, as Tamanaha suggests, general jurisprudence should confront the relationship between law and society, how should it do so? And how has that relationship been conceived to date? According to Tamanaha, legal theory commonly accounts for the law–society relationship in terms of two basic, often unarticulated, propositions. The first is that law is a *mirror* of society, that is that the content, aims, and general normative underpinnings of law reflect the particular society in which it operates. The second is that law functions to maintain social order. These two propositions together capture prevailing attitudes about how law and society interrelate. However, according to Tamanaha, neither is necessarily true and both are often simply wrong. Empirical evidence reveals the existence of a gap between social and legal norms, particularly in contexts in which other normative schemes exercise considerable influence, for example, religious or customary norms, or where law has been imposed from the outside, for example, as a consequence of colonization. In addition, the assumption that law functions to maintain social order is problematic for a whole host of reasons; sometimes law is not concerned with social order at all or at least not in the sense of providing a fair and effective system for the resolution of disputes. Sometimes law is deployed as a weapon to oppress or contain certain elements of the population in order to advance the interests of others. Sometimes law is simply dysfunctional and/or ineffectual and fails to achieve anything much at all. (Again this is more likely to be the case where 'competing' normative systems are also operative.)

Having rejected these two key propositions as *necessary* assumptions about the law–society relationship, Tamanaha proceeds to explore in greater depth the various ways in which that relationship has been depicted in legal and social theory. He traces the origins of the mirror thesis to the legal theory of Ancient Greece, particularly the writings of Plato and Aristotle,[87] while the idea that law—in its human, that is, positive form—functions to preserve social order is located in the natural law theory of Thomas Aquinas.[88] Tamanaha also highlights the natural law commitment to a necessary connection between law and morality, which, in the case of Aquinas, ties the validity of law effectively to a divine will but, in broader conceptualizations of natural law theory, aligns law with nature so that the law and society relation becomes situated within a discursive frame governed by what nature, natural rights, human nature, and so on dictate. Moving on to modern theoretical traditions, Tamanaha argues that legal positivism may seem perhaps to be less committed to the mirror thesis and more committed to the idea that law functions to maintain social order. At the same time, because legal positivism ties the validity of a legal system to its social efficacy, it remains reliant upon the mirror thesis to some extent.

Tamanaha also explores historical, anthropological, and sociological accounts of law and society, exemplified by the work of Maine, Durkheim, and Weber, among others, each of whom have 'formulated highly influential accounts of the way in which the form and content of law is intimately linked to the nature of social organization—the mirror thesis in a different form'.[89] Maine's account is particularly interesting for our purposes because it accords gender a place of sorts in the course of legal development. Maine views the progression from ancient to modern law as entailing a shift from social arrangements in which the family/local community constitute the core social unit to a conception of social life in which individuals are at the heart of social organization. In the former kind of arrangement, hierarchy and status are crucial and authority is generally vested in the patriarch/father, while in the latter, individuals are regarded as formally equal and authority derives from their free

[87] Tamanaha, *A General Jurisprudence of Law and Society*, 14.
[88] Tamanaha, *A General Jurisprudence of Law and Society*, 16.
[89] Tamanaha, *A General Jurisprudence of Law and Society*, 32.

agreement to submit to law to preserve social order.[90] As we saw in Chapter Four, Maine sees the loosening of legal restrictions on women as part of this process of progression.

Weber's account of the law-society relation places greater weight on the influence of economic factors in shaping law. His approach relies upon the construction of four ideal types of law which correspond to different kinds of social and economic arrangements.[91] Weber identifies the modern legal order as 'formally rational'; formal in the sense that it relies exclusively on considerations internal to law to determine legal outcomes, and rational because it relies upon logical analysis and the application of rules and principles. Weber argues that formal rationality is best suited to a capitalist social order because it provides the highest degree of stability and predictability. By so doing, Weber links ideas about law's autonomy and rationality directly to the economic and social order. To put it another way, in Weber's analysis, the concept of law articulated by Hart and others is a historically specific legal manifestation of industrial capitalism.

This leads on neatly to Tamanaha's account of what he describes as the 'selective mirror tradition'[92] of social theory, in which category he locates critical perspectives on law such as feminism, Marxism, and critical race theory. A selective mirror approach basically posits the law and society relationship in terms of the interests of a particular dominant group—men, white people, capitalists and so forth. In such a legal system, legal norms reflect the values and interests of the dominant social group and not the population as a whole. The selective mirror tradition also problematizes the notion that law functions to maintain social order. Benign accounts of law in terms of social order typically invoke the idea of agreement or social contract to justify the imposition of a normative order on otherwise free individuals. Selective mirror theories on the other hand locate

---

[90] Maine, *Ancient Law*.

[91] Weber's ideal types draw on the dichotomies of form and substance, and rationality and irrationality: Rheinstein, *Weber on Law in Economy and Society*, 61–4.

[92] Tamanaha, *A General Jurisprudence of Law and Society*, 40–4.

the origins of legal authority in power and domination rather than agreement. Technically, the extent to which law mirrors the social in such contexts could be very selective indeed, as where the indigenous population is colonized and oppressed by an external force. The selective mirror thesis also accommodates or gives way easily to instrumentalist accounts of law-accounts which see law as a tool to be deployed for particular purposes, that is, as a technique of social engineering.[93] Again instrumentalist accounts may but do not necessarily have to reflect social norms and customs—everything depends upon the ends to which law is put. Similarly, while the effectiveness of law as an instrument is likely to depend to some extent on its functionality as a social ordering mechanism, this requires a view of social order tied directly to social ends. The function of law, in other words, becomes to deliver whatever end law is called upon to fulfil.

So where does all this leave us—and Tamanaha—in terms of accounting for the relation between law and society? First, Tamanaha concludes that on close exploration neither the mirror thesis nor the social function thesis hold as necessary features of law. Law *may* reflect society and *may* function to maintain social order but it does not have to do so to be law. Moreover, for various reasons, the mirror thesis in particular is far less applicable to law now than in the past. Tamanaha cites as evidence in this regard: the very fact that law has assumed a formally rational form in which an internal logic rather than external social factors tends to determine legal outcomes; the influence of a specialized body of internal experts (legal practitioners) who shape law in their own interests not those of society; the increasing use of legal transplantation (whereby laws from one jurisdiction are incorporated in the legal system of another); and the general growth of legislation and instrumentalism in law. In fact, Tamanaha suggests, what counts as law varies so much between time and place and depends upon social and legal configurations which are highly specific and contingent that it is not possible to identify in isolation any

---

[93] Pound, *Introduction to Philosophy of Law*, 47.

necessary or sufficient properties which might be said to signal the presence of law in any and every given context. What law is or is not depends entirely upon what we treat as law as a matter of social practice. Simply put, Tamanaha maintains: 'the term "law" has no essence'.[94]

At first glance this would seem to kick the project of general jurisprudence well and truly into the long grass. Not so. Tamanaha seeks to hold onto the idea of general jurisprudence (albeit a 'general jurisprudence of law and society') and to at least some of the tenets of legal positivism. In particular, he still thinks it is worthwhile to 'ask the law question' although only in the context of socially grounded and empirically supported enquiry. Tamanaha styles this approach 'socio-legal positivism'. It is an approach to the study of law and legal phenomena which is bare in the assumptions it makes about law in advance but still provides a frame in which questions about the nature of law, contextually situated, can be explored:

Instead of dictating what law is [socio-legal positivism] asks how groups of people talk about law. Instead of assuming what law does, it examines what people do with law. It creates a framework for the identification of law accepting that there may be more than one phenomenon that goes by the name of law, then leaves the rest to be filled in by actually existing social practices. If law is indeed a human social creation, only a flexible, open approach can capture the myriad forms and manifestations that law(s) take(s).[95]

5.4.2 THE PLACE OF GENDER IN A GENERAL JURISPRUDENCE OF LAW AND SOCIETY

Tamanaha's general jurisprudence recognizes that law and society tend to be closely interrelated but that the nature of that relation can vary in time and place. He also suggests that an exploration of that relation can tell us more about the nature of law by focusing on how it is apprehended in particular contexts.

---

[94] Tamanaha, *A General Jurisprudence of Law and Society*, 204.

[95] Tamanaha, *A General Jurisprudence of Law and Society*, 156. Of course it remains debatable to what extent this general critique of legal positivism can be accurately directed at particular legal positivist accounts.

It is in this sense, for example, that Hart's analysis of law tells us a lot about the nature of a modern Western legal system in the mid-20th century.

Can we use Tamanaha's approach to tease out the place of sex/gender in a general jurisprudence? Anthropological studies show that sexual divisions are a characteristic feature of almost all societies. This is hardly surprising given that sexuality is likely to be central to the reproduction of any social unit. At the same time, the way in which sexuality is socially organized varies considerably so that the social conventions and practices which support the sex/gender regime in any given society will also vary. In other words, while social arrangements are almost always characterized by some degree of sex/gender stratification, the nature and implications of that stratification will be socially contingent.

Were we to adopt the mirror thesis we might then conclude that the place of gender in law is dependent upon its place in social organization: law reflects social arrangements and changes in the latter are likely over time to produce changes in the former. However, as Tamanaha points out the mirror thesis does not always hold. The mirror may be only partial, as, for example, when law reflects the interests and concerns of men and not women. Or the law may take a turn which is out of line with indigenous gender norms, as for example, when a colonizing power brings its own assumptions and values about gender relations to bear upon the legal regime of a conquered country. Alternatively, law and the social gender regime may be out of sync because of the normative grip of religious fundamentalism, positing a very different conception of appropriate gender relations than that enshrined in law.

All the considerations above go some way to explain why sex/gender is likely to be a significant substantive feature of law in any given context and why law is almost certainly structurally implicated in the support of particular sex/gender regimes. If we reflect upon the history of the common law, for example, we immediately see that law has been called upon at various times to adapt to significant social changes in the relations between the sexes. *R v R* might be cited as an example of this process, and indeed, this is very much how the case was viewed by the courts who considered it. Bringing this analysis back within a Tamanaha frame, the place of gender in law will vary in time and space and will very much depend upon how sex/gender is socially constituted *and* how the law-society relationship is configured in a given society. Moreover, within this general jurisprudential framework, gender *may* be conceptually linked to law, that is, integral to how law is apprehended and understood, or, on the other hand, it may not; it all depends upon what conventions and beliefs comprise the population's general understanding of law in a particular context. In any event, given the centrality of sex/gender to social organization, gender considerations are likely to feature prominently in any system of law.

Are we there yet? Not quite. There is more still to be said. First, let us return to the relation between law and society and the tendency to view the former as a mirror of the latter. Tamanaha has already offered a range of reasons why this assumption does not universally hold. However, in addition to the reasons he puts forward, one of the main difficulties with the mirror thesis is that it posits the law–society relationship as unidirectional: the legal *reflects* the social and law is reduced to a passive reproduction of the real. One of the most important contributions of (post)modern critical legal theory is to challenge this assumption of unidirectionality. We have seen already in Chapter Three how Michel Foucault's notion of discourse has been deployed, inter alia, by feminists, to emphasize the active, constituting operations of law. Law does not merely *reflect* the social (understood widely to include political, economic, cultural, and so on) but helps to construct it. Law is no shy imitator of some 'external' reality; as an authoritative form of knowledge which presents itself as scientific and objective, law directly influences how we see and make sense of the world. The categories of law become part of the cognitive armoury upon which we call to order and interpret our experiences, while legal values and assumptions, by virtue of being legally enshrined, carry greater weight and purchase in discursive navigation.

To return the focus to gender, law is no mere reflection of the sex/gender order but actively involved in its construction and maintenance. Moreover, law does not simply 'mirror' gendered norms and assumptions but may be their primary source and legitimation. Again this will vary in time and space and will depend in particular upon the degree of authority law wields and the extent to which it is normative integrated into everyday life. The greater the grip law has on social and cultural consciousness, the greater its likely cognitive significance, including its significance in shaping and informing gender norms and perceptions. It follows that in a society in which law's discursive influences and effects are widespread and pervasive, the social constructionist importance of law is likely to be greater. Moreover, in seeking to challenge social arrangements which are unfair or unjust, law in such a context will be a key site of contestation. Finally, the subject of contestation will not just be formal legal norms, as for example, the rules currently governing marriage in the UK, but the whole discursive legal framework within which they are located, including underpinning ideas, assumptions, categories, textual conventions, advocacy techniques, and core values. From a gender perspective then, whether and to what extent to invest in law as a strategy for bringing about social change, will depend significantly upon the nature of the relationship between law and society in a given time and space and the degree to which law is integrated into processes of social cognition and valuation.

Before concluding this engagement with jurisprudence there is one final issue to flag up and introduce with a view to embarking on an exploration in the chapter that follows. One of the important themes to emerge from Tamanaha's general jurisprudential reconstruction is that law may take a range of different forms and still count as law if that is how that form is understood in a given society. This raises questions about what kind of form law takes in particular contexts, including, for example, contemporary Western societies. It also brings into potential play enquiry into the relation between legal form and substance, in a gendered context, between the form of law and the place of gender therein. For example, Weber argued that the formally rational character of modern law was best suited to the needs and imperatives of a capitalist social order; but what, if any, are the gendered implications of formal rationality? Similarly, Maine maintained that the evolution of law from ancient to modern times is marked by the decreasing prominence of a hierarchal family form and the increased significance of individualism; but where does the modern family form fit into this individualist model? How does modern law reconcile the individual as the core unit of law with legal constructions of the family? To the extent that either Weber or Maine's characterizations still hold true, they have been subject to extensive interrogation by feminists. A wealth of feminist legal scholarship, for example, has been devoted to exploring how the discourse of public and private has been deployed in law to facilitate the co-existence of an ideology of individual sovereignty, on the one hand, and the gendered family form, on the other.[96] Similarly, feminists have paid considerable attention to understandings and applications of legal reasoning and the gendered implications of an emphasis on formal abstract logic and adherence to discursive norms of universality, coherence, and objectivity.[97] Working through the gendered implications of Tamanaha's analysis allows us to locate these kinds of theoretical engagements within the broader jurisprudential enterprise, while at the same time confirming both their relevance to legal theory and their strategic importance to feminists and other scholars seeking to harness law to the pursuit of progressive social aims.

[96] See in particular here, N Naffine, *Law and the Sexes: Explorations in Feminist Jurisprudence* (Sydney: Allen & Unwin, 1990).

[97] See further, §6.6.

6

THE SIREN CALL OF LEGAL REASON

6.1 INTRODUCTION: 'BUT DARLING— YOU'RE NOT THINKING LIKE A LAWYER!'

My father bears responsibility for setting me upon the path of legal study. He was a lawyer, as was his father before him, and various other relatives were, in one way or another, associated with that venerable profession. Thus from an early age I learned that to think like a lawyer was to think in a very special way, and since daughters so often seek the approval of their fathers, I made the acquisition and cultivation of legal intellectual skills my keenest aspiration. It did not help that thinking like a lawyer more often than not went against my natural inclinations, causing more than a fair share of arguments at the family dinner table. I was vaguely aware too that my gender stood against me—it was still not uncommon to encounter the view that women were intellectually inferior to men. I gradually realized that to think like a lawyer required me to be on constant state of alert to prevent my femininity from slipping in undetected to contaminate my otherwise smoothly functioning intellectual processes. Gender, I discovered, was alien to reason. Therefore to bring the particularities of my female experience to bear upon any discussion in which sex or gender was not the direct focus was immediately to compromise the intellectual credibility of my position. This did not seem quite fair because in the cut and thrust of intellectual debate, the experiences and attitudes of men appeared subject to no similar embargo, were, in fact, presumed to be typical and gender-less. Masculinity rarely found itself at odds with reason. In any event, I learned that to be rational was not so much to think like a lawyer but rather to think like a man; to contain my femininity whenever the forces of reason came into play.

Pierre Schlag observes that legal training demands nothing less than 'the eclipse of self'.[1] To think like a lawyer, he suggests, is to invoke a distinct, unitary mind-set purged of all personal and contextual influences and capable of apprehending the world in a particular way common to all other lawyers. Schlag is suggesting that the process of thinking like a lawyer entails some degree of self-repression regardless of sex. I agree. However, there is little doubt that gender, and more specifically, femininity, presents particular challenges in this respect, given the historically masculine derivations of legal thought, practice, and culture. Studying cases like *Best v Fox*[2] only served to reinforce a sense that part of me—the feminine part—did not quite fit into the world of law. While I learned how to speak the language and acquire the necessary skills to support a sound legal mind, I never quite got over that early sense of dislocation and dissonance. In truth, my 'eclipse of self' was rather more simulated than real; in that respect, I fear, my legal education failed me.

The purpose of this chapter is to take these old anxieties and neuroses of mine and reformulate them as an object of intellectual enquiry. That, after all, is the rational way to approach such issues. Moreover, doing so presents an opportunity to probe the relationship between law and gender by examining what we understand as reason in law. What does it mean to 'think like a lawyer'? In what sense is lawyering a special or distinct way of thinking or doing? What role, if any, does gender play with respect to ideas of legal reason and modes and techniques of legal reasoning? Within feminist legal scholarship it has often been argued that legal reasoning relies upon a model of rationality which privileges masculinity and excludes or marginalizes the feminine. Is this argument sustainable? Can the ideal of legal reason survive the scrutiny of a gender-based critique or is it irretrievably mired in the patriarchal culture which produced it? Most importantly, are my long-held anxieties and neuroses well-founded? Or is it time I put them to rest?

---

[1] P Schlag, *The Enchantment of Reason* (Durham: Duke University Press, 1998), 126, and generally ch 6.

[2] [1952] AC 716.

6.2 REASON RULES

Most people will agree that reason is important to law. Indeed, most people will insist it is a crucial aspect of what we understand by legality. Underpinning this insistence is recognition of the power and authority of law; the capacity it holds to compel conduct and perpetrate violence. Without reason, law has limited appeal. With reason, it has a good deal more to recommend it. Law offers a means of regulating the inevitable conflict which accompanies human sociability, but, tempered by reason, it also promises a kind of justice. Government by laws and not by men, which is the essence of the Rule of Law ideal, presupposes a legal order premised upon rationality, expressed in the systematic application of general and pre-determined rules, equally and impartially, to the conduct of human affairs. Reason and the Rule of Law then go hand in hand.[3]

Reason provides law both with an overarching frame and an internal disciplinary mechanism. It supports the presentation of law as orderly and systematic. It also positions law as benign and progressive by aligning it with a conception of human nature in which reason serves as a key indicator of human worth. Reason also brings law directly into contact with desirable qualities such as objectivity and impartiality and offers a much sounder justification for legal authority than provided by tradition or convention. This is recognized by Sir William Jones, an 18th-century legal commentator, who observes:

If *law be a science*, and really deserve so sublime a name, it must be founded on principle, and claim an exalted rank in the empire of *reason*; but if it be a *merely* unconnected series of decrees and ordinances, its use may remain, though its dignity be lessened, and he will become the greatest lawyer who has the strongest habitual, or artificial *memory*.[4]

Reason helps to 'exalt' law to the status of a science, transforming it into a discourse which can promise certainty and deliver truth.

---

[3] N MacCormick, *Legal Reasoning and Legal Theory*, revised edn (Oxford: Clarendon Press, 1994), xi–xii; Schlag, *Enchantment*, 20.

[4] Sir W Jones, *Essay on the Law of Bailments* (London: J Nichols, 1781), 123–4.

Aside from lending law such powerful normative legitimacy, reason also assumes responsibility for keeping law in good order. Reason, as Schlag tells us 'is the formative medium through which the field of law is organized and represented'.[5] Reason puts the system we recognize as law together, constructing the external frame and configuring the internal structure. Reason also provides the primary tools of legal navigation. To find one's way around law, one must be familiar with the content of particular rules and doctrines and the concepts and classifications which house and distinguish them. But this is not enough—one must also know how all the different elements fit together and have a firm grasp of the dynamics that underpin law as an operating system. This demands the application of a trained legal mind. Sir Edward Coke famously distinguished between the 'natural' reason which inheres in each and every one of us and the 'artificial reason' required for the proper application of the common law. The latter, he insisted, is necessarily the product of long study and experience. Even the King in all his wisdom (and much to his annoyance) could not adjudicate on a question of law unless he was properly 'learned in the laws of his realm'.[6] Such a high level of technical proficiency ensures that, among other things, law remains a discrete field of professional expertise. At the same time, the focus on law not as something that *is* but as something one *does*—emblematically depicted in the expression 'thinking like a lawyer'—shifts attention away from the substantive content of legal rules (with all their values, assumptions, and contentions) towards an emphasis on legal method and approach, so that the *reason* of law—and thereby its standing as an objective, science-based way of knowing—is seen to lie not in its substance but in its form. This has led Lon Fuller, among others, to embrace the idea that 'forms liberate', affirming not just the distinctiveness of law as a formally rational mode of governance but also its virtue (in Fuller's terms, 'inner morality') as a social

---

[5] Schlag, *Enchantment*, 15.
[6] E Coke, *Prohibitions del Roy* (1607) 12 Co Rep 65, cited in M Davies, *Asking the Law Question*, 3rd edn (Sydney: Thomson Lawbook Co, 2008), 50.

organizing framework which enables the free exercise of individual human agency.[7]

This insistence on formal rationality as the central feature and virtuous core of legality is not unqualified. Indeed, more recent thinking about the Rule of Law signals a shift away from a predominant emphasis on legal form towards the articulation of some minimum substantive content to the Rule of Law ideal. Forms, it seem, do not liberate enough. Thus, the late Lord Bingham has argued that adequate protection for fundamental human rights should be recognized as an essential element of the Rule of Law.[8] Hilary Charlesworth has made a similar argument, stressing attention to human rights as important part of the process of instituting the Rule of Law in post-conflict situations.[9] The late Neil MacCormick, while originally espousing a value-sceptical approach to legal reasoning in his classic exposition in 1978, has since remarked: 'Now however it seems to me that the whole enterprise of explicating and expounding criteria and forms of good legal reasoning has to be in the context of fundamental values that we impute to legal order'.[10] What all this suggests is that ideas of the Rule of Law—and of legal rationality—are undergoing reassessment. Legal reason, understood in narrow formalistic terms, may be giving way to broader elaborations asserting a direct relation between reason and fundamental values. More generally, it seems that what passes for reason depends at least in part on the kind of work reason is called upon to do. It is difficult therefore to disassociate reason from its applications. At the same time, ideas of reason have emerged from and are identifiable with particular philosophical

---

[7] On the origins and the significance of Fuller's pronouncement that 'forms liberate' see K Rundle, *Forms Liberate: Reclaiming the Jurisprudence of Lon Fuller* (Oxford: Hart Publishing, 2012), especially 1–3. For an account of law's 'inner morality' see L Fuller, *The Morality of Law* (New Haven: Yale University Press, 1965).

[8] T Bingham, *The Rule of Law* (London: Penguin, 2010), ch 7.

[9] H Charlesworth, 'Human Rights and the Rule of Law after Conflict' in P Cane (ed), *The Hart-Fuller Debate in the Twenty-first Century* (Oxford: Hart Publishing, 2010), 43.

[10] N MacCormick, *Rhetoric and the Rule of Law: A Theory of Legal Reasoning* (Oxford: OUP, 2005), 1.

and political traditions. The kind of reason traditionally associated with law, for example, is very much an expression of Enlightenment ideals and aspirations. Could it be that the postmodernist disenchantment with Enlightenment values is prompting the articulation of a new kind of legal reason? If so, (where) does gender feature in this reconstructive process? To answer these questions requires some closer consideration of how reason in law is currently understood and deployed. However, before doing so, let us briefly traverse the general theoretical landscape in which reason resides.

6.3 THE TOPOGRAPHY OF REASON

Simply understood, reason is a faculty of the mind. This tells us very little. It tells us little about what reason entails or how it fits with other cognitive faculties, for example, memory, imagination, or sensory perception. It offers us no insight into how reason interacts with bodily processes and the world at large or whether reason has any inherent value other that as a tool which can be put to various uses, good and bad. The history of philosophical enquiry into reason is a history of enquiry into any and all of these concerns. However, first and foremost, reason is viewed as the quality which distinguishes human beings from other life forms. Against the backdrop of a vast, complex, and unpredictable natural world, the capacity to reason stands out as that which sets humanity apart and enables some degree of human control over the natural environment. Robert Nozick suggests that reason is 'a crucial component of the self-image of the human species'.[11] While it is true that opinions diverge over how to conceive our relations with other species and the natural environment—the view that man is at the top of the evolutionary ladder and master of all he surveys no longer goes unchallenged—most people tend to accept that our intellectual faculties distinguish us, qualitatively or quantitatively, from other life forms. Reason is thus a commonly agreed marker of humankind.

[11] R Nozick, *The Nature of Rationality* (Princeton: Princeton University Press, 1994), xii.

One consequence of seeing reason in this way is that it lends support to claims of human exceptionality: because we are capable of reason, we occupy a unique place in the universe. In a religious context, this generates links between reason and the possession of a soul. Descartes saw reason as a capacity which humans shared (albeit in a more limited fashion) with God.[12] However, even in a secular context, reason serves to single humanity out. It is no coincidence that the historical period known as the 'Age of Reason' (broadly speaking, the late 17th and 18th century) is also the period in which natural rights discourse emerged and took tangible form in the revolutionary politics of the rights of man.[13] It is the shared possession of reason which supports the assertion of equality implicit in natural rights claims. In contemporary times, human rights are a quintessential expression of ideas of human exceptionality.

In this way, reason becomes entangled in philosophical speculation about the value of human life and ideals of human flourishing. In particular, because, as humans, we possess the capacity to reason, we are also capable of exercising moral agency. This leads to questions about how we *ought* to act and the role of reason in relation to conceptions of virtue and the good life. We have moved from an idea of reason as a common marker of humanity to reason as a virtue or path to virtue: reason holds out the possibility of providing a foundation for articulating standards for good (virtuous) living. Aristotle is credited with offering one of the earliest versions of this rational ideal of the good life. For Aristotle, the best—and most ethical— way to live was to aspire to full realization of the distinctive human power of rationality, understood in terms of cultivating habits of reflective contemplation and careful deliberation.[14] Hegel offers a more recent take on the importance of reason to

[12] R Descartes, 'Fourth Meditation: Truth and Falsity' in *Meditations on First Philosophy*, trans M Moriarty (Oxford: OUP, 2008 [1640]).

[13] The works of Thomas Paine notably include both *The Age of Reason* (London: DI Eaton, 1794) and *Rights of Man* (London: JS Jordan, 1791).

[14] Aristotle, *Nicomachean Ethics*, revised edn, trans J A K Thomson (London: Penguin, 2004) and discussion thereof by M Homiak, 'Feminism and Aristotle's Rational Ideal' in L M Antony and C Witt (eds) *A Mind of One's Own: Feminist Essays on Reason and Objectivity* (Boulder, CO: Westview Press, 1993), 1.

human fulfilment. Like Aristotle, Hegel offers a teleological account of the human condition in which reason steers a steady and progressive course towards consciousness of freedom.[15] Intellectual development, the process by which the mind comes to know itself, thus becomes the ultimate goal and purpose of human life.

 Interestingly, both Aristotle and Hegel considered women as less capable of achieving the virtuous heights of a fully developed rationality. Even Marcia Homiak, a feminist defender of Aristotelianism, declares that 'Aristotle's views on women's nature are, without exception, objectionable'.[16] For Aristotle, women, along with slaves, simply lacked sufficient deliberative capacity to participate in the *polis* (in crude terms, the public sphere). While Hegel's view on women may seem marginally less objectionable,[17] it is clear from his account of the development of consciousness in *Phenomenology of Spirit* that Hegel does not consider women to be capable of achieving the same level of intellectual and spiritual maturity as men. Indeed, it is in relation to this point that Hegel invokes the tragic fate of Antigone: it is her inability as a woman to rise above the particularity of family ties and grasp the universal issues at stake that spells her demise.[18]

Putting these gender considerations to one side for the moment, what Aristotle and Hegel both articulate in different ways is an ideal of rationality closely aligned with virtuous living. This tells us something about the work reason can do in philosophical and political discourse; it gives purpose and value to reason but does not really endow it with tangible content or form. Can we

---

[15] Freedom in Hegelian terms is being free when we act in accordance with our reason. See, in particular, G W F Hegel, *Elements of the Philosophy of Right*, trans H B Nisbet (Cambridge: CUP, 1991 [1820]) and *Lectures on the Philosophy of History* (published posthumously in 1837).

[16] Homiak, 'Feminism and Aristotle's Rational Ideal', 6.

[17] But only marginally; for example, in *Philosophy of Right* Hegel draws attention to the rational and ethical significance of differences between men and women by observing that 'the difference between men and women is like that between animals and plants' (para 166).

[18] G W F Hegel, *Phenomenology of Spirit*, trans A V Miller (Oxford: OUP, 1977), ch 6. For a detailed discussion of Hegel's analysis of Antigone's dilemma, see §3.4.

understand reason other than in vague terms which equate it with our intellectual faculties? One way of going about this is to identify what reason is not. Indeed, it is quite common to account for reason in this way: reason is other than prejudice, faith, superstition, intuition, emotion, desire, tradition, and any number of other predicates one might call upon to ground belief and inform decision-making. Moreover, it is common to encounter the positive associate of reason with certain qualities, attributes, or ideals and its disassociation from others, often through the construction of hierarchically imbued dichotomous pairings. We have already encountered the operation of oppositional pairings in the Pythagorean Table of Opposites.[19] While reason is not explicitly included in the Pythagorean Table, accounts of reason frequently take oppositional form and much philosophical discussion has been devoted to explaining how reason interacts with its various 'others'. For example, Francis Bacon, in discussing the relationship between reason ('mind') nature, invokes the metaphor of marriage to express the ideal which should govern their association: 'Let us establish a chaste and lawful marriage between Mind and Nature'.[20] As Genevieve Lloyd points out, the marriage metaphor serves to depict the mind/nature relationship in unequal terms in which mind is clearly the master.

Another distinction which crops up repeatedly is between reason and emotion (or in Humean terms, 'the passions').[21] From the Ancient Greeks onwards, philosophers have sought to differentiate intellectual processes—logic, memory, and critical reflection—from feelings or emotions—desire, hate, love, anger, and so forth. While philosophical texts diverge on the precise nature and dynamics of the relation between these (the Ancient Greeks tended to see reason and passion as working in

[19] See §3.4.

[20] F Bacon, 'The Refutation of Philosophies' in *The Philosophy of Francis Bacon: An Essay on its Development from 1603 to 1609 with new translations of fundamental texts*, trans B Farrington (Liverpool: Liverpool University Press, 1964), 131, quoted in G Lloyd, *The Man of Reason: 'Male' and 'Female' in Western Philosophy* (London: Methuen & Co, 1984), ch 1.

[21] See §6.4.

alignment whereas the Enlightenment tendency was to draw a much sharper line between these different kinds of cognitive operations), the use of gendered imagery, equating reason with masculinity and passion/emotion with femininity, is undeniably widespread throughout the history of philosophical thought.[22] A related distinction here and perhaps the most famous and influential illustration of the constitution of reason through dichotomization is Cartesian dualism. According to Descartes, mind and matter were radically different kinds of substance: matter was material, what Descartes described as 'extended stuff', while the mind comprised a wholly immaterial substance.[23] The mind/matter distinction forms the basis of a host of other distinctions now well entrenched in philosophical and indeed popular discourse, including the recurring distinctions between reason and emotion and mind and body. For Descartes, the body played no role in intellectual processes other than to house the mind. The mind itself was non-corporeal—disembodied. Cartesian dualism thus constructs a frame in which reason is distanced from bodily processes, including sensory perceptions—touch, feel, sight—and, of course, the emotions. The disembodiment of reason also lends support to the view that intellectual ideas can be detached from the contexts—cultural, political, and historical—which give rise to them so that the 'products' of reason emerges as ahistorical and universally applicable.

Sexuality and desire fall firmly within the remit of materiality. Cartesian reason thus emerges as thoroughly and completely sexless; the realm of ideas is marked as a sex-free space. However, because the formal implications of the mind/body distinction are that sexual difference has no bearing on intellectual processes, Descartes' ideas were potentially liberating for women in that they presented an opportunity to assert the capacity to reason for the female sex. Indeed, some women, for example,

---

[22] See generally Lloyd, *The Man of Reason*.
[23] R Descartes, *Meditations on First Philosophy* (1640), see in particular Meditation VI: 'Concerning the Existence of Material Things, and the Real Distinction between Mind and Body'.

the feminist essayist, Mary Astell, did precisely this.[24] At the same time, because Descartes' mind/body distinction located sex in materiality, and because sexual difference was largely perceived in terms of women's deviation from a male corporeal norm, it takes no great leap of intellectual prowess to see how the mind/body dichotomy often worked in practice to disassociate femininity from reason's operations. The recurrent assumption was that because women's bodies were different from—or inferior versions of—men's, so also were their minds. An example of this process of association occurs in James Fitzjames Stephen's well-known refutation of Mill's arguments regarding the subjection of women. Stephen, a 19th-century barrister and judge, was firmly of the view that natural differences between men and women precluded the desirability of social and legal arrangements based on gender equality:

The physical differences between the two sexes affect every part of the human body, from the hair of the head to the soles of the feet, from the size and density of the bones to the texture of the brain and the character of the nervous system. Ingenious people may argue about anything . . . but all the talk in the world will never shake the proposition that men are stronger than women in every shape. They have greater muscular and nervous force, greater intellectual force, greater vigour of character.[25]

However, perhaps the most important consequence of Cartesian dualism is that it has resulted in a failure to take seriously the full implications for reason of our embodied condition. What if, contrary to the Cartesian vision, corporeal context *is* relevant to the exercise of reason? Recent developments in cognitive science suggest that the relationship between brains, bodies, and bodily experience is far more intricate and involved than the Cartesian model would suggest. This is not, as George Lakoff and Mark Johnson observe '. . . the innocuous and obvious claim that we need a body to reason; rather it is the striking

[24] For a discussion of Astell's use of Descartes' ideas, see M Atherton, 'Cartesian Reason and Gendered Reason' in Antony and Witt, *A Mind of One's Own*, 19.
[25] J F Stephen, *Liberty, Equality, Fraternity*, RJ White (ed) (Cambridge: Cambridge University Press, 1967, [1874]), 193–4.

claim that the very structure of reason itself comes from the details of our embodiment'.[26] According to Lakoff and Johnson, the concepts we deploy (including legal concepts) are grounded in and shaped by our perceptual and motor systems. Moreover much of our understanding relies on metaphors derived in this way: 'There is a logic of our bodily experience that is imaginatively appropriated in defining our abstract concepts and reasoning with them'.[27] The gendered implications of these insights are not really explored by Lakoff and Johnson, but they are potentially significant. In particular, if processes and outcomes of abstract thought are tied to embodied experience, what does this say about fields of knowledge which are almost entirely constructed by men? Lakoff and Johnson's analysis enhances the value and relevancy of the kind of metaphysical reimagining undertaken by philosopher, Christine Battersby, in which she posits the female subject position as the paradigm model of the self in philosophical thought;[28] for surely, if the mind *is* embodied then sex is no longer outside the domain of reason but rather firmly within its purview. In this way, current trends in the cognitive sciences threaten wholly to disinter the ideal of Abstract Universal Reason which is the Enlightenment inheritance and continues to serve as an important fount of legal authority and legitimacy.

6.4 *SAPERE AUDE!*

At this point it is necessary to consider more closely the particular ideas about rationality which characterize Enlightenment thought. The starting point once again is Descartes whose legacy to the empire of reason goes well beyond the cultural institutionalization of an ideal of the disembodied mind. Descartes also

---

[26] G Lakoff and M Johnson, *Philosophy in the Flesh: the Embodied Mind and its Challenge to Western Thought* (New York, NY: Basic Books, 1999).

[27] M Johnson, 'Mind, Metaphor, Law' (2006–2007) 58 *Mercer LR* 845, 846. Johnson offers a selection of examples to illustrate his point: 'affection is warmth'; 'intimacy is closeness'; 'bad is stinky' (860). All of these evidence the use of bodily processes as metaphors for abstract ideas.

[28] C Battersby, *The Phenomenal Woman* (London: Polity Press, 1998), and discussion at §5.4.

helped to bequeath to posterity an approach to rationality which champions the view that the proper application of reason can yield outcomes which are beyond contestation. In this sense, his work prefigures the 18th century 'triumph' of reason as a political ideal, captured in the slogan, *sapere aude* ('dare to think')[29] and expressing an aspiration to be free to think for oneself rather than be directed by custom, tradition, or religion.

To understand how Descartes approached reason, it is helpful to know that from an early age, he demonstrated a pronounced aptitude for mathematics and the physical sciences. This produced in adulthood a thinker very much preoccupied with establishing the kind of certainty generally only obtainable in the mathematical world: the threshold Descartes sets for validating knowledge is very high, his object to devise a method of thought—a form of rationality—which, is capable of yielding knowledge which is more or less infallible. This concern to identify the best way in which to apply the intellectual faculties is reflected in the title of one of Descartes' most famous works, *Discourse on the Method for Rightly Conducting the Reason and Searching for Truth in Science*, published in 1637 and now generally referred to as *Discourse on Method*. This text, along with *Meditations*, contains the bulk of Descartes' ideas on the nature of reason.[30]

In approaching reason as method,[31] Descartes invokes a tradition, dating back to the Greeks, of attempting formally to articulate the intellectual procedures by which one is able to arrive at sound conclusions. Descartes sees his method as applicable across the sciences; it is not an approach the application of which is context-dependent. It requires first that the knower purge his mind of any kind of knowledge which does not already meet Descartes' exacting requirements of certainty, and to approach problems in a wholly detached and dispassionate

---

[29] I Kant, *What is Enlightenment?* trans H B Nisbet (London: Penguin, 1991 [1784]).

[30] Although see also Descartes' unfinished manuscript, *Rules for the Direction of the Mind*, which is similarly focused.

[31] The following elaboration relies primarily on Descartes' accounts of his four 'precepts' or 'laws' in Part 2 of *Discourse on Method*.

fashion. Relevant data should be abstracted from the messiness of practical living and reduced to a series of simple propositions which can then be subject to the same intellectual moves as one applies to a mathematical equation. In the same vein, the components of a problem should be broken down into as many separate parts as possible and then approached individually, taking the simplest first and gradually progressing in step-by-step fashion to the resolution of complexities. Finally, Descartes emphasizes that in the course of such endeavours it is vital to pay close attention to and record each step taken so that nothing of relevance is missed. If all these steps are followed correctly, the conclusions they produce will be genuinely and demonstrably proved.

Descartes' rationalism bears many of the hallmarks of contemporary cultural understandings of reason, commonly informing, inter alia, ideas about the objectivity and neutrality of legal reasoning. It requires the separation of the knower from the context in which things are known and the adoption of a sceptical methodological stance. It prescribes that knowledge be broken down and reconstructed in a reduced form free of messiness and extraneity. It deploys a formal and sequential analytic approach paying due attention to detail and methodological rigour. Above all, it supports the idea of a universal rationality which is abstract, not situated, and resides innately in the human mind. At the same time, Descartes distinguishes between reason as the intellectual faculty existing 'whole and complete in each one of us',[32] and the development of good reasoning skills through education, practice, and attention to methodological finesse. This latter, more exalted form of reason requires dedication, discipline, and rigorous application. The demands placed upon our intellectual processes inevitably constrain the practical uses of Descartes' method. While Descartes aspired to discover a method of reasoning which would allow 'even' to women[33] the opportunity to enhance their knowledge

---

[32] *Discourse on Method*, Part 1.

[33] See discussion of Descartes in Lloyd, *The Man of Reason*, 39–49 which includes reference to Descartes' correspondence on the subject of women's reasoning capacities (fn 8).

and understanding, in practice, his approach contributed to the narrowing of reason to a technical proficiency from which all traces of humanity had been erased. Genevieve Lloyd describes the contracting effect on reason of Descartes's arguments in the following terms:

Descartes' method transformed Reason into a uniform undifferentiated skill, abstracted from any subject matter. This loss of differentiation gave rise to a crucial change. Reason lost the strong motivational force it had in earlier thought. In the lack of inner direction to specific ends, Descartes's Reason became an inert instrument needing direction from an extraneous will.[34]

The relegation of reason to the status of an instrument finds further confirmation in the moral philosophy of David Hume. One of the classic debates of Enlightenment thought is between rationalists, such as Descartes, who claim that true knowledge is rationally derived and empiricists, for example, John Locke and David Hume, who argue that the basis of knowledge is empirical, that what we know derives primarily from our experience, and, in particular, from our sensory perceptions. Thus, in his *Treatise of Human Nature* (1740) Hume rejects any grand ambitions for reason, emphasizing that knowledge is primarily experience based. Both our moral sense and our understanding of the natural world derive from the 'passions' (by which Hume means sensations and feelings, including emotions). It is the passions, not reason, which provide motives for action and justify ends. Reason plays no role in determinations of value: "'Tis not contrary to reason to prefer the destruction of the whole world to the scratching of my finger'.[35] The role of reason is thus limited to engagement with formal questions of fact (that is, determinations of truth and falsity) and processes of relating ideas to form a sound basis for the drawing of inferences (essentially, conceptual concerns). In this way, Hume argues, reason can exert some control over the exercise of the passions by aiding

---

[34] Lloyd, *The Man of Reason*, 50.

[35] D Hume, *A Treatise of Human Nature: Being an Attempt to introduce the Experimental Method of Reasoning into Moral Subjects* (London, Penguin Classics, 1985), 463.

the assessment of how to achieve a desired end. Ultimately, however, reason is in the service of that end: 'reason is and ought only to be the slave of the passions, and can never pretend to any other office than to serve and obey them'.[36] Hume's famous distinction between fact and value, or the 'is/ought distinction' which was to become such a central feature of legal positivism, slots neatly into an overall conceptual framework in which reason is thought to provide no foundation for moral claims.

The most systematic account of Enlightenment reason is offered by the great German philosopher, Immanuel Kant. Kant comes onto the scene in the aftermath of the demotion of reason to 'slave' status by Hume. While in some ways sympathetic to empiricism, Kant seeks to rescue reason from its Humean shackles while resolving the apparent deadlock between rationalism and empiricism. In a series of *Critiques* written mainly in the 1780s, Kant presents a detailed elaboration of reason and its operations. He begins by distinguishing between the conditions which allow us to ascertain what is true, those which determine how we should act, and those which inform the making of evaluative or aesthetic judgements. These three distinctions mirror sequentially the focus of Kant's three main critiques: *Critique of Pure Reason* (1781), *Critique of Practical Reason* (1788), and *Critique of the Power of Judgment* (1790).[37] The distinction between 'pure' and 'practical' reason in the first two titles is somewhat misleading not least because Kant recognized that pure reason might be applied in practical reasoning contexts. More significant is Kant's differentiation of theoretical and practical reason, the former being concerned with the cognitive processes involved in the acquisition of knowledge, and the latter addressing the capacity to select goals or ends and

---

[36] Hume, *A Treatise of Human Nature* (1985), 462.

[37] For an accessible introduction to Kantian theory, see S Gardner, *Routledge Philosophy GuideBook to Kant and the Critique of Pure Reason* (London: Routledge, 1999). For an analysis in a legal context, see A Barron '(Legal) Reason and its "Others": Some Recent Developments in Legal Theory' in J Penner, D Schiff and R Nobles, *Jurisprudence and Legal Theory* (London: Butterworths, 2002), 1035. The account which follows draws from both these sources.

work out best how to achieve them. In his account of theoretical reason, Kant acknowledges the importance of both sense-based perceptions and rationality in the acquisition of knowledge. Kant's account of cognition is detailed and in its time quite revolutionary. The gist of it is that the objects we perceive do not determine how we perceive them; rather how we perceive objects determines how they appear. Thus, we can only ever know the world as it appears to us, not how it really is. At the same time, Kant argues that how things appear to us is, ultimately, the product of certain universal laws of understanding which order our experience. Underpinning processes of cognition, in other words, there is knowledge which is just true, independent of and prior to the senses, a set of first principles which transcend our experience. This is the essence of Kant's 'transcendental idealism'.[38]

For Kant, 'pure' reason is transcendental; it is not based on the evidence of the senses. Pure reason produces knowledge and prescriptions for action which are innately derived and universally applicable. In this way Kant retains an idea of universal reason as a foundation for thought but not as the exclusive or necessarily most significant foundation. Reason plays a role along with other processes of cognition to aid determinations of what can be known, how one should act, and how to make judgments. Unlike Hume, Kant also sees reason as being able to ground and support moral deliberations. Pure reasoning in particular can serve as a foundation for the articulation of universal moral principles although only when it is properly deployed. The purpose of 'critique', Kant asserts, is to identify the conditions for the appropriate and legitimate use of reason.

Kant's account of reason has had a profound influence on categories of thought and feeds directly into the structuring and delineation of modern disciplinary boundaries. It also offers perhaps the most detailed map of reason's operations in philosophical thought. This is an articulation of reason which, under the right conditions, can yield objective knowledge, ground moral principles, and aid practical reasoning. It also heralds the

[38] On transcendental realism, see Gardner, *Guide to Kant*, ch 5.

rejection of political absolutism, the espousal of scientific and social progress, the rise of secularism, and the pursuit of political and legal arrangements which ensure (or purport to ensure) that everyone is free to 'dare to think'.[39] There is a direct correlation between the emergence of liberal political philosophical ideas premised on values of individual autonomy, freedom of choice, and limited state intervention, and the shared human capacity to reason. The triumph of Enlightenment reason has clear and significant implications for law. In particular, it generates the need for a legal order which is capable of supporting and sustaining the empire of reason. Modern legal reasoning thus emerges as the product of a confluence of historical contingencies yielding a particular, historically specific instantiation of reason with deep roots in Enlightenment values and aspirations.

6.5 TRAVERSING THE EMPIRE OF LEGAL REASON

How do we know what to do? This is the essential question in law which reason is called upon to answer: conventionally understood, legal reasoning is a form of practical reasoning, the branch of reasoning which aids determinations about how to act. Of course in a general sense, we may act for all sorts of reasons—desire, envy, self-love, and so forth. While any of these may provide a 'reason' for acting, they are not usually regarded as 'reasoned'. Linguistically speaking then, there are clear differences between reasons for acting and reasoned action, that is, action which is the result of considered reflection and careful deliberation. Practical reasoning concerns the latter; it is what MacCormick describes as 'the application by humans of their reason to deciding how it is right to conduct themselves in situations of choice'.[40]

---

[39] The Enlightenment legacy was far from uniformly benign. For example, on the relationship between Enlightenment ideas, the construction of race, and the spread of colonialism, see Davies, *Asking the Law Question*, 288–93 and 300–1.

[40] MacCormick, *Legal Reasoning and Legal Theory*, iv.

Thus understood, legal reasoning is merely a particular instantiation of a more generic form of reasoning. James Penner observes that when students first encounter legal reasoning they quickly find that they are being taught to deploy moves with which they are already familiar. Most of us become acquainted at an early age with the notion of rules, the authority commanded by past practice, and the need to provide good reasons to support a position. According to Penner, legal reasoning is simply 'human practical reasoning with a vengeance',[41] a sort of *uber*-practical reasoning which is the peculiar province of the legally initiated: there is nothing really distinctive about legal reasoning other than perhaps an annoying tendency to nit-pick excessively.

Accepting this for the moment, what does practical reasoning in law entail? Formal accounts of legal reasoning are many and quite varied. Some take the form of skills-based or 'how to' introductions to legal reasoning, generally tailored to the needs of new law students. Others are more jurisprudential, for example, Neil MacCormick's classic and influential account, *Legal Reasoning and Legal Theory*, which first appeared in 1978. Unsurprisingly, jurisprudential accounts of legal reasoning tend to be strongly influenced by particular jurisprudential allegiances. MacCormick, for example, identifies his analysis with legal positivism, describing it 'as something of a companion volume to H L A Hart's *The Concept of Law*'.[42] Edward H Levi's mid-20th century exposition is widely recognized as a reflection of the American Realist tradition.[43] Depending on jurisprudential stance, accounts of legal reasoning are likely to take a more or less strict approach to the determinacy of legal rules, the scope for judicial discretion, the extent to which legal materials may be subject to interpretation (or manipulation), and the role of more informal approaches to legal decision-making, involving, for example, the deployment of rhetoric, the use of narrative, and appeals to that judicial weapon of last resort, common sense.

---

[41] J Penner, 'Legal Reasoning' in Penner, Schiff, and Nobles, *Jurisprudence and Legal Theory* (2002), 649 and 651.

[42] MacCormick, *Legal Reasoning and Legal Theory*, xiv.

[43] E H Levi, *An Introduction to Legal Reasoning* (Chicago: University of Chicago Press, 1948).

Accounts of legal reasoning can also be more or less 'critical'. It is perhaps helpful to envisage conceptions of legal reasoning in terms of a wide spectrum of approaches. At one end is a stance of extreme formalism, in which rules are thought to govern outcomes mechanically and incontrovertibly within a fixed and finite framework in which everything is known or anticipatable. At the other end of the spectrum, legal reasoning is understood as a discursive camouflage which conceals the uncertainty and openness which actually characterizes legal doctrine: legal rules are indeterminate and manipulable and the apparent autonomy of law a sham which disguises the fact that legal outcomes are the result of political and/or personal choices. In practice, few legal scholars adhere to either extreme and most will acknowledge that notwithstanding the permeability of legal boundaries and the (relative) elasticity of legal concepts, law is a field within which discursive operations are subject to particular constraints. The nature of those constraints and the extent to which they determine legal outcomes remains the subject of intense juris-prudential contestation.

One of the fullest and most influential jurisprudential accounts of legal reasoning as practical reasoning is provided by Neil MacCormick. According to MacCormick, at the heart of legal reasoning processes lies the syllogism, which is a form of deduc-tive reasoning (that is reasoning which proceeds from general premises to a particular conclusion). In syllogistic form, a valid rule of law combined with the proven operative facts to which the rule applies will justify a particular outcome. To present it in formulaic terms: if p then q, p therefore q (where 'p' = rule(s) + proven operative facts and 'q' = correct legal outcome). Take, for example, the doctrine of vicarious liability which includes the rule that when an employee commits a tort in the course of employment, the employer will be liable. If, on the proven operative facts, a tort *is* committed, then the employer is liable: rule + facts = outcome.

Of course, matters are rarely so simple. MacCormick fully acknowledges that while deductive reasoning forms the logical core of a rule-based system of legal rationality, it is by no means the only way in which legal outcomes are determined: the rule may be ambiguous and require interpretation; the facts may present difficulties in terms of identifying what is relevant and therefore making the appropriate classification; there may be a clash of rules requiring an evaluative choice to be made about which is the better rule to apply. Sometimes, there may be no rule at all so that one must be invented. What does one do in these circumstances? It is at this point that the legal reasoning process turns away from pure deduction to harness a wider range of deliberative techniques. What becomes crucial in such contexts is the ability to identify a good argument capable of supporting the preferred legal outcome. But how do we know what *is* a good argument to aid the interpretation of rules, the classification of facts, the choice between conflicting rules, or the invention of new rules? According to MacCormick, we must invoke principles and values: 'Deductive reasoning from rules cannot be a self-sufficient, self-supporting mode of legal justification. It is always encapsulated in a web of anterior and ulterior reasoning from principles and values'.[44]

What are these principles and values and where do they come from? MacCormick tells us that they emerge over time from the practice of law and acquire legitimacy through their institutional acceptance as legally relevant. They do not however emerge in a vacuum but within the context of the functioning needs of law as a system concerned with the regulation of human conduct. 'Legal' principles and values develop within a framework of general structural constraints which also serve as justificatory devices in legal argument. One such constraint is presented by *consequences*. If law is concerned to encourage some kinds of conduct and deter others, it follows that attention to the consequences of imposing a particular rule, particularly in situations of choice, is likely to feature significantly in justificatory arguments. A consideration of consequences will often involve making evaluative judgements, for example, about the costs and benefits of one legal outcome over another and this in turn will lead to the gradual embedding of particular value choices into the normative fabric of law. Consequences are

---

[44] MacCormick, *Legal Reasoning and Legal Theory*, xiii.

also likely to play a significant role in decisions about whether to extend the scope of a legal rule to new fact situations.[45]

A second institutional constraint is posed by the need for *consistency* in decision-making. The principle that like cases are treated alike is identified by MacCormick as a requirement of formal justice compelling the legal decision-maker to ensure that consistency across decisions is maintained as far as possible. The decision-maker must also be mindful that any decision she takes will apply not just to the case in hand but to all other like situations. Therefore, notwithstanding the particularity of the immediate situation, the justifying reason must be capable of universal application. The doctrine of precedent is one important expression of formal justice requirements but the commitment to consistency in law goes well beyond the technical requirements of precedent rules. Among other things it serves to enshrine a formal Aristotelian conception of equality as the preferred or default model of equality in legal discourse.[46]

A final constraint identified by MacCormick which shapes the development of 'good' arguments in law (and the values and principles which support them) is *coherence*. Any decision rendered has to make sense within the context of the broader fabric of the legal order. The system as a whole must be intelligible. This is more than an obligation to act consistently. It is a rather a commitment to ensuring that the decision, and more particularly, its justification, coheres with—does not contradict, undermine, or render out of place—the kinds of justificatory norms which have already found institutional acceptance. In other words, coherence requires that legal argumentative positions should fit as seamlessly as possible within the broad frame of norms already in place.[47]

---

[45] See generally MacCormick, *Legal Reasoning and Legal Theory*, ch 6. MacCormick also offers a more recent analysis of legal reasoning, *Rhetoric and the Rule of Law*, including a discussion of reasoning from consequences in ch 6.

[46] MacCormick, *Legal Reasoning and Legal Theory*, ch 4 and *Rhetoric and the Rule of Law*, ch 5.

[47] MacCormick, *Legal Reasoning and Legal Theory*, ch 7 and *Rhetoric and the Rule of Law*, ch 10.

The quest for coherence often prompts the deployment of inductive reasoning in law, that is, reasoning from particular instances to general principle. Where, for example, there exists an assortment of apparently conflicting and contradictory decisions on a particular issue, inductive reasoning can be applied to identify and abstract a common thread which can unite the decisions or render them more intelligible, thereby assisting future decision-making. An example of just such a process is the judgment of Lane CJ in *R v R*.[48] After a trawl of recent cases Lane CJ pulls from the case law three different solutions to the dilemma posed by the marital rape exemption. He then considers each in turn, and determines which should apply. In making his determination, Lane CJ has due regard to concerns of consistency and coherence. His approach is also strongly consequentialist in that he is simply not prepared to accept an outcome which upholds the principle that a man can rape his wife with legal impunity. Ultimately, Lane CJ (and subsequently the House of Lords) makes an evaluative choice to eschew the exemption in part because it does not conform to the contemporary realities of the marital relationship but also because it no longer 'fits' the general legal framework governing marriage and, particularly, divorce.[49] In this way, and notwithstanding the clear break from the past which *R v R* enacts, the decision can just about be seen to comply with acceptable modes of legal justification.

It is useful at this point quickly to recap the gist of MacCormick's argument. At the heart of legal reasoning, he maintains, is the syllogistic logic of rule application. However, the business of identifying and applying rules is often fraught with complexities which make the job of the decision-maker a lot more difficult than is the case when simple deductive reasoning can be deployed. In tackling these complexities, the decision-maker must make evaluative judgements: MacCormick is not denying that values inhere in law; nor is he suggesting that they are not relevant to the disposition of legal problems. Values (and

---

[48] [1992] 1 AC 599 (CA and HL).
[49] *R v R* [1992], 609–10 per Lane CJ (CA). See also discussion at §2.3.1 and §2.3.2.

principles), he argues, undergird rules and come into play to support their operation within the structural constraints of the normative order as a whole. MacCormick therefore distinguishes between rules—which function syllogistically in law— and legal values and principles which, because they are recognized as such, carry weight as explanatory or justificatory norms but do not logically *entail* a particular outcome. Moreover, these may operate at various levels of generality. For example, at a very general level, law respects and protects property rights. Therefore, when confronted with what looks like a new form of property, the legal decision-maker is likely to extend the idea of what constitutes property 'by analogy' and recognize a right to protection. Other forms of principled justification may be particular to doctrinal fields. In tort law, for example, there are lots of general principles flitting about to tilt the decision-making process in particular instances: no liability without fault, liability for acts not omissions, and so forth. These principles tend to inform the articulation and application of rules. They also influence the extension of rules to new situations (again, often through the use of analogical reasoning) or the creation of new rules when gaps are identified in the doctrinal network. Whether we understand these norms as principles, values, or expressions of public policy (and they may be any and all of these things—MacCormick sensibly does not get too worked up about how precisely we classify them), their authority derives from the historical fact of their institutional acceptance which, taken with the requirement of coherence, consistency, and attention to consequences, ensures their continued influence on decision-making.[50]

6.6 A (GENDERED) CRITIQUE OF LEGAL REASONING

MacCormick offers what is among the very best of conventional analyses of the structural dynamics underpinning legal reasoning

---

[50] MacCormick observes: 'What gives a principle *legal* quality . . . [is] its actual or potential explanatory or justificatory function in relation to law as already established'. See *Legal Reasoning and Legal Theory*, 238.

and decision-making. This is not a mechanistic account which insists upon the rigid determinacy of rules or the impenetrability of the law/politics boundary. Nor does it deny the value-laden character of legal reasoning or the openness of categories. At the same time, it manages to show that legal decision-making takes place within circumstances of genuine constraint. At the heart of MacCormick's analysis is a commitment to the idea that identifiable criteria *do* exist to distinguish good from bad, acceptable from unacceptable, types of argument in law; that some line, in other words, between the legal and non-legal can be drawn. Is he right in this assertion? And if so, what is the significance of recognizing this in terms of understanding the place (or lack thereof) of gender in law? Is there anything male or gendered about MacCormick's analysis? How does the application of the gender lens help to throw light on aspects of his account which might not otherwise become apparent?

The first thing to point out is that MacCormick's framework is not inconsistent with a substantive legal regime which enshrines values and assumptions about gender roles and relations that place women in a position of systematic social and legal disadvantage. Indeed, MacCormick would probably not deny this. He is after all open about the fact that particular values enter and infuse law and acquire a privileged status, generally in the form of legal principles. Many of the values and principles in tort law, for example, which feminist legal scholars have identified as 'male', whether in the sense of being associated, socially and culturally, with masculine behaviour and attributes or being symbolically aligned with ideas of masculinity, are well-respected elements of the normative legal landscape. Tort doctrines exposed to this form of feminist critical appraisal have included the duty of care, the rules governing assessment of damages, the distinction between acts and omissions, and the related 'no duty to rescue' doctrine.[51] The gender dimension of such norms is not

---

[51] Whether or not one agrees that these doctrines are 'male', at the very least, feminist scholarship has drawn attention to their gendered associations and effects. For a sustained gender and race informed critique of tort law, see M Chamallas and J B Wriggins, *The Measure of Injury: Race, Gender, and Tort Law* (New York, NY: NYU Press, 2010).

always apparent, particularly when incorporated into formal categorical schemes and structures. For example, Martha Chamallas
and Jennifer Wriggins contend that the well-established and
seemingly 'innocent' distinction in negligence law between
physical and emotional or psychological injury has problematic
gender connotations and implications. They suggest that the
prioritizing of physical injury in the doctrinal framework and
the scepticism and suspicion with which emotional harm as a
category of tortious injury is typically treated reflect an implicit
hierarchy of value with a gendered impact: '[the distinction]
tends to place women at a disadvantage because important and
recurring injuries in women's lives are more often classified as
lower-ranked emotional or relational harm'.[52] In similar vein,
Chamallas and Wriggins argue that the pedagogic and doctrinal
preoccupation with negligence as the 'core' of the field of tort
law contributes to the masking and trivializing of intentional
harms (particularly those occasioned by trespass to person) and,
by so doing, constrains the development of tort law as an
appropriate remedial vehicle in the context of sexual harassment
and abuse and domestic violence.

The argument here is not so much that legal decision-makers
are biased (although Chamallas and Wriggins do offer substantial
evidence of judicial bias in the disposition of tort claims, particularly historically) but rather that a cognitive bias with gender—
and race—implications, is already built into the relevant legal
categories. Again, MacCormick is unlikely to deny this, at least
as a possibility. It should be recognized that in expounding his
analysis of legal reasoning, MacCormick aligns himself with the
Humean tradition which rejects the idea that moral premises can
be generated by purely rational processes. Underpinning his
articulation is an assumption that the values which populate
law are at root the result of 'affective' judgements and preferences, the product of sentiment, passion, [and] predisposition'.[53]
Their authority is derived from a consensus as to their legal
quality existing at a given time and within a given legal interpretative community. This does not mean, MacCormick insists,

[52] Chamallas and Wriggins, *Measure of Injury*, 92.
[53] MacCormick, *Legal Reasoning and Legal Theory*, 2.

that the values which law privileges cannot be subject to reasoned scrutiny or are not, in some meaningful sense, reasonable. In this respect, MacCormick distinguishes his position from Hume's:

... That our adherence to ultimate principles in the evaluative and normative spheres is not derived by reasoning from ulterior factual and scientific knowledge... nor justifiable by reasoning of that sort, does not show that our adherence to such principles is other than a manifestation of our rational nature.[54]

While values are not ultimately susceptible to the kind of demonstrable proof that a chain of logical reasoning can yield, efforts to impose some principled order on decision-making processes, as reflected in the enterprise of law, do manifest a kind of rationality. Moreover, the tools of practical reasoning are clearly capable of supporting legal arguments based on normative premises although, inevitably, MacCormick concedes, such reasoning can never be wholly conclusive.

In his subsequent writing, MacCormick seeks to distance himself somewhat from the value-scepticism he originally espoused, observing that 'some arguments are genuinely better than others although it is often possible for reasonable and highly experienced judges to differ about the right conclusion to reach'.[55] However, for our purposes and in terms of MacCormick's formal framework, which he deems to have survived his Humean renunciation more or less intact, the substantive content of legal norms is less a question of reason and more a matter of legal convention. In a society in which inequalities of power, based, inter alia on gender, thrive, this is likely to yield legal norms which support and legitimate existing power relations and the resulting distributive disparities.

Perhaps, however, MacCormick's strong commitment to the Rule of Law precludes an outcome in which men are systematically privileged? We have seen that historically the Rule of Law has co-existed quite comfortably with formal gender-based legal distinctions. While one might insist that—notwithstanding the

[54] MacCormick, *Legal Reasoning and Legal Theory*, 6.
[55] MacCormick, *Rhetoric and the Rule of Law*, 2.

historical position—such distinctions are clear violations of Rule of Law principles, feminist analyses highlighting the gendered values and assumptions which can lurk undetected beneath the patina of formal legal neutrality, suggest that, at best, the Rule of Law, certainly in its more traditional manifestations,[56] places limits on the form which gendered legal norms can take by adopting a stance of suspicion or downright hostility towards formally discriminatory gender-based categorizations.

As an active and committed social democrat, MacCormick might well respond that the way forward here is to work towards the incorporation within law of more inclusive values and principles. Law is not immutable and legal norms only hold their authority so long as they are recognized to do so. MacCormick's identification of an 'intermediate *terra incognita* of principles struggling for legal recognition'[57] reflects a clear understanding on his part that the normative content of law changes over time. However, aspects of MacCormick's account mediate against the practical likelihood of the kind of change needed to purge law of, inter alia, its problematic gendered implications and effects. In particular, the structural constraints identified by MacCormick as placing necessary limitations on how legal reasoning is conducted—the constraints posed by coherence, consistency, and the need to take account of consequences—inhibit to varying degrees progressively-driven efforts to reconstruct the legal architectural landscape. The coherence requirement is particularly problematic here. If law as a whole is to be rendered intelligible, the decision–maker must ensure that the decision she takes *fits* within the framework of decisions already taken. Thus, she is required constantly to reaffirm the conceptual and categorical structures already in place. As Oliver Wendell Holmes observes: '. . . the substance

---

[56] On attempts to invest the Rule of Law with greater normative substance, see §6.2. Mayo Moran has argued that the principle of equality which underpins the Rule of Law is capable of capturing at least some of the kinds of disparate impact which Chamallas and Wriggins, among others, identify as resulting from the 'neutral' application of legal categories. See M Moran, *Rethinking the Reasonable Person: An Egalitarian Reconstruction of the Objective Standard* (New York, NY: OUP, 2003), especially ch 5.

[57] MacCormick, *Legal Reasoning and Legal Theory*, 238.

of law at any given time pretty nearly corresponds so far as it goes with what is then understood to be convenient but its form and machinery . . . depend very much on its past'.[58] In this way the legal past continues to exercise a strong influence on the legal present, not just in terms of the content of particular rules and doctrines, but, more importantly, in the way in which that content is formulated, represented, and arranged.

Returning for a moment to Chamallas and Wriggins' critique, the problematic distinctions they target, for example between physical and emotional harm or between negligent and intentional acts, are deeply embedded in the doctrinal architecture of tort law and not easily displaced. One might contend that the difficulty here is not so much with the distinctions themselves but with the valorizations they inscribe in legal discursive practices. The distinction between physical and emotional/psychological harm, for example, clearly privileges the former over the latter, certainly in the context of negligence claims. However, if we opt simply to treat both categories of injury in the same way, the need for the distinction itself (effectively to limit the scope of negligence liability) falls away. This might not be a bad thing because the physical/emotional injury distinction is arguably a highly suspect reaffirmation of Descartes' mind/body distinction. The sharp distinction which negligence law draws between physical and emotional injury seems quite out of line with contemporary cultural-medical understandings in which trauma to the mind and body tend to be apprehended as interconnected. At the same time, undoing categorical schemes so deeply entrenched in the doctrinal framework threatens the stability and sustainability of the schema as a whole making the whole enterprise fraught with institutional risk.

At the heart of this issue there emerges a recurring tension in law and legal argument between change and tradition. To what extent does a commitment to the past prevent law from developing in ways which are more conducive to contemporary social mores? It would be quite wrong to suggest that the

---

[58] O W Holmes, *The Common Law* (Boston, MA: Little, Brown, & Co, 1881), 1–2.

traditional character of law is an insurmountable barrier to change. On the contrary, and as Martin Krygier points out, legal traditionalism yields a process of slow but continuous change as old norms, confronting new circumstances, undergo repeated reconfiguration. It is quite impossible, Krygier argues, for traditions to survive endless processes of transmission wholly unchanged.[59] At the same time, and like Holmes, Krygier acknowledges that certain kinds of change in law are more difficult to obtain than others:

> ... All who use law inhabit and manipulate traditions whose general intellectual structures, underlying conventions, canons of authority and standards change glacially and in ways which individuals rarely have power to affect radically. They may innovate within these traditional idioms ... but at the level of underlying assumptions and presuppositions, change within legal systems is a more complicated, supra-individual, and usually supra-generational affair.[60]

In other words, in so far as the normative underpinnings of entrenched categorical orderings and conceptual schema in law are implicated in gender-based disadvantage (innocently or otherwise) and/or help to reproduce, through ideological or symbolical alignments, problematic understandings of sex and sexual difference, the extent to which these effects can be countered by deploying more progressive legal arguments remains seriously constrained. To put it another way, if as Naffine and others have maintained 'a problem of sex *is* built into the very forms of law',[61] then feminists really do face a long and uphill struggle.

For many of the same reasons as coherence inhibits feminist reconstructive efforts, so also does consistency. However, the difficulties here are arguably less challenging. *R v R* demonstrates how a bad law combined with the expression of a level of judicial dissatisfaction sufficient to pose a serious threat to the normative legal order can lead to the abandonment of a precedent,

---

[59] M Krygier, 'Law as Tradition' (1986) 5 *Law and Philosophy* 237, 251–4.

[60] Krygier, 'Law as Tradition', 248.

[61] N Naffine, *Law of the Sexes: Explorations in Feminist Jurisprudence* (Sydney: Allen & Unwin, 1990), x (my emphasis); see also discussion at §1.1.

however well entrenched and canonically endorsed. At the same time, such radical steps can only rarely be taken if law is to be seen to be able to retain its commitment to formal justice, which, as MacCormick identifies, is at the heart of the consistency requirement. Nor is MacCormick alone in stressing the importance of a basic legal commitment to the principle that like cases are treated alike. John Rawls describes the principle of 'justice as regularity' as the 'least controversial element of the common sense idea of justice'.[62] And, as we have seen, Dicey viewed legal equality as a core principle of the Rule of Law.[63]

Just how much constraint *is* imposed by the requirement that like cases are treated alike? Surely in determining whether things are alike or different everything depends on the measure selected: if the standard of measure is shape, apples and oranges are alike; if it is colour, they are not. In the case law leading up to *R v R*, a number of courts sought to get round the marital exemption by finding a measure which enabled them to 'distinguish' the case in hand from the circumstances caught by the rule.[64] This is a standard judicial move when confronted by the undesirable consequences of rule application. Of course in taking this approach—that is, by identifying a criterion (or criteria) which can justify the non-application of the rule—one is hardly allowed free rein. In working the legal materials the decision-maker operates within limits imposed by the texts before her and they are, in turn, subject to the conventions which govern the discursive field, in particular, the hierarchy of courts and the hierarchy of parts within the texts themselves. As Peter Goodrich observes, legal texts are not neutral sources from which the decision-maker can pick and choose. Their content, structure, and interpretation are shaped by their institutional context and they undoubtedly exhibit a certain kind of coercive power.[65] However, because there is always discretion in relation to the

---

[62] J Rawls, *A Theory of Justice* (Cambridge, Ma: Harvard University Press, 1971), 504–5.

[63] See further §3.2 and §4.4.1.

[64] See eg *R v Clarke* [1949] 2 All ER 448.

[65] P Goodrich, *Reading the Law: A Critical Introduction to Legal Method and Techniques* (Oxford: Basil Blackwell, 1986), ch 4.

selection of measure, that is, on the criterion used to classify
similarity and difference between cases, the principle that like
cases be treated alike is far less constraining than it appears. Even
the formality of the system of precedent (barely) conceals the
lack of precision which riddles its practical application. In particular, there is extensive theoretical contention within legal
scholarship about how to identify the *ratio decidendi* of a case.[66]
In a common law context, in which decisions may consist of a
number of different judgments expressing various levels of judicial (dis)agreement, the task of extracting a *ratio* is rendered even
more problematic.

There is yet a further issue here. Some legal scholars argue
that like cases are never really treated alike in law, that every
new decision effectively yields the creation of a new rule. An
engaging account along these lines is offered by Edward Levi.
Levi presents legal reasoning as a simple three-step process: first,
identify a similarly between the case at hand and one that has
already been decided; second, identify the rule of law inherent
in the first case; and third, 'make' the rule of law applicable to
the case in hand. In the course of this process of applying old to
new, Levi argues, some change in the rule will always occur:

. . . This change in the rules is the indispensable dynamic quality of law.
It occurs because the scope of the rule of law, and therefore its
meaning, depend upon a determination of what facts will be considered similar to those present when the first rule was announced. The
finding of similarity or difference is the key step in the legal process.[67]

Levi goes on to apply this three-step approach, which he describes as 'reasoning by example' to a range of leading cases in
American law, demonstrating that through the repeated reclas-
sification of facts in terms of similarity and difference, rules are
remade from case to case. Levi thus rejects the 'pretense that law
is a system of known rules applied by a judge'.[68] It is, he
acknowledges, a system of rules, but not in the formal sense
captured by the Rule of Law. For the same reason, Levi also

[66] See generally, MacCormick, *Rhetoric and the Rule of Law*, ch 8.
[67] Levi, *Introduction to Legal Reasoning*, 2.
[68] Levi, *Introduction to Legal Reasoning*, 1.

rejects the assertion that legal reasoning is, strictly speaking, an exercise in logic. MacCormick's claim that deductive reasoning lies at the heart of legal reasoning processes is not one Levi would endorse.[69] Indeed, Levi emphasizes that comparisons between legal reasoning and logic are unhelpful and do both forms of reasoning a disservice.[70] Moreover, Levi views the ambiguity and changeability inherent in legal reasoning processes as a virtue. That more than one analogy might be drawn to resolve a case invites the presentation of competing analogies, thereby ensuring that a wider range of arguments come before the court. This in turn allows for the entry into legal argument of new ideas which are reflective of wider changes in social and cultural norms. In this way, legal reasoning, Levi-style, assumes a democratic hue as it provides a forum through which new ideas can compete with old orthodoxies and gradually find favour.

In many ways Levi's analysis offers a better—more realistic—account of how rules operate in law. He does this by according far greater significance than MacCormick does to the indeterminacy injected into legal reasoning processes by the need to rely upon classifications of similarity and difference in the context of rule-based operations. By so doing he presents a serious challenge to MacCormick's emphasis on the importance of deductive reasoning. Theoretically speaking, Levi's account does not completely eliminate deductive reasoning from legal argumentation but it certainly calls into serious question its centrality as a legal reasoning technique. Margaret Davies, in considering MacCormick's account of the legal syllogism, observes that she is inclined to say 'so what?': 'Such a rule is purely abstract and tautologous: stated as a logical proposition it is boringly obvious'.[71] She goes on explain, in terms which correspond, though not explicitly, with Levi, that everything depends upon what constitutes 'p', that is, how the proposition which logically dictates the consequences 'q', is arrived at; and this, she insists—as do Levi, Kant (whom she quotes directly), and even MacCormick—is a non-logical operation of judgement which

---

[69] Levi, *Introduction to Legal Reasoning*, 28.
[70] Levi, *Introduction to Legal Reasoning*, 104.
[71] M Davies, *Delimiting the Law* (London: Pluto Press, 1996), 33.

involves the application of a standard of evaluation in terms of similarity and difference which, abstractly conceived, is quite empty. It is only when the decision-maker identifies the criteria upon which determinations of similarity and difference are to be made that the standard assumes substance. Notwithstanding the constraints presented by the facts themselves as well as the legal materials with which the decision-maker must work, there is still too much room for choice in this context to be able to claim with any real confidence that legal reasoning is primarily or fundamentally a logical process.

To this extent, consistency is less constraining in a legal decision-making context than coherence, certainly in terms of the range of legally sanctioned techniques available to aid the avoidance of a rule the application of which will yield undesired consequences. What is perhaps more problematic, particularly from a gender perspective, is that consistency enshrines in law an aesthetic of similarity and difference. Everything which comes before the law is reformulated in terms of this aesthetic so that legal reasoning comes to entail endless determinations of what is within and what is without a sameness-difference framework. In the course of such assignments of interiority and exteriority, the rich complexities of social life must be made conform to what Schlag describes as a 'unitary conceptual matrix' so that reason can perform its operations: 'the subjugation of the many to the one, of pluralism to monism, of difference to sameness ... is an essential requirement of the rule of reason'.[72] As a result, a suspicion of difference, a tendency to view it as beyond or other than law, is etched into the legal discursive landscape. Moreover, the designation of difference is always reliant upon the existence of a prior norm from which sameness is derived. Law thus assumes a discursive form in which norms of sameness are repeatedly re-inscribed. There is a performative dimension to legal reasoning which is normatively reiterative. The gender implications of this need little spelling out. Sameness and difference remains the primary discursive framework within which considerations of gender are situated, particularly in law.[73] In making gender-related

---

[72] Schlag, *Enchantment*, 44. [73] See generally §3.2.

arguments, women invariably find themselves on the 'difference' side of legal argumentation, confronted by a norm of sameness the express purpose of which is to exclude.

One of the best examples of this dynamic in operation is the debate which has developed in recent years around the idea of the 'woman judge'. The tendency to frame this issue in terms of the positive *difference* that women can make to processes of adjudication is enough without more to cast such arguments in a suspicious light. The gendered alignment of styles of adjudication, prompted in particular by Carol Gilligan's research indicating that men and women seem to approach moral reasoning and problem-solving differently,[74] has not helped matters, encouraging the reproduction of already problematic gender stereotypes about differences in men and women's reasoning capacities. These difficulties notwithstanding, the *perception* of difference which accompanies representations of the woman judge serves to highlight the extent to which common sense ideas of adjudication are already gendered.[75] This is more than simply acknowledging the reality that, in the UK certainly, the gender composition of the judiciary remains deeply skewed in men's favour. It is also to highlight the role gender plays in the presentation of judges in terms of sameness and uniformity, giving support to the idea that who the judge is does not matter. According to Erika Rackley, women judges help to flush out the still operative power of this belief:

...their real significance lies in exposing the myth of the default judge: the judge without politics, without personality, without preference.... Her gender puts us on notice. But what it puts us on notice of is not simply the difference of the woman judge, but the dependence of *all* judges on their background, values and experiences.[76]

Rackley is one of a number of legal scholars currently arguing for a more diverse and open judiciary. Given the general

---

[74] C Gilligan, *In a Different Voice: Psychological Theory and Women's Development* (Cambridge, MA: Harvard University Press, 1980).

[75] E Rackley, *Women, Judging and the Judiciary: From Difference to Diversity* (London: Routledge-Cavendish, 2013), ch 4.

[76] Rackley, *Women, Judging, and the Judiciary*, 163–4.

acceptance that law is indeed a value-laden enterprise, it is truly remarkable that an argument for diversity has to be made at all. Once we acknowledge, as MacCormick does, that law is a space of genuine normative contestation, legitimacy requirements surely demand an inclusive approach to involvement in legal decision-making processes. The debate which judicial diversity has generated, particularly in directing attention towards ideas of difference in a judicial context, forces us to confront the uniqueness and particularity of the individual legal decision-maker. And once we recognize that who the decision-maker is, *is* likely to be a factor in the legal reasoning process, the case for diversity becomes close to unanswerable.

These kinds of issues emerge again when we look at consequentialist reasoning in legal decision-making. According to MacCormick, legal decision-makers often pay attention to the likely consequences of their decision, both in making their determination and justifying it. As a matter of description this is probably true: it is not difficult to find examples of judges invoking consequences to inform their deliberations. For example, Birkett LJ in *Best v Fox* expressed deep concern about the likely consequences of recognizing the divisibility of consortium: 'if consortium is capable of separation into many and extremely diverse elements, so that the impairment of any element, however, slight, will give a cause of action, then the prospects are overwhelming'.[77]

MacCormick further argues that to be capable of justifying legal decisions, consequentialist arguments must be capable of taking universalized form. It is not enough to justify a decision purely on the basis of the facts at hand. While the immediate implications of the decision for the parties involved are not irrelevant, the kind of consequentialist argument which can serve as a sound legal justification must be cast in terms of universals not particulars.[78] Moreover, the point at which it is appropriate to invoke consequentialist considerations is when there is a genuine choice between two otherwise equally legally supportable alternatives.[79]

---

[77] *Best v Fox* [1952] (CA), 665.
[78] MacCormick, *Rhetoric and the Rule of Law*, ch 5.
[79] MacCormick, *Rhetoric and the Rule of Law*, 102 and generally, ch 6.

Consequentialist arguments very often take policy form. For example, in determining whether or not to extend the duty of care in negligence to a new situation, the courts will often consider the policy implications of doing so, generally under the doctrinal rubric of the third 'prong' of the *Caparo* test: is it just and reasonable to impose a duty.[80] In this context the courts have repeatedly invoked policy considerations to limit the liability of public authorities (particularly the police) for their negligent acts and omissions. However, consequentialist arguments can also invoke matters of principle and human rights. MacCormick, for example, cites with approval the arguments of Lord Hope in *A v State for the Home Department* (the '*Terrorist Suspects*' case),[81] warning against the risks to democracy posed by preventing the courts from exercising oversight of the power of the state to imprison people suspected of terrorist acts.

While arguments from consequences are indeed unavoidable and generally desirable in a legal decision-making context, there can be little doubt that they introduce yet a further element of subjectivity and choice into the decision-making process. The consideration of consequences is inevitably an evaluative process in which some values or policies simply trump others depending on the preferences of the decision-maker. The institutional and cultural setting can of course help to mould those preferences achieving some degree of normative consistency. For example, concern about the implications for criminal investigative processes of imposing too heavy a burden of potential liability on the police has now become a familiar judicial refrain. However, in my view, too little judicial attention has been given to the consequences of recognizing such a wide band of civil immunity in terms of a lack of police accountability. I raised this point some years ago in the context of an analysis of *Waters v Metropolitan Police Commissioner*, in which a former female police officer who had been subject to a sustained campaign of harassment by her colleagues after reporting being raped by another police officer, struggled to establish that her employer, the

<hr />

[80]   *Caparo Industries plc v Dickman* [1990] 2 AC 605.
[81]   *A (FX) and others v State for the Home Department* [2004] UKHL 56, see in particular para 100.

Metropolitan Police Commissioner, owed her a duty of care.[82]
More recent events in the UK—the mishandling of the investigation into the criminal activities of the 'Black-cab rapist', John
Worboys, finally convicted in 2009 and the conviction in 2012 of
a detective from the elite Sapphire sex crimes unit for perverting
the course of justice in his handling of rape complaints—do little
to inspire the confidence of rape victims in the Metropolitan
Police. Whether or not the victims of crimes, including rape
victims, should be able to bring claims against the police in
relation to negligence in the conduct of criminal investigation
is undoubtedly a tricky issue.[83] However against an evidentiary
background of systemic investigative failures in the context
of some kinds of crime, the policy reasons for imposing a duty
of care are surely worthy of greater consideration.

Of course in making these kinds of evaluative assessments
between different kinds of policy considerations, the experience
and general outlook of the judge come into play. A judge
concerned about the relatively low rate of rape convictions in
the UK as opposed to most other European countries might
well place greater weight on a legal outcome which encourages
the better conduct of rape cases by the police. However, it may
be that the judge is unaware that the rape conviction rate is an
issue of contention in the UK. The judge may also have little
knowledge about the recent record of the Metropolitan Police
with regard to the handling of rape investigations. This brings us
to the issue of know-ability. In order to evaluate the consequences of deciding in one way and not another, those consequences must be known. Moreover, what is known and
what is valued are very closely connected: we are more likely
to know about things we think are important or that matter to

---

[82] *Waters v Metropolitan Police Commissioner* [2000] 1 WLR 1607 and analysis
in J Conaghan, 'Law, Harm and Redress: A Feminist Perspective' (2002) 22
Legal Studies 319.

[83] Although in Canada, a duty of care has been recognized, and indeed held
to be broken, in circumstances where the police failed properly to investigate
rape allegations suggesting that a serial rapist was operating in the area, as a result
of which further women were raped: *Doe v Metropolitan Toronto (Municipality)
Commissioners of Police* (1998) 160 DLR (4th) 289.

us. Thus, when speculating about the consequences of taking a particular decision, a lot depends on what the decision-maker knows and the relative value she accords to different kinds of consequences. Any balance she strikes will, at least to some extent, be subjective. This subjective element is somewhat disguised by the deployment of legal idioms such as 'reasonable-ness' and 'fairness' to support the balance reached. Moreover, the representation of consequences in universal terms also helps to deflect any hint of subjectivity. Framing consequences in universalized form can also serve to justify an apparent neglect of particularity. One might speculate that the poor record of the Metropolitan Police with regard to rape investigations is unfor-tunate but not relevant to the general consideration of whether or not the police should be civilly liable for negligence in the course of criminal investigations. This is not however an insur-mountable problem. The judge so inclined can simply articulate a universalization of the consequences which takes account of relevant specifics so that, in the example under consideration, one could express concern about recognizing a civil immunity wherever there is a likely risk (supportable by empirical evi-dence) that it will encourage a culture of impunity with regard to the execution of professional and/or public duties. That works for me.[84]

What all this reveals is that arguing from consequences in the circumstances identified by MacCormick is not necessarily a bad thing. Nor must it lead to results which, from a gender equality point of view, are undesirable. However, much turns here on who is taking the decision and on their background, experience, and values. If legal decision-makers are to engage in the ade-quate assessment of the consequences of their decisions, knowl-edge must be shared and values and priorities openly debated. Once again we confront the issue of who takes the decisions. A close critical look at how processes of legal reasoning operate provides, in my view, a close to unassailable argument for supporting judicial diversity.

---

[84] See MacCormick's discussion of this point in *Rhetoric and the Rule of Law*, 97–100.

6.7 CONCLUSION

In 2010 I was a minor collaborator in the Feminist Judgments project. *Feminist Judgments: from Theory to Practice* comprises a collection of simulated judgments on leading cases by UK feminist legal scholars, each accompanied by separate legal commentary. The object of the project was to explore whether it was possible to be a judge and a feminist by subjecting key cases to feminist scrutiny while adhering strictly to the practices and conventions governing legal reasoning and judgment writing in the UK. Commenting on the judgments in a foreword to the book, Lady Hale observes: 'it is remarkable how plausible they mostly are, not only as judicial writing but also as examples of how a different judgment might properly have been written in that case at that time'.[85] (What for example, might a feminist judge have made of *Best v Fox*?)

It is still commonplace to present legal reasoning as a formal, logical, and objective process by which the legal mind is able to reason its way towards a correct legal outcome. Supporting this idea is a cluster of assumptions about reason and reasoning processes which find their most concrete and detailed expression in Enlightenment philosophy, although their pedigree extends a good deal further back in time. These assumptions include the idea that through the proper deployment of our faculty of reason we can adopt a position which is wholly outside—detached—from the circumstances in which we find ourselves and which shapes who and what we are; that the categories and concepts which we deploy are the product of a sexless disembodied mind; that reducing the complexity and messy contextuality of living to abstract features and propositions which can be reformulated in universal terms is generally the best way to approach problem-solving and decision-making; and that the results of reason's applications are as certain and as right as results can be. In a legal context, these ideas have encouraged an understanding of legal reasoning as an essentially logical process which yields objectively defendable answers except when the

---

[85] B Hale, 'Foreword' to R Hunter, C McGlynn, and E Rackley (eds), *Feminist Judgments: From Theory to Practice* (Oxford: Hart Publishing, 2010), v.

decision-maker is confronted with hard cases, at which point some value judgements do have to be made. However even here, the formal constraints which structure legal reasoning processes ensure that the range for discretion is slim and the opportunities to inject subjective values and preferences into the legal process strictly limited. A judge, for example, could not legitimately act on the basis of a personal political agenda, whether informed by feminism or some other ideological position:[86] there is no such thing—or there ought to be no such thing—as a feminist judgment.

However, a close analysis of the nature and dynamics of legal reasoning suggests otherwise. While legal reasoning is indeed a loosely structured process, it is characterized far less by logic and far more by evaluation, in which context the room for differences of opinion is considerable, as are the opportunities to determine outcomes in accordance with one's own values and preferences. This is not to say that legal reasoning does not take place within circumstances of genuine constraint—clearly it does. Nor is it to suggest that these constraints are easily navigated. My analysis of MacCormick suggests that in a gender context for example, some discursive constraints place more obstacles in the way of progressive modes of legal argumentation than others. My analysis also suggests that in seeking to free law from its patriarchal inheritance (still very much a work-in-progress), attention has to be paid not just to legal rules and doctrines, and not just to the values and assumptions, principles and policies, which underpin them. The conceptual structures and categorical schemes which support law, and which derive their authority from the past and their legitimacy from their association with reason, also need to be scrutinized and, where appropriate, reconfigured or abandoned. It does seem likely that, to a degree at least, Naffine is right and a problem of sex *is* built into the very forms of law. Understanding and accepting this is a first step towards truly tackling the problem. While the difficulties should not be underestimated, the Feminist Judgments project illustrates that, even within the existing contours of legal

---

[86] See T Bingham, 'The Judges: Active or Passive' (2006) 139 *Proceedings of the British Academy* 55, 70.

convention, there is more room for manoeuvre than might at first glance be thought. In an optimistic moment American critical legal scholar, Karl Klare, observed that 'there is no necessary contradiction between working for social transformation within adjudication and embracing the commitments and obligations of legality'.[87] I agree; but, then again, nobody said it was going to be easy.

---

[87] K Klare, 'The Politics of Duncan Kennedy's *Critique*' (2001) 22 *Cardozo LR* 1073, 1088.

7

CONCLUDING THOUGHTS

This book opened with many questions about the relationship between gender and law. Condensing them into as succinct a form as possible they basically consist of two: What is the place of gender in law? And why does it appear to have little or no place at all? The time has now come to pull together the various threads of argument in the book and represent them in a way which might provide answers to these two key questions. Inevitably such answers are provisional, incomplete, and offered only as tentative hypotheses. Moreover, I would be deceiving myself and my readers if I did not acknowledge that as the book draws to an end, I am confronted by far more questions than I have answers. That the law-gender relationship emerges as complex and multi-faceted should be obvious to all. That there are no simple, good-for-all-time answers to the core questions posed should go without saying. And yet this seems a somewhat unsatisfactory state in which to leave things. Perhaps if I begin by focusing first on a fairly straightforward question posed at the beginning of this book—why is justice almost always portrayed as a woman?—I might be able to deliver something resembling a concrete answer. So, has the exploration I have undertaken brought me any closer to an understanding of this curiously incongruous depiction of the female form in legal terrain?

Lady Justice, or in her Roman form, Justitia, is undoubtedly one of the most ubiquitous images in legal iconography. She has a long and august history which reaches back (at least) to the civilizations of Ancient Egypt, in which context she was known as Ma'at, and also Ancient Greece, where she was personified by Themis and her trio of virtuous daughters ('the Three Fates'), Dike, Eirene, and Eunome. In both Egyptian and Greek mythology, ideas of justice were almost always allied with notions of balance and order in the universe. Themis's daughters, for example, were variously associated with law and justice (Dike), peace (Eirene), and good order (Eunomia). Women's key role as creators of life was also of significance here as it helped to connect ideas of law and justice with natural processes of life-renewal.

During the early Middle Ages, and notwithstanding the deep misogynistic vein running through the life blood of much Christian theology, Justice emerged as a Virtue alongside her three sisters, Prudence, Temperance, and Wisdom. These ladies together comprised the four Cardinal Virtues, and, with the theological virtues of Faith, Hope, and Charity, they presented an impressive array of feminine goodness. Judith Resnik and Dennis Curtis document the frequent depiction of the female virtues in medieval and Renaissance art, pointing out that the image of Justice with which we are most familiar today is largely a product of that period. Resnik and Curtis also highlight the continued contemporary purchase of Lady Justice, relative to her sisters. This they account for by emphasizing the role of Justice as a successful tool of political propaganda: a statue of Justitia above a courthouse or outside a place of government is a way of capitalizing upon the lady's virtuous reputation and associations to invest political power with a greater degree of legitimacy and 'natural' authority.[1]

Of course none of this tells us *why* justice is almost always depicted as a woman and, in fact, there is a surprising lack of attention to this question in accounts of justice in female form. No conclusive explanation thus jumps out from the welter of speculation I have come across. Marina Warner perhaps rather mundanely suggests that the answer to the mystery may simply lie in linguistic convention: it is a common feature of Indo-European languages to cast certain abstract nouns of virtue in the feminine gender. While linguistic gender classifications themselves, Warner emphasizes, do not necessarily equate to gender understood in terms of sexual difference, depictions of justice, and indeed the virtues generally, in female form may at least in part be explained by their prior linguistic designation as

---

[1] J Resnik and D Curtis, 'Representing Justice: From Renaissance Iconography to Twenty-first Century Courthouses' Henry Law Barred Jayne Lecture, (2007) 151 *Proceedings of the American Philosophical Society* 139, 145.

feminine nouns.[2] Certainly, it is unlikely, particularly in a medieval context, that justice emerged as female because of any belief that women were thought to be better at dispensing justice than men. This is simply not a position which accords with the operational realities of justice systems at the time.

And yet one can identify certain perceived features of femininity which are not out of a place in a justice context, particularly the idea of justice as mercy which is frequently contrasted with the sterner side of justice as upholding the law. Shakespeare's Portia from the *Merchant of Venice* is often represented as an embodiment of justice as mercy although it is arguable that this is a rather simplistic and even sexist depiction of Portia which fails to recognize her skill and strategic acumen when confronting a tricky legal problem.[3] Motherhood can also assume significance in relation to justice. It is mothers after all who are most likely to forgive. Mothers also dispense punishment to guide and direct their wayward offspring but always as an act of love. Robin West is among a number of feminist scholars who have argued that caring should be an indispensable part of justice, that justice without care, compassion, and some commitment to nurturing the community is an inferior form of justice which we should eschew.[4]

Finally, the sheer historical out-of-placeness of women in the world of law is almost certainly a factor in accounting for the persistent portrayal of justice as female. Her gender sets Lady Justice apart from law, locating justice beyond the gritty realities of day-to-day legal practice. Justice is the exotic Other of law, a muse and source of inspiration to the legal mind. Justice fires the ambitions and stokes the desires of the men of law, setting them off on a perpetual quest in her pursuit.[5] When Sir Frederick Pollock depicted the common law as a medieval lady, protected

---

[2] M Warner, *Monuments and Maidens: the Allegory of the Female Form* (London: Random House, 1996), xxi and generally ch 4.

[3] E Rackley, 'Reassessing Portia: the Iconic Potential of Shakespeare's Woman Lawyer' (2003) 11 *Feminist Legal Studies* 25.

[4] R West, *Caring for Justice* (NY: New York University Press, 1997), especially ch 1.

[5] F Pollock, *The Genius of the Common Law* (New York: Columbia University Press, 1912). On our lady of the common law, see further §1.1.

and pursued by the knights of law, he was surely drawing upon chivalrous ideals to invest in his audience a sense of the nobility of law as a path to pursue. Similarly when Benjamin Cardozo advised a class of graduands that 'Our Lady of the Common Law has no lack of wooers',[6] his purpose was to instil in a new generation of gallant suitors the importance of approaching law with an appropriate level of fidelity, respect, and restraint. In both these depictions the common law emerges as mysteriously and alluringly feminine. At the same time, we are being told that with proper handling, the lady is controllable.

The gendered imagery which Cardozo and Pollock invoke to depict the common law, along with the myriad examples of the broader portrayal of justice as female, evidence the metaphorical or symbolic deployment of gender in legal contexts to confer meanings and assign value. In Pollock's account, for example, gender functions as a coding mechanism; the 'coding' of the common law as feminine helps to reinforce particular ideas not just about law but also about the lawyer's relationship to law.[7] The power of this gendered legal imaginary, however, is derived from the associations it creates between ideas of law and social and cultural perceptions of gender difference. Our lady of the common law can only serve as an object of chivalrous desire to a roomful of lawyers with an assumed sexual preference for the feminine form. Similarly, it is precisely because women have not traditionally been involved in the dispensation of justice that feminization works to set justice apart from—beyond—the law. In this sense, the use of feminized imagery in law may best be understood, certainly historically, as an expression of women's exclusion from the legal realm. Such gendered invocations help to flush out the masculine self-image which often lurks beneath the gender-neutrality of legal form. They remind us too that we have inherited a gendered legal legacy which still struggles fully to erase itself from the topography of modern law. Whether we

[6] B Cardozo, 'Our Lady of the Common Law', originally a speech given in 1928 to the first graduating class of St John's law school, and reproduced in (1972) 18 *Catholic Lawyer* 276.

[7] On the use of gender to 'code' meanings, see generally J W Scott, *Gender and the Politics of History*, revised edn (New York: NY University Press, 1999).

like it or not, gender is an operative factor in processes of knowledge production and particularly prominent in the contexts of efforts to articulate, naturalize, and/or legitimate difference. And law, as we have seen, is all about determinations of sameness and difference.

Where does this leave things? What can be said about the place of gender in law? Here then are my tentative conclusions. First, gender is not *inherent* in law in any absolute sense. I say this because I share Brian Tamanaha's view that nothing inheres in law as such.[8] While empirically speaking, there may be a wide range of identifiable factors which converge in what we choose to label as 'law', and, moreover, there may well be value in gathering these factors together to get a better of sense of how law is apprehended in practice, *essentially* speaking, law is whatever we conventionally recognize as such. Therefore the nature of the relationship between law and gender is contingent rather than necessary or absolute. That said, that gender is deeply woven into the fabric of law as it is understood and practiced in modern Western cultures is undeniable. It inheres in the values and assumptions that underpin legal doctrine. It slips into and shapes the evaluative operations of legal decision-makers. It is consistently a factor implicated in the legal distribution of power and resources: without a doubt and notwithstanding a stance which is formally gender-neutral, law delivers outcomes which, more often than not, are gendered. In addition, gendered patriarchal configurations remain an intrinsic part of a legal heritage in which tradition features centrally. It is an inescapable fact that the past can never be fully excised from a discursive frame in which it continues to exercise a significant level of power in the present.

Moreover, that the law–gender relationship is contingent rather than necessary does not preclude a determination that gender is indeed built into the very forms of law—as we currently know and understand it. Close scrutiny suggests that the extent of gender's involvement in legal terrain goes well beyond the bricks and mortar to encompass significant aspects of legal

---

[8] See generally §5.4.1.

architectural design. In particular, many of the conceptual and categorical structures of law have been revealed to have gender dimensions or implications: the distinction between public and private, the paradigmatic model of the legal subject, and tortious conceptualizations of harm, to name but a few. That gender is to some degree implicated in these contexts is not to adduce clear evidence of the precise nature of involvement. Indeed, in general terms the nature of the relationship between law and gender is best understood to operate interactively, at multiple levels simultaneously, and rarely in terms of any simple alignment of cause and effect. The important point to recognize is that, whether understood as a body of knowledge or as a practical activity, law is an important source of meaning and value. As a central category of social organization, gender also features prominently in processes of meaning conferral and value assignment. And it is in the operation of these processes in the context of law that gender is likely to be found.

Why then does gender appear to have little or no place in law at all? One of the things I have tried to tease out during the course of this book is the nature of the difficulties legal scholars confront when they attempt to excavate gender from the dimensions of law. Simply put, they are too often required to eschew conventional jurisprudential approaches in order to do so. They have to reject the assumption that the person is, legally speaking, an abstract, disembodied, universal expression of everyone and no one and highlight the particular features and characteristics with which the person of law is invariably endowed. They have to introduce and place considerable weight upon factors which are deemed to be beyond the realm of the strictly legal to explain or account for legal outcomes. Finally, they have to challenge and disrupt the categorical ordering schemes which give law its coherence and credibility as a neutral forum for the resolution of disputes. In other words, because law self-presents as a gender-free zone, it is difficult to engage gender in legal discursive argumentation without seriously disturbing that self-image.

A range of legal conventions and practices conspire to ensure the continuance of this self-image. Chief among these is the formal exclusion of gender as a category of legal relevance, in particular through adherence to an ideal of the Rule of Law which emerged at a critical juncture in law–gender relations and is very much a product of specific historical circumstances and demands. There also continues a predilection for conceptualizing law as a relatively discrete and autonomous field of knowledge in relation to which meaningful boundaries can be drawn. While contemporary legal theory better recognizes the difficulties with such conceptualizations and, indeed, demonstrates a receptiveness to a wider diversity of approaches to law than it has exhibited in the past, there is still, I would suggest, a tendency to downplay the difficulties which attach to such boundary-drawing efforts and thereby, a failure to recognize the significance of those difficulties in terms of what they tell us about law. In this sense, I share the view of legal scholars such as Tamanaha that general jurisprudential enquiry needs to be significantly re-oriented.

At the same time, I would encourage feminists and other critical legal scholars to take seriously the discursive constraints that operate to structure and shape forms of legal argumentation. To take the view that legal rules are hopelessly indeterminate is to ignore the existence and operation of legal ordering schemes which genuinely require negotiation. To collapse law into politics gets one nowhere. To recognize that law and politics occupy a lot of the same space, albeit differently configured, is quite another matter. We return to the idea that law is not just something that *is* but also something one *does*. And it is in the doing that change may be brought into effect. The change I want to help bring about is a simple one. I want to encourage legal scholars to rethink their understanding of what it means to say law is gendered. I say law is gendered, not absolutely or inherently, but historically, contemporaneously, and above all, multi-dimensionally. Moreover, in making this assertion, my purpose extends beyond engaging in mere description. Rather by deploying gender as an evaluative tool in legal contexts, I am seeking to harness processes of meaning conferral to prompt a better (more inclusive) understanding of law in which gender considerations come more easily to the fore. Within the contours of legal discourse ideas of gender have traditionally been contained within a straightjacket of suppositions about the nature and operation of the field, most of which are no longer sustainable, if indeed they ever were. This is already widely recognized, but most scholars would probably acknowledge that the implications are far from fully considered. I hope that the analysis here may go some small way towards bringing additional theoretical clarity to the issues while at the same time opening up space for new explorations of law as a field of study.

INDEX

Printed and bound by CPI Group (UK) Ltd, Croydon, CR0 4YY